GRINGO LOVE

ethno GRAPHIC

This groundbreaking series realizes ethnographic and anthropological research in graphic form. The series speaks to a growing interest in comics as a powerful communicative medium and to the desire for a more creative and public anthropology that engages with contemporary issues. Books in the series are scholarship-informed works that combine text and image in ways that are conceptually sophisticated yet accessible to broader audiences, open-ended, and aesthetically rich, to encourage conversations that build greater cross-cultural understanding.

Series Editors: Sherine Hamdy (University of California, Irvine) and Marc Parenteau (comics artist)

Series Advisory Board: Juliet McMullin (University of California, Riverside), Stacy Pigg (Simon Fraser University), Nick Sousanis (San Francisco State University), and Fiona Smyth (OCAD University)

OTHER BOOKS IN THE SERIES

Gringo Love

STORIES OF SEX TOURISM IN BRAZIL

WRITTEN BY MARIE-EVE CARRIER-MOISAN
ADAPTED BY WILLIAM FLYNN
ILLUSTRATED BY DÉBORA SANTOS

UNIVERSITY OF TORONTO PRESS
Toronto Buffalo London

© University of Toronto Press 2020
Toronto Buffalo London
utorontopress.com
Printed in Canada

ISBN 978-1-4875-9453-4 (cloth)   ISBN 978-1-4875-9454-1 (EPUB)
ISBN 978-1-4875-9452-7 (paper)   ISBN 978-1-4875-9455-8 (PDF)

Library and Archives Canada Cataloguing in Publication

Title: Gringo love : stories of sex tourism in Brazil / written by Marie-Eve Carrier-Moisan ;
adapted by William Flynn ; illustrated by Débora Santos.
Names: Carrier-Moisan, Marie-Eve, 1976–, author. | Flynn, William, 1974–, adapter. |
Santos, Débora, 1989–, illustrator.
Series: ethnoGRAPHIC.
Description: Series statement: ethnoGRAPHIC | Includes bibliographical references and index.
Identifiers: Canadiana (print) 20200213725 | Canadiana (ebook) 2020021389X |
ISBN 9781487594534 (cloth) | ISBN 9781487594527 (paper) |
ISBN 9781487594541 (EPUB) | ISBN 9781487594558 (PDF)
Subjects: LCSH: Sex tourism – Brazil – Natal – Comic books, strips, etc. | LCSH: Prostitutes –
Brazil – Natal – Social conditions – Comic books, strips, etc. | LCSH: Women – Brazil – Natal –
Social conditions – Comic books, strips, etc. | LCGFT: Graphic novels.
Classification: LCC HQ175.N38 C37 2020 | DDC 306.740981/32 – dc23

We welcome comments and suggestions regarding any aspect of our
publications – please feel free to contact us at news@utorontopress.com or visit
us at utorontopress.com.

Every effort has been made to contact copyright holders; in the event of an error or
omission, please notify the publisher.

University of Toronto Press acknowledges the financial assistance to its publishing
program of the Canada Council for the Arts and the Ontario Arts Council, an agency of
the Government of Ontario.

Canada Council   Conseil des Arts
for the Arts   du Canada

ONTARIO ARTS COUNCIL
CONSEIL DES ARTS DE L'ONTARIO
an Ontario government agency
un organisme du gouvernement de l'Ontario

Funded by the   Financé par le
Government   gouvernement
of Canada   du Canada

Canadä

MIX
Paper from
responsible sources
FSC® C016245

In memory of Jojo and Susan, who both taught me a great deal about the art of conversation. – Marie-Eve

For Flávio. – Billy

I dedicate this graphic novel to the women of northeast Brazil, may they always have strength. – Débora

CONTENTS

ACKNOWLEDGMENTS

Gringo Love has long been in the making; as such, many people, institutions, and organizations have contributed their guidance, vision, encouragement, and support. First, this book would not have been conceivable without the superb artwork of Débora Santos; it has been an honor for Marie-Eve and Billy (William) to work alongside her on this project and to witness the materialization of academic research into a graphic story through her drawings. Débora would like to take this opportunity to thank her best friend and companion, Márcio Moreira, who always encouraged her to draw, as well as her family, who accompanied her in the process and tried to understand how one makes a graphic novel.

In its current form, *Gringo Love* exists as an ethno-graphic novel in large part thanks to the relentless support of past executive editor at the University of Toronto Press Anne Brackenbury and her innovative vision for telling anthropology otherwise. We owe a great deal to Anne's commitment both to the ethnoGRAPHIC series she launched and to our project. We are also deeply grateful to cartoonist Marc Parenteau for his generous and incredibly helpful advice during key moments as we struggled to craft *Gringo Love*. Anthropologist Sherine Hamdy, co-author of the first book published in the ethnoGRAPHIC series, also provided fabulous suggestions for reorganizing the story, contributing greatly to a better version of the narrative structure. We are also very grateful to the anonymous reviewers for their enthusiastic support, generosity, and critical engagement with our work during both the proposal and the first draft stages. *Gringo Love* has also involved a complex process of production; at the University of Toronto Press, we want to thank design and production manager Ani Deyirmenjian for her patience in the process of formatting the graphic story for printing. We're also grateful to

Jenn Harris and Janice Evans for their excellent and thorough editorial work on the final manuscript. And a big thanks to our new editor, Carli Hansen, for supporting us and bringing us to the finishing line despite the hurdles!

We received financial support from the Social Sciences and Humanities Research Council of Canada, in the form of an Insight Development Grant, for both the graphic story and the ethnographic research conducted during the 2014 World Cup. This funding was essential to the making of *Gringo Love*. At Carleton University, we benefited from various kinds of support, including initial funding to conduct research through a Faculty of Arts and Social Sciences Junior Research Grant and receiving interest and encouragement from colleagues and students, especially in Billy's and Marie-Eve's home Department of Sociology and Anthropology. Thanks to both Pablo Mendes, at Carleton University, and Fiona Jeffries, at the University of Ottawa – besides their genuine curiosity for this project, they have been fabulous interlocutors about virtually everything and have provided me (Marie-Eve) with the opportunity to share my work in their respective graduate seminars, where I received invaluable feedback. I would also like to thank the Pauline Jewett Institute of Women's and Gender Studies, at Carleton University, for the invitation to present early drafts of this work as part of their 2016–17 Feminist Futures Lecture Series. In Ottawa, I am lucky to engage with many inspiring intellectual companions and friends who have modeled for me critical forms of engagement with the world. In particular, I want to thank Sonya Gray, Danielle DiNovelli-Lang, Karen Hebert, Corrie Scott, Karine Geoffrion, Jen Ridgley, Jackie Kennelly, Alexis Shotwell, Jill Wagle, Lorena Zarate, Emilie Cameron, Megan Rivers-Moore, Ummni Khan, Rena Bivens, Stacy Douglas, Kamari Clarke, Blair Rutherford, Kat Van Meyl, and Kayleigh Thompson. I am also grateful to Alexandrine Boudreault-Fournier and Stacy Pigg, who have pioneered ethnographic engagements with the graphic form, for the various opportunities they offered, over the years, to exchange about our respective projects. Many graduate and undergraduate students have offered support and inspiration to continue on with the imperfect project of doing anthropology – thank you! Two research assistants – Sabrina Fernandes and Lauren Montgomery – have also been tremendously resourceful, inspiring, and helpful. Much gratitude, as well, to both Fazeela Jiwa and Karen Caruana for their copy editing on various sections of the textual materials.

The making of *Gringo Love*, however, began many years before its current configuration as a graphic story in the form of a doctoral dissertation, and so I owe a great debt to those who have mentored me, starting with *minha companheira* Sally Cole at Concordia University, who opened up for me a path forward in anthropology with my first field trips to Brazil during my MA. I also received enormous support as a doctoral student while at the University of British Columbia (UBC), including in the Department of Anthropology and the Lui Institute for Global Issues. Alexia Bloch, my PhD supervisor, helped me craft a legitimate space for my work in feminist anthropology and mentored me far beyond the dissertation, while Becki Ross profoundly shaped my engagement with scholarship through her unique ability to instill both intellectual rigor and humility. Thanks also to Gastón Gordillo for his teachings, especially about the anthropology of space and place that has deeply influenced my understanding of the world. At UBC, I was part of a rich, formative, nurturing community of peers that profoundly shaped me, including Oralia Gómez-Ramírez, Rafael Wainer, Ana Vivaldi, and the late Susan Hicks, all of whom lifted me up when I needed it most, as well as Robin O'Day and Rachel Donkersloot, members of my writing group, who provided a supportive space to share our work.

In Natal, I would like to thank the Coletivo Leila Diniz–Ações de Cidadania e Estudos Feministas for their institutional support during the field research in 2007–8 that led to some of the content in the graphic story – special appreciation to Joluzia Batista and Analba Brazão Teixeira for their kindness, hospitality, friendship, and generosity, and to Claudia Gazola, who provided help during the 2014 fieldwork. I am also grateful to anthropologist Elisete Schwade, at the Federal University of Rio Grande do Norte, for all the intellectual and emotional support during the two field trips in 2007–8 and 2014 – including the doctor referral and help during a medical emergency, *obrigada!* A warm and heartfelt thanks to Lucas, Carol, Maria de Lucia, Flávio, and Lita for friendship and support in the field. And to the protagonists – the women and men I have fictionalized – this ethnography feels like a long time coming to term; I feel I am writing of another time, but I still hope I do represent your experiences in fairness and in a way that feels like recognition. I am so grateful for your generosity and willingness to share with me about your lives.

Merci à mes amies et à ma famille for your curiosity, encouragement, and support, and for being there all along: Marie-Claude Asselin and Fred Amyot (and all your questions!), *les filles* – Mélanie Normand, Isabelle Côté, Mathilde Côté, and Karine Blouin – and my family of keen supporters: my two brothers, two pillars in my life in their own distinct ways, Philippe and David Carrier-Moisan; my father, John Moisan, and his wife, Danielle Gaulin; my sister-in-law, Julie Paquet, and my nieces and nephews, Léa-Maude, Maïka, Émile, and Éloïse Moisan, as well as my extended family, including, especially, Julie Carrier and the gang, Lise, Jacques and Claire, and Pierre Carrier.

Finally, the idea for *Gringo Love* started some time ago, and its coming to fruition is, in great part, because of the willingness of Billy to jump on the wagon with me and explore this new medium while also standing behind me both intellectually and emotionally. The first roots of *Gringo Love* are to be found, perhaps, in the drawings that Billy included in his dissertation, drawings made by his daughter, Laurynn Kearney. I would like to end by thanking her – her cartoonish drawings, so expressive, have certainly planted the seeds of our current experiment with drawings (and a nod to Tom Kemple for reminding us about this).

NOTE TO THE READER

When a Portuguese term is used for the first time within the graphic story, a translation is available at the bottom of the page. A full lexicon appears immediately before the graphic pages.

Readers curious to learn more about the making of *Gringo Love*, the practice of anthropology, the study of "sex tourism," or the context in which Brazilian women seek to meet foreign men may find it useful to refer to the appendices prior to, during, or after reading the graphic novel. While the graphic story can be understood and made meaningful without this additional content, the appendices aim to provide contextualization and analytical discussion and to open up spaces for further conversations and engagements with the key themes discussed.

LEXICON

bem-vindo ao Brasil	welcome to Brazil
brasileiros/as	Brazilian men/women
cafuçu	cheap and rude man (colloquial, slang term)
coroa	literally translates as crown; colloquially used to refer to an older, richer, whiter man. Close to a "sugar daddy."
de graça	for free
essa vida	this life
favela	shantytown
festinha	little party; colloquially used as a euphemism for sex
filhinha(s) de papai	daddy's girl(s)
garota(s)	diminutive of *garota(s) de programa*; literally translates as girl(s)
garota(s) de programa	softer term for prostitute(s); sometimes associated with middle-class escort(s)
gringo/a	male/female foreigners. While elsewhere (e.g., Mexico, Costa Rica) the term commonly denotes "American," in Natal it also denotes "European."

gringo para casar, brasileiro para transar	gringos to marry, Brazilian men to have sex with
hola, guapo	hi, handsome (in Spanish)
meu amor	my love (*meu* = masculine for my)
meu corpo não é mercadoria	my body is not a commodity
mineiraço	national shame, how Brazil's loss against Germany came to be known
minha querida	my dear (*minha* = feminine for my)
morena(s)	literally translates as brown woman (women); a context-dependent category that may refer to a brunette, Indigenous woman, or mixed-race woman.
mulata	a shorthand translation would be mixed-race woman; it has a sexual connotation, too.
namorado	boyfriend
namoro	dating, courtship
oi	hi
patrão/patroa	male/female boss
pousada	cheap accommodation/bed-and-breakfast style
programa	an explicit arrangement to exchange sex for money
puta	whore
putaria	whoring, whoring around
real/reais	Brazilian currency
sair dessa vida	to get out of this life
sem futuro	without a future

PART 1: ARRIVALS

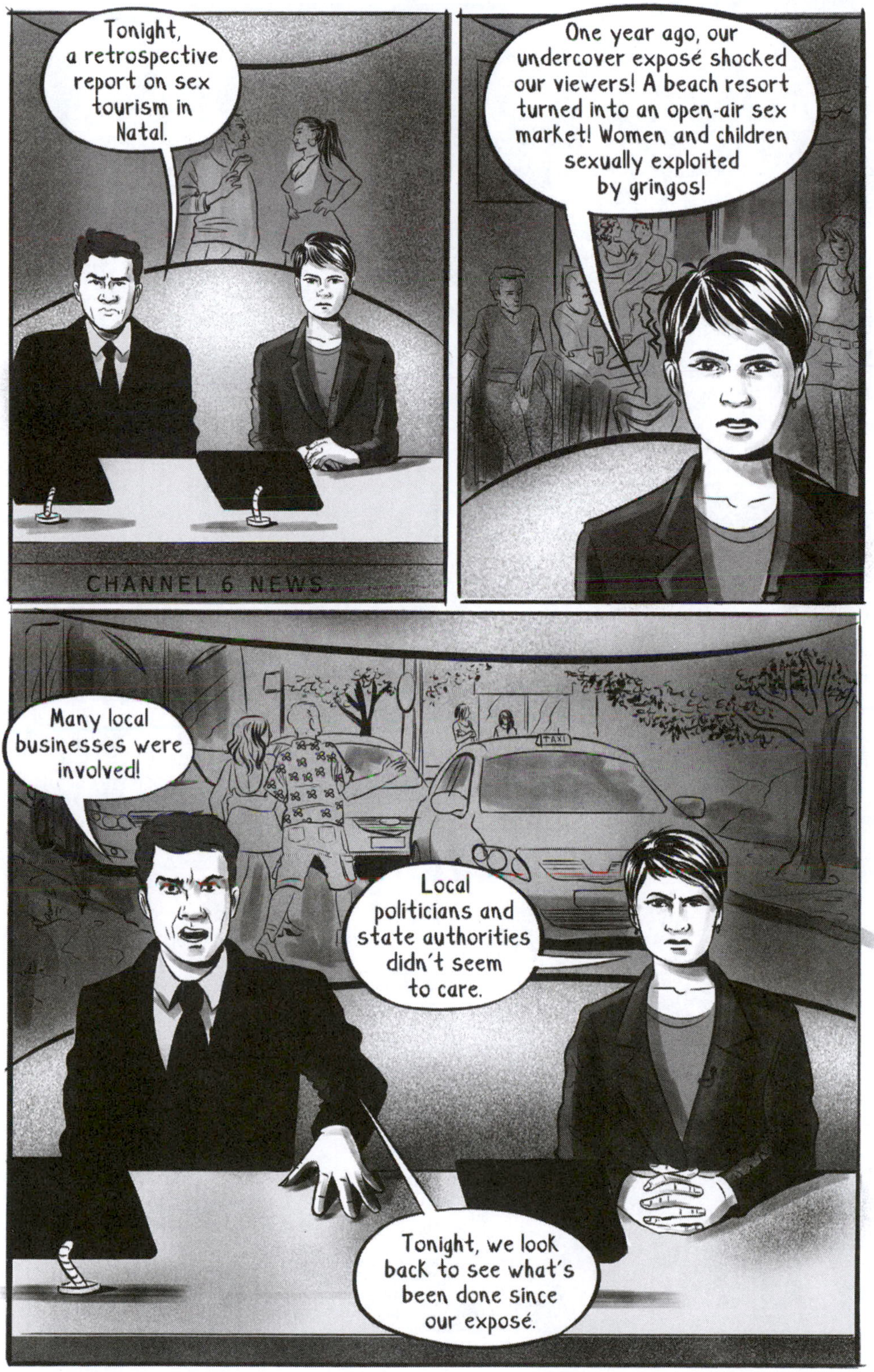
Tonight, a retrospective report on sex tourism in Natal.
CHANNEL 6 NEWS
One year ago, our undercover exposé shocked our viewers! A beach resort turned into an open-air sex market! Women and children sexually exploited by gringos!
TAXI
Many local businesses were involved!
Local politicians and state authorities didn't seem to care.
Tonight, we look back to see what's been done since our exposé.

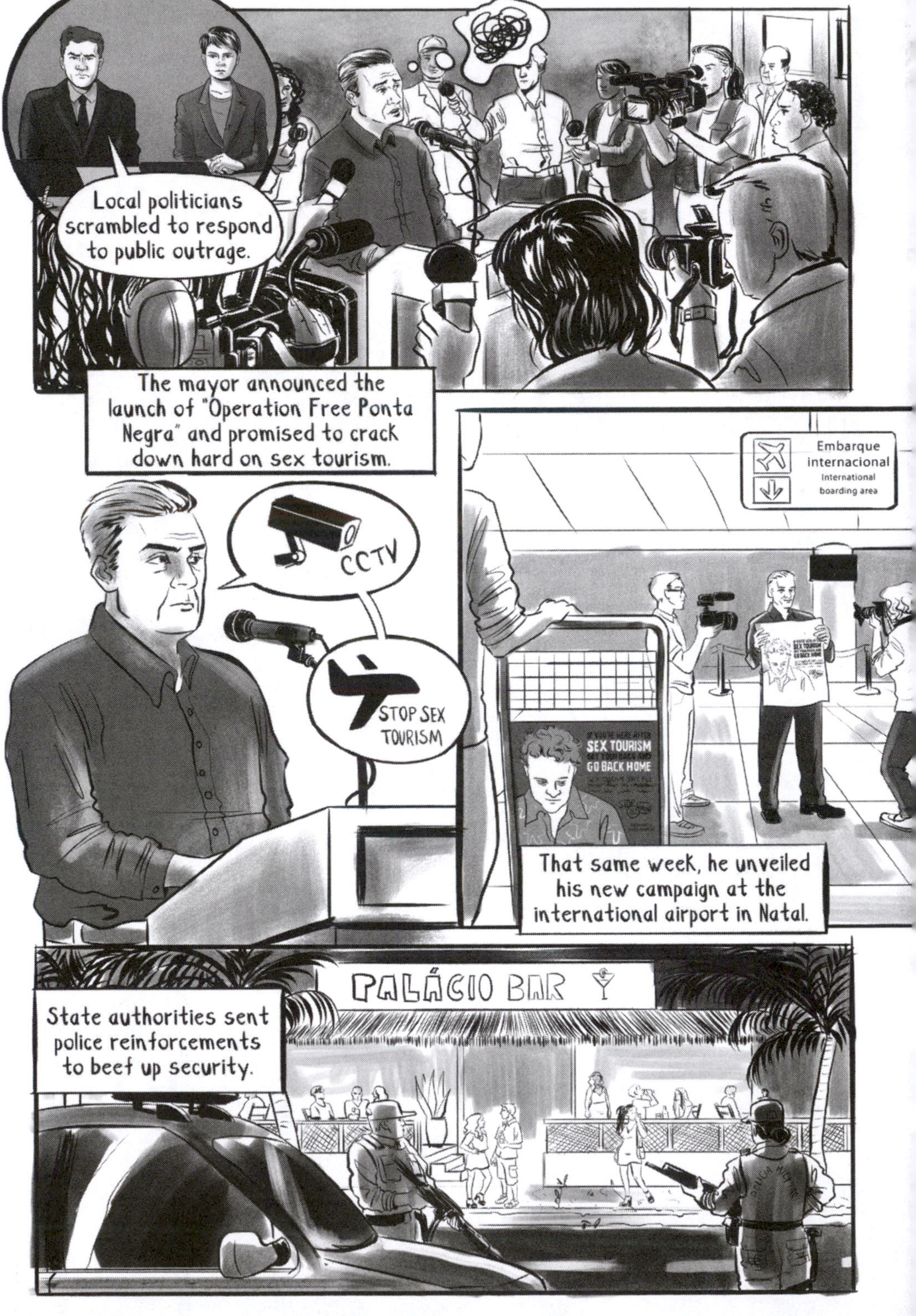
Local politicians scrambled to respond to public outrage.
The mayor announced the launch of "Operation Free Ponta Negra" and promised to crack down hard on sex tourism.
CCTV
STOP SEX TOURISM
Embarque internacional
International boarding area
SEX TOURISM
GO BACK HOME
That same week, he unveiled his new campaign at the international airport in Natal.
PALÁCIO BAR
State authorities sent police reinforcements to beef up security.

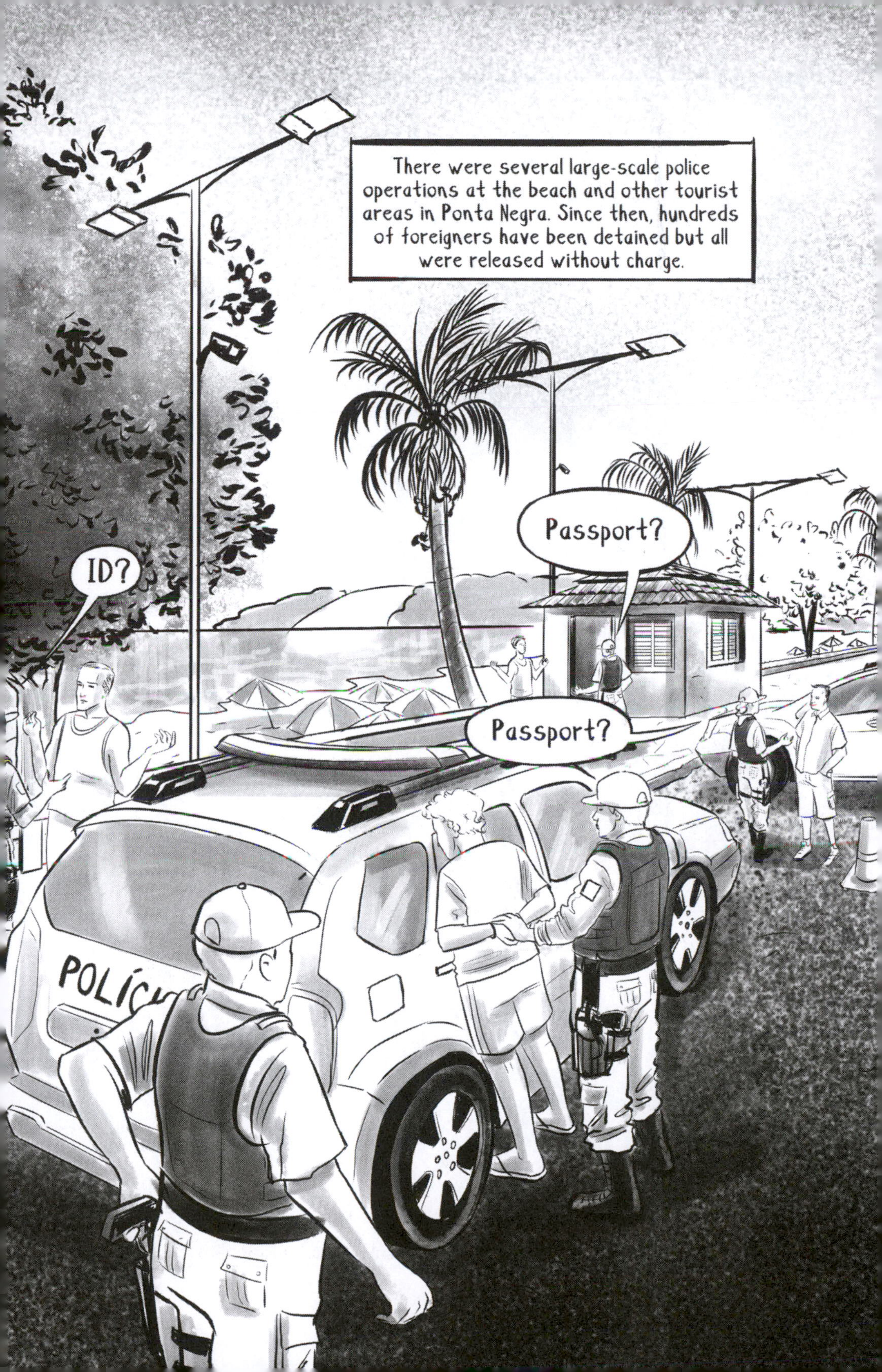
There were several large-scale police operations at the beach and other tourist areas in Ponta Negra. Since then, hundreds of foreigners have been detained but all were released without charge.
Passport?
ID?
Passport?
POLÍC

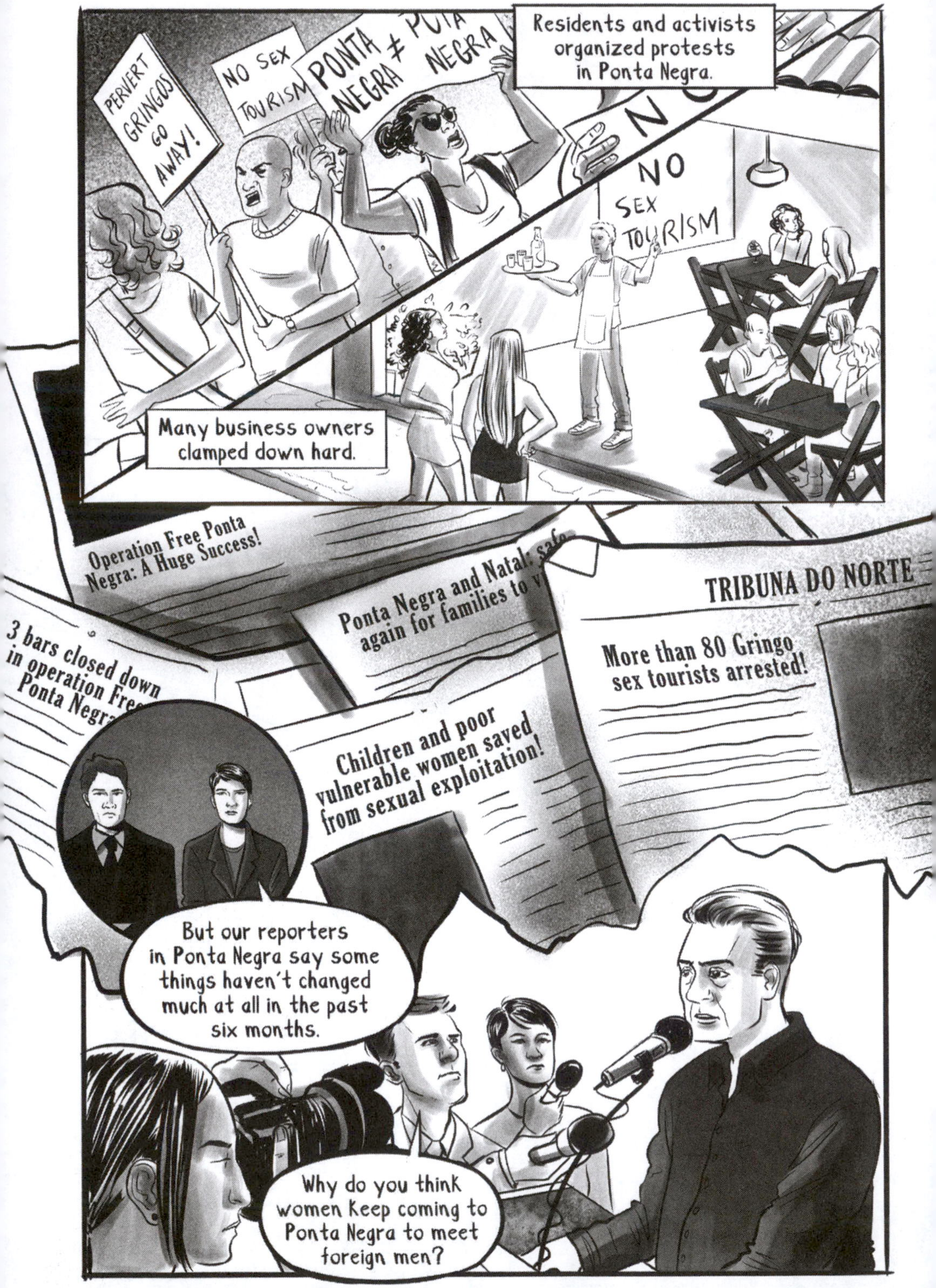

Residents and activists organized protests in Ponta Negra.
PERVERT GRINGOS GO AWAY!
NO SEX TOURISM
PONTA NEGRA ≠ PUTA NEGRA
NO
NO SEX TOURISM
Many business owners clamped down hard.
Operation Free Ponta Negra: A Huge Success!
Ponta Negra and Natal: safe again for families to
TRIBUNA DO NORTE
More than 80 Gringo sex tourists arrested!
3 bars closed down in operation Free Ponta Negra
Children and poor vulnerable women saved from sexual exploitation!
But our reporters in Ponta Negra say some things haven't changed much at all in the past six months.
Why do you think women keep coming to Ponta Negra to meet foreign men?

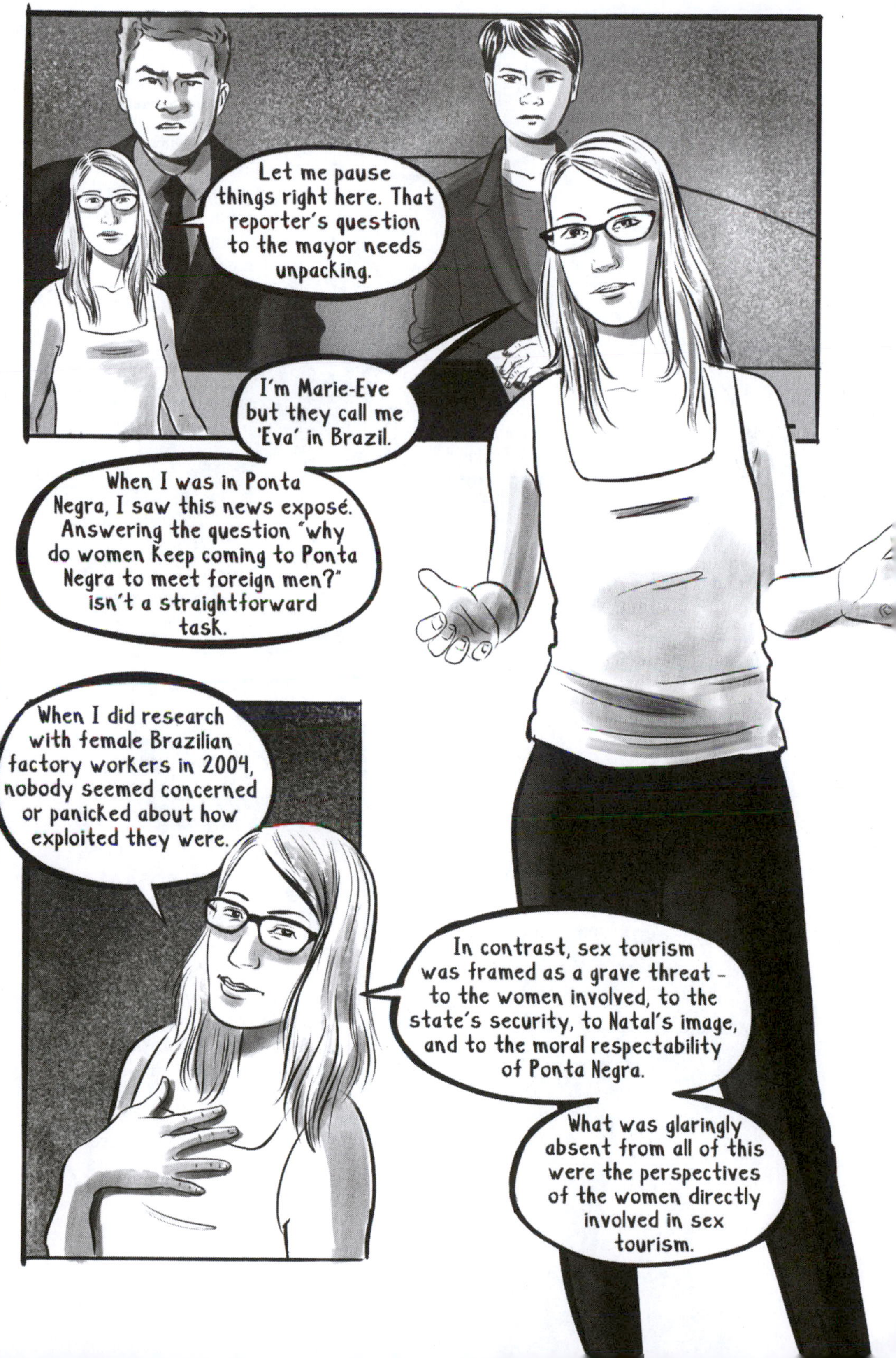
Let me pause things right here. That reporter's question to the mayor needs unpacking.
I'm Marie-Eve but they call me 'Eva' in Brazil.
When I was in Ponta Negra, I saw this news exposé. Answering the question "why do women keep coming to Ponta Negra to meet foreign men?" isn't a straightforward task.
When I did research with female Brazilian factory workers in 2004, nobody seemed concerned or panicked about how exploited they were.
In contrast, sex tourism was framed as a grave threat - to the women involved, to the state's security, to Natal's image, and to the moral respectability of Ponta Negra.
What was glaringly absent from all of this were the perspectives of the women directly involved in sex tourism.

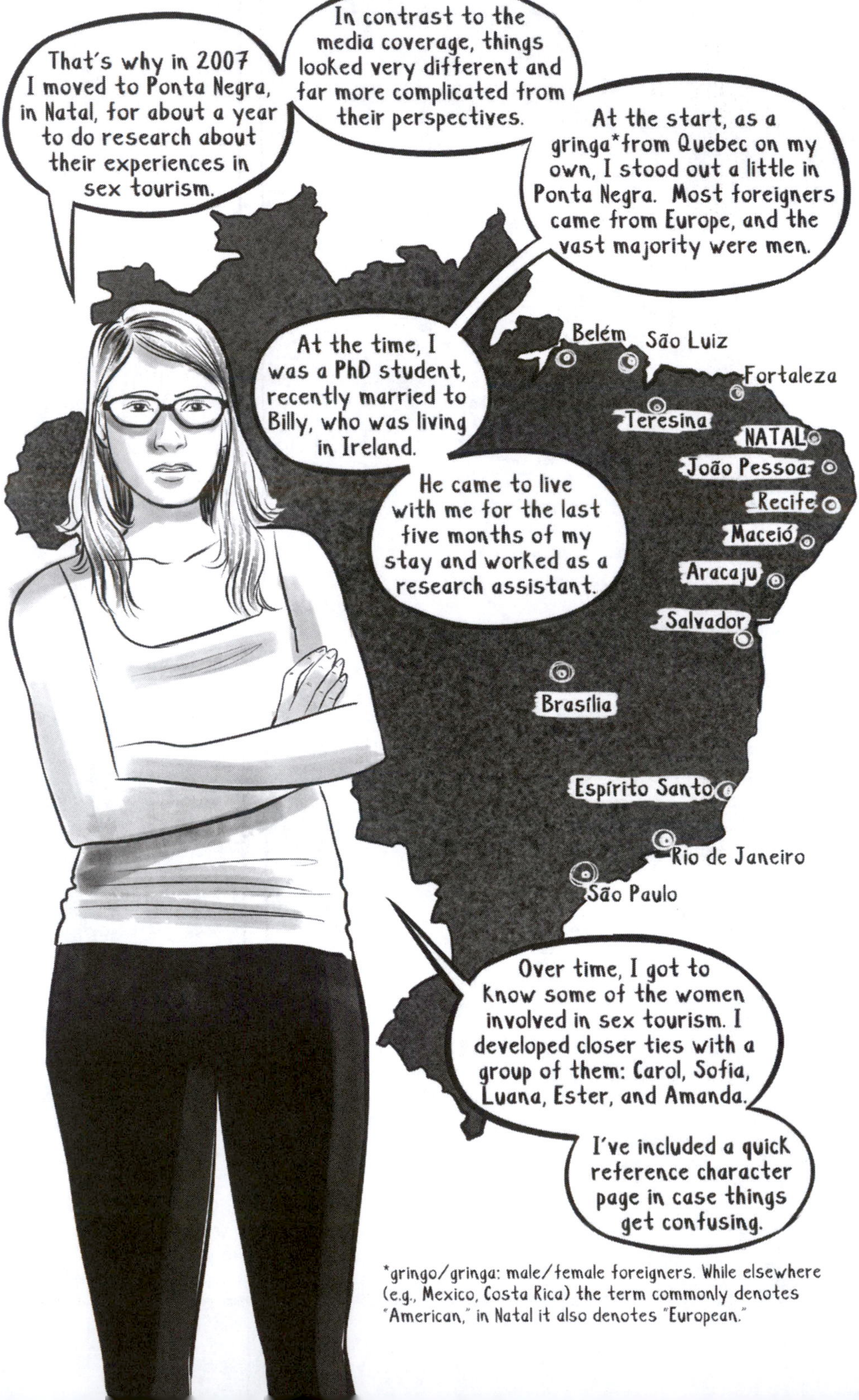
That's why in 2007 I moved to Ponta Negra, in Natal, for about a year to do research about their experiences in sex tourism.
In contrast to the media coverage, things looked very different and far more complicated from their perspectives.
At the start, as a gringa*from Quebec on my own, I stood out a little in Ponta Negra. Most foreigners came from Europe, and the vast majority were men.
At the time, I was a PhD student, recently married to Billy, who was living in Ireland.
He came to live with me for the last five months of my stay and worked as a research assistant.
Belém
São Luiz
Fortaleza
Teresina
NATAL
João Pessoa
Recife
Maceió
Aracaju
Salvador
Brasília
Espírito Santo
Rio de Janeiro
São Paulo
Over time, I got to know some of the women involved in sex tourism. I developed closer ties with a group of them: Carol, Sofia, Luana, Ester, and Amanda.
I've included a quick reference character page in case things get confusing.

*gringo/gringa: male/female foreigners. While elsewhere (e.g., Mexico, Costa Rica) the term commonly denotes "American," in Natal it also denotes "European."

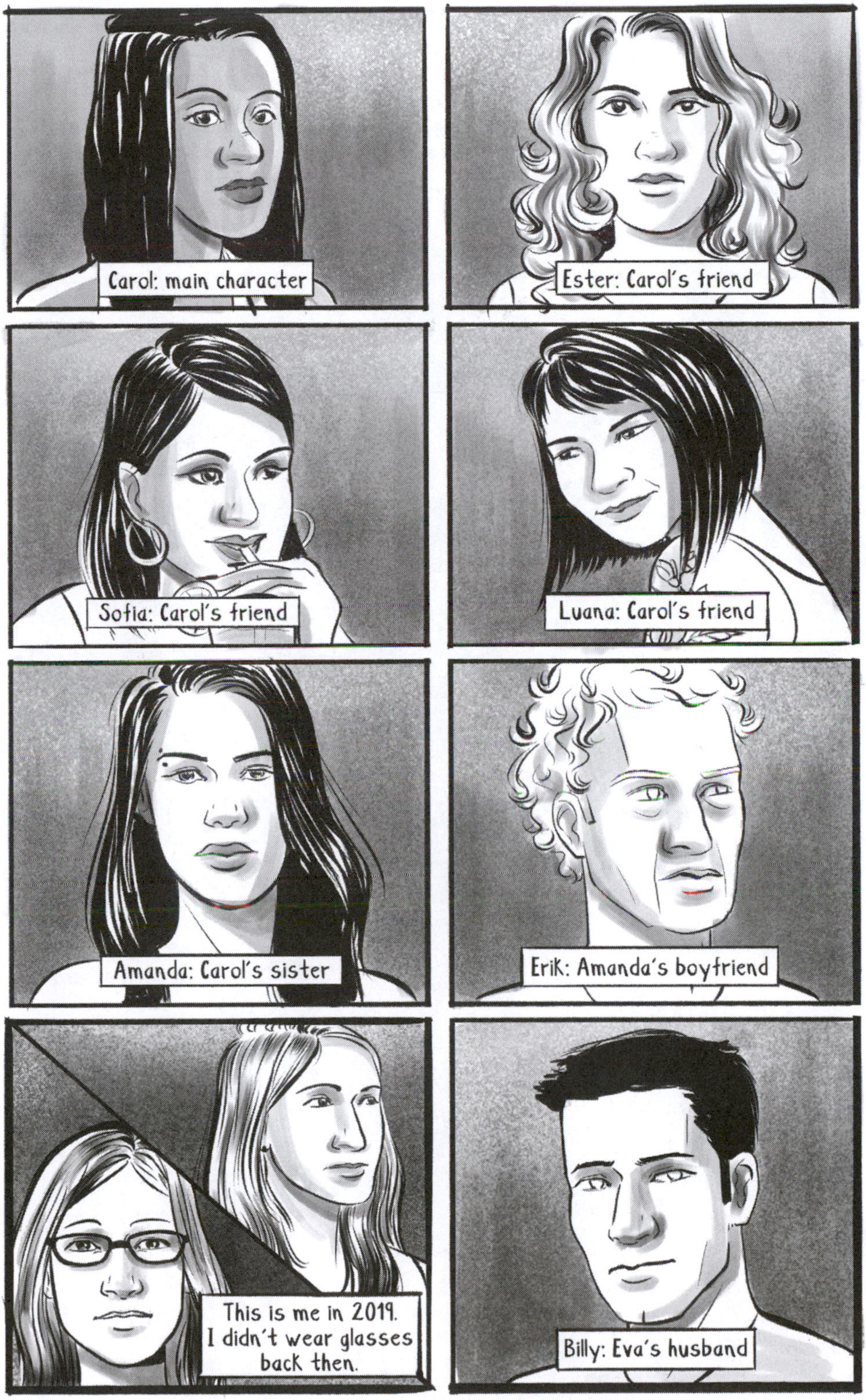
Carol: main character
Ester: Carol's friend
Sofia: Carol's friend
Luana: Carol's friend
Amanda: Carol's sister
Erik: Amanda's boyfriend
This is me in 2019. I didn't wear glasses back then.
Billy: Eva's husband

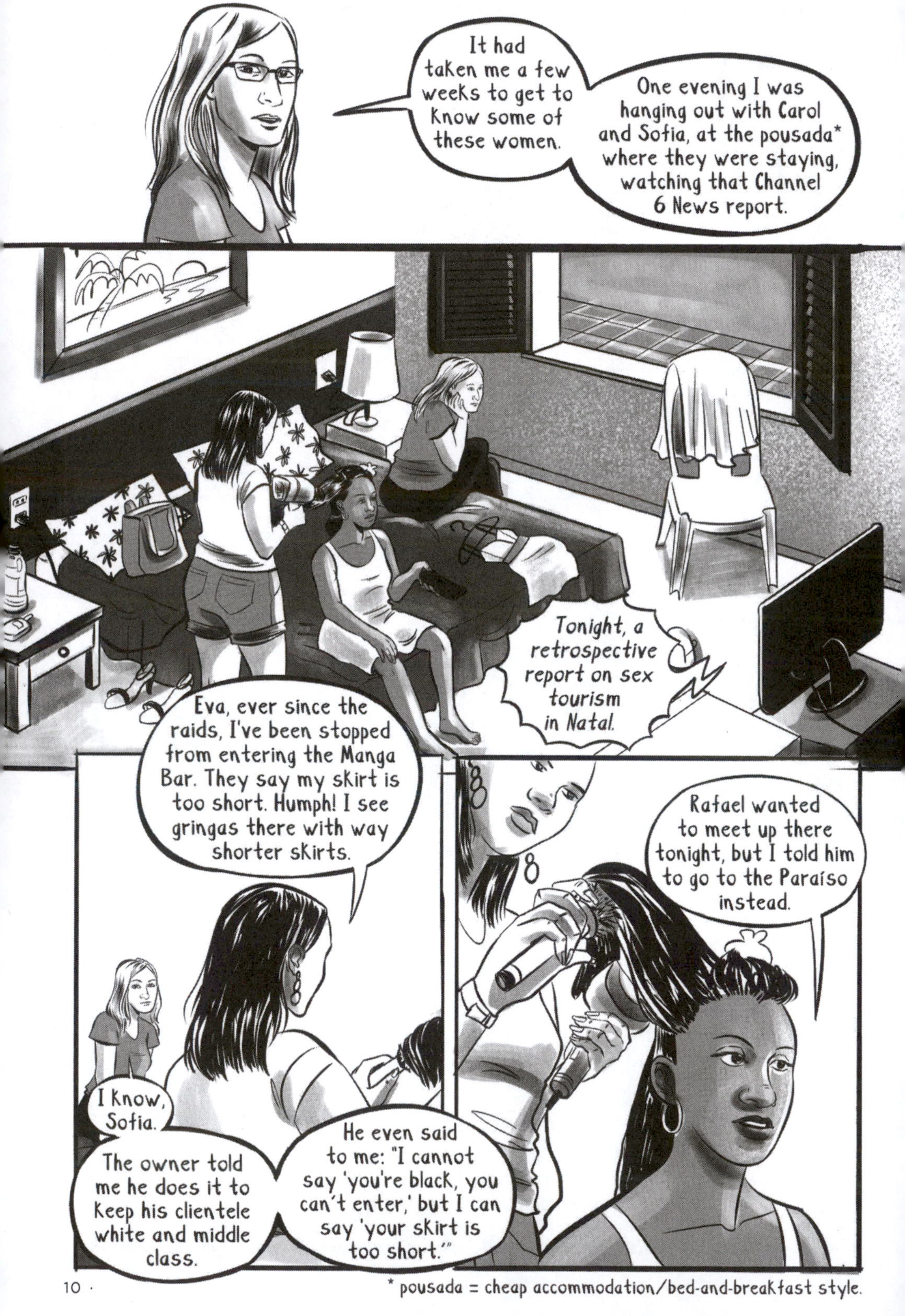
It had taken me a few weeks to get to know some of these women.
One evening I was hanging out with Carol and Sofia, at the pousada* where they were staying, watching that Channel 6 News report.
Tonight, a retrospective report on sex tourism in Natal.
Eva, ever since the raids, I've been stopped from entering the Manga Bar. They say my skirt is too short. Humph! I see gringas there with way shorter skirts.
Rafael wanted to meet up there tonight, but I told him to go to the Paraíso instead.
I know, Sofia.
The owner told me he does it to keep his clientele white and middle class.
He even said to me: "I cannot say 'you're black, you can't enter,' but I can say 'your skirt is too short.'"

* pousada = cheap accommodation/bed-and-breakfast style.

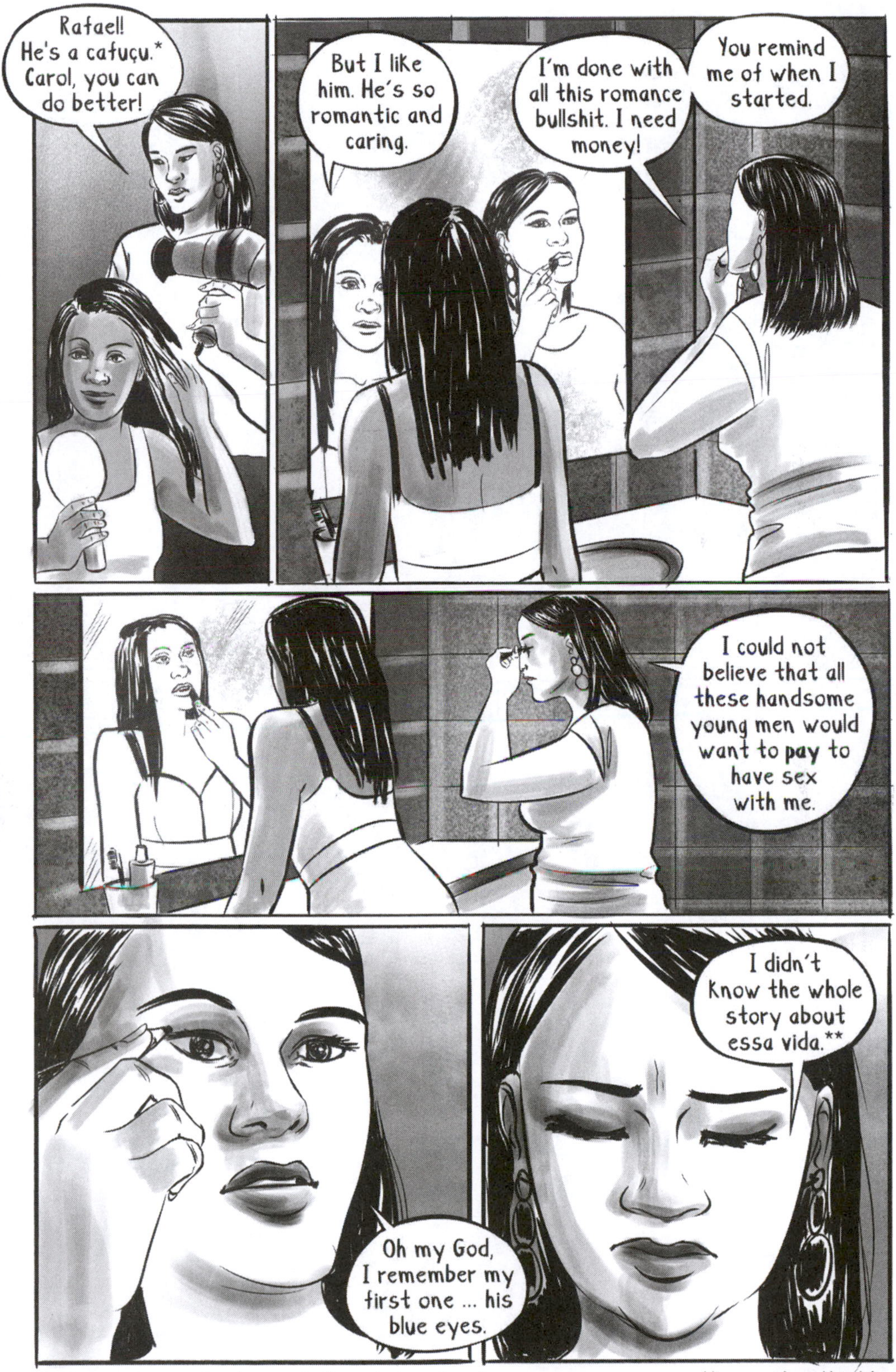
Rafael! He's a cafuçu.* Carol, you can do better!
But I like him. He's so romantic and caring.
I'm done with all this romance bullshit. I need money!
You remind me of when I started.
I could not believe that all these handsome young men would want to **pay** to have sex with me.
Oh my God, I remember my first one ... his blue eyes.
I didn't know the whole story about essa vida.**

*cafuçu = cheap and rude man (colloquial, slang term)

**essa vida = this life

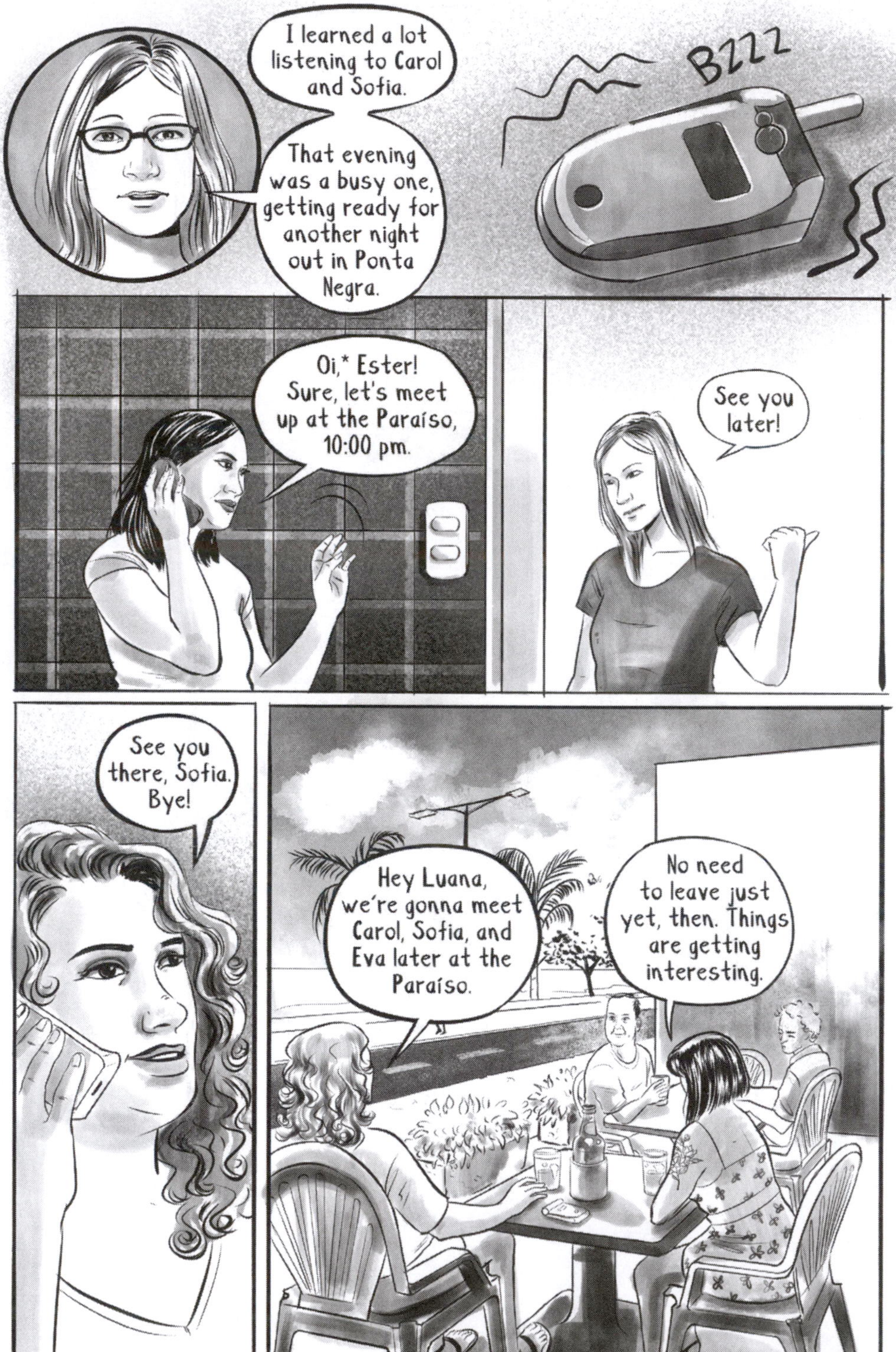
I learned a lot listening to Carol and Sofia.
That evening was a busy one, getting ready for another night out in Ponta Negra.
BZZZ
Oi,* Ester! Sure, let's meet up at the Paraíso, 10:00 pm.
See you later!
See you there, Sofia. Bye!
Hey Luana, we're gonna meet Carol, Sofia, and Eva later at the Paraíso.
No need to leave just yet, then. Things are getting interesting.

*Oi = hi

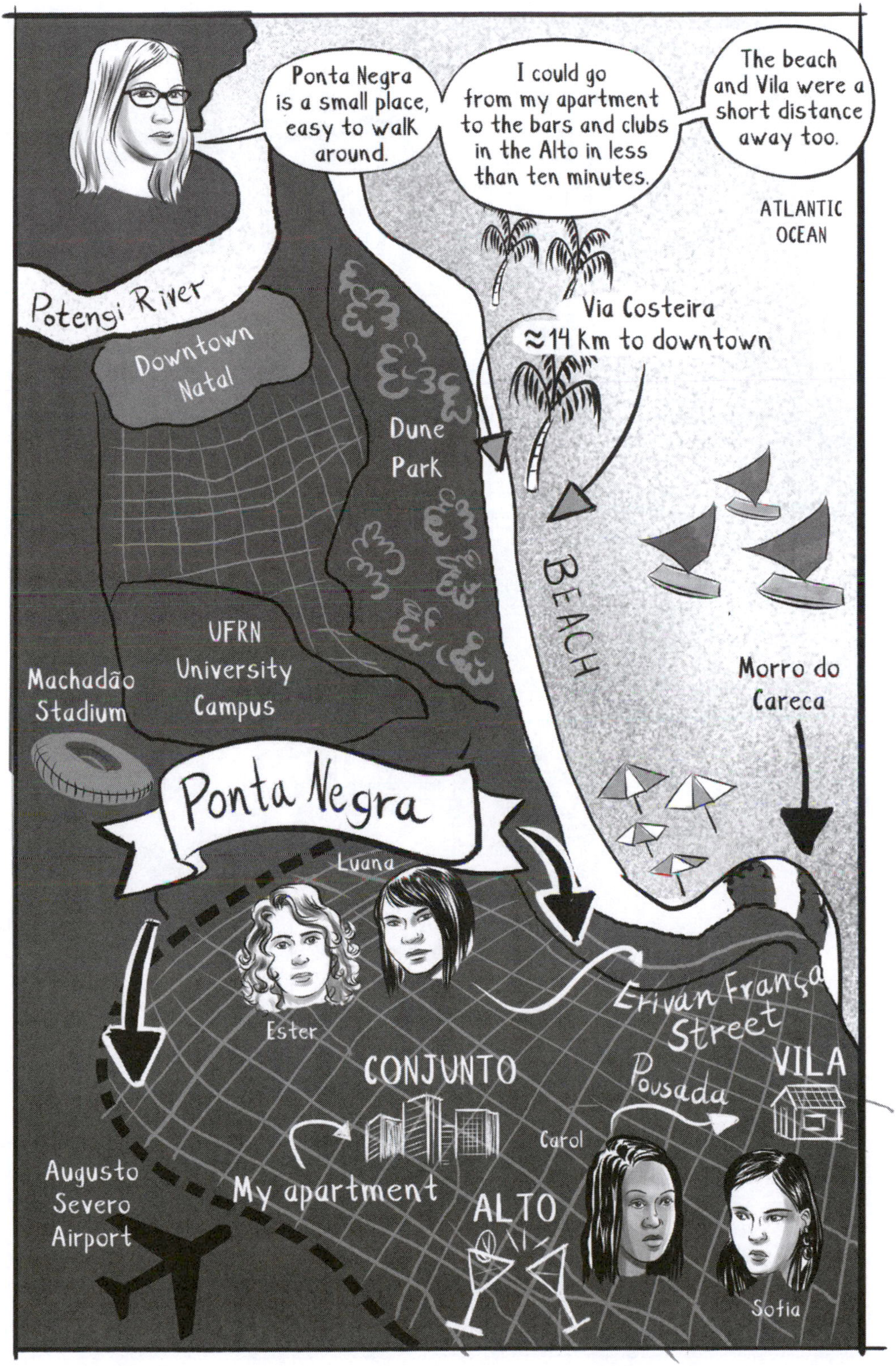
Ponta Negra is a small place, easy to walk around.
I could go from my apartment to the bars and clubs in the Alto in less than ten minutes.
The beach and Vila were a short distance away too.
ATLANTIC OCEAN
Potengi River
Downtown Natal
Dune Park
Via Costeira ≈14 Km to downtown
BEACH
UFRN University Campus
Machadão Stadium
Morro do Careca
Ponta Negra
Luana
Ester
Erivan França Street
CONJUNTO
Pousada
VILA
Carol
My apartment
ALTO
Augusto Severo Airport
Sofia

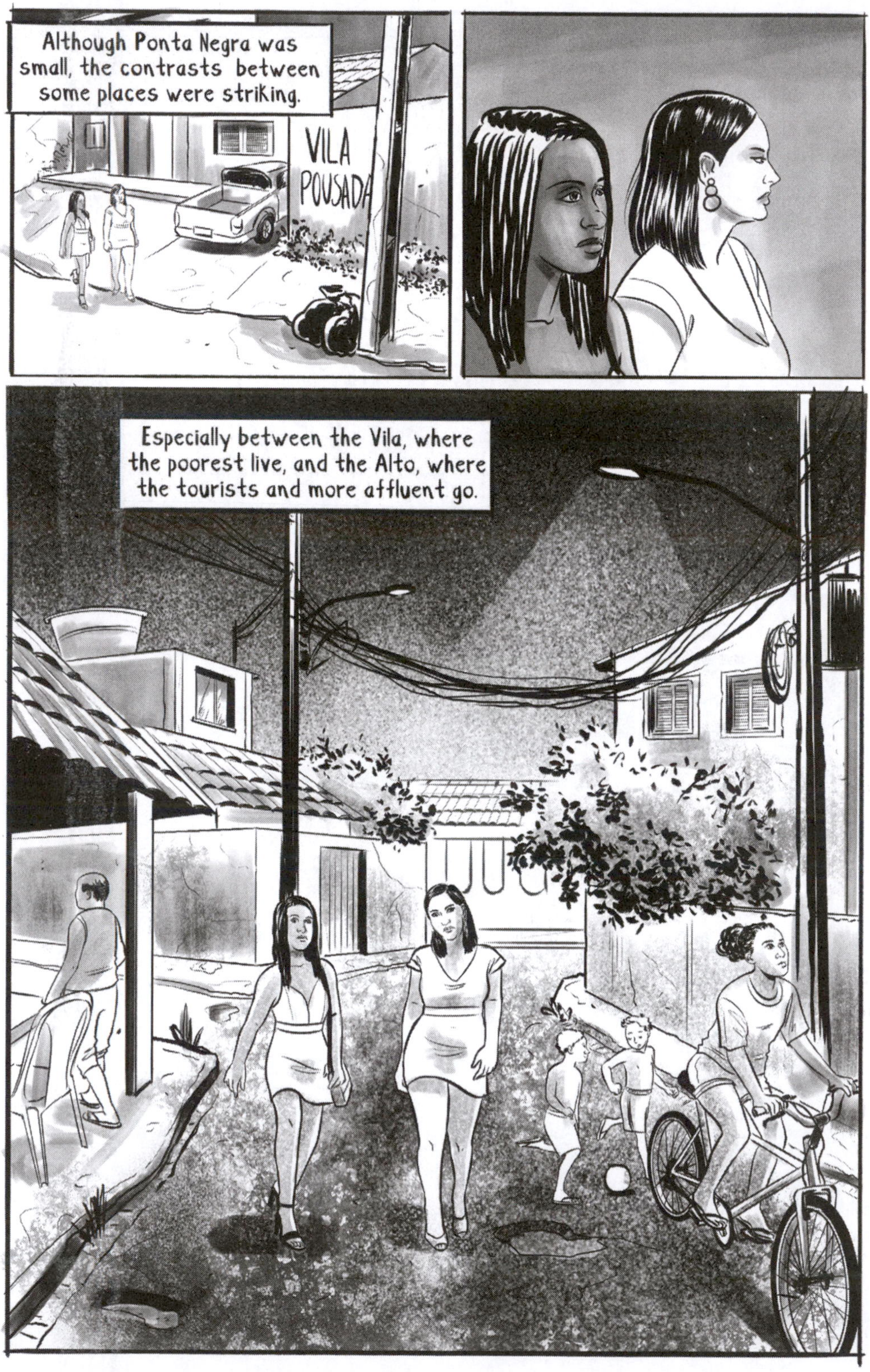
Although Ponta Negra was small, the contrasts between some places were striking.
VILA POUSADA
Especially between the Vila, where the poorest live, and the Alto, where the tourists and more affluent go.

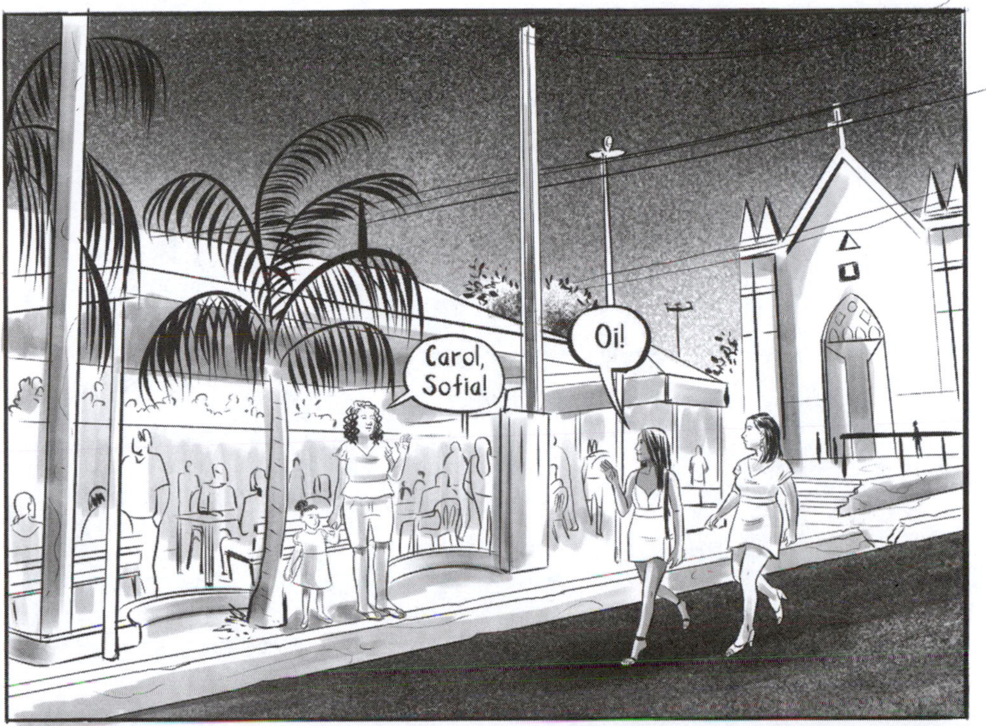
Carol, Sofia!
Oi!

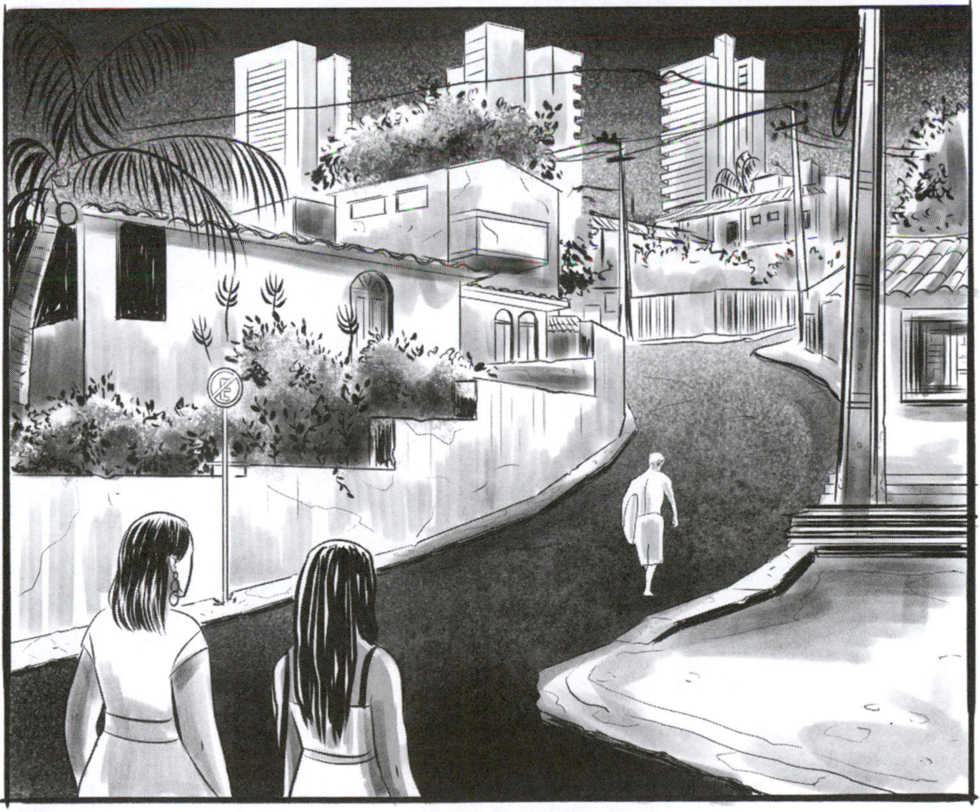

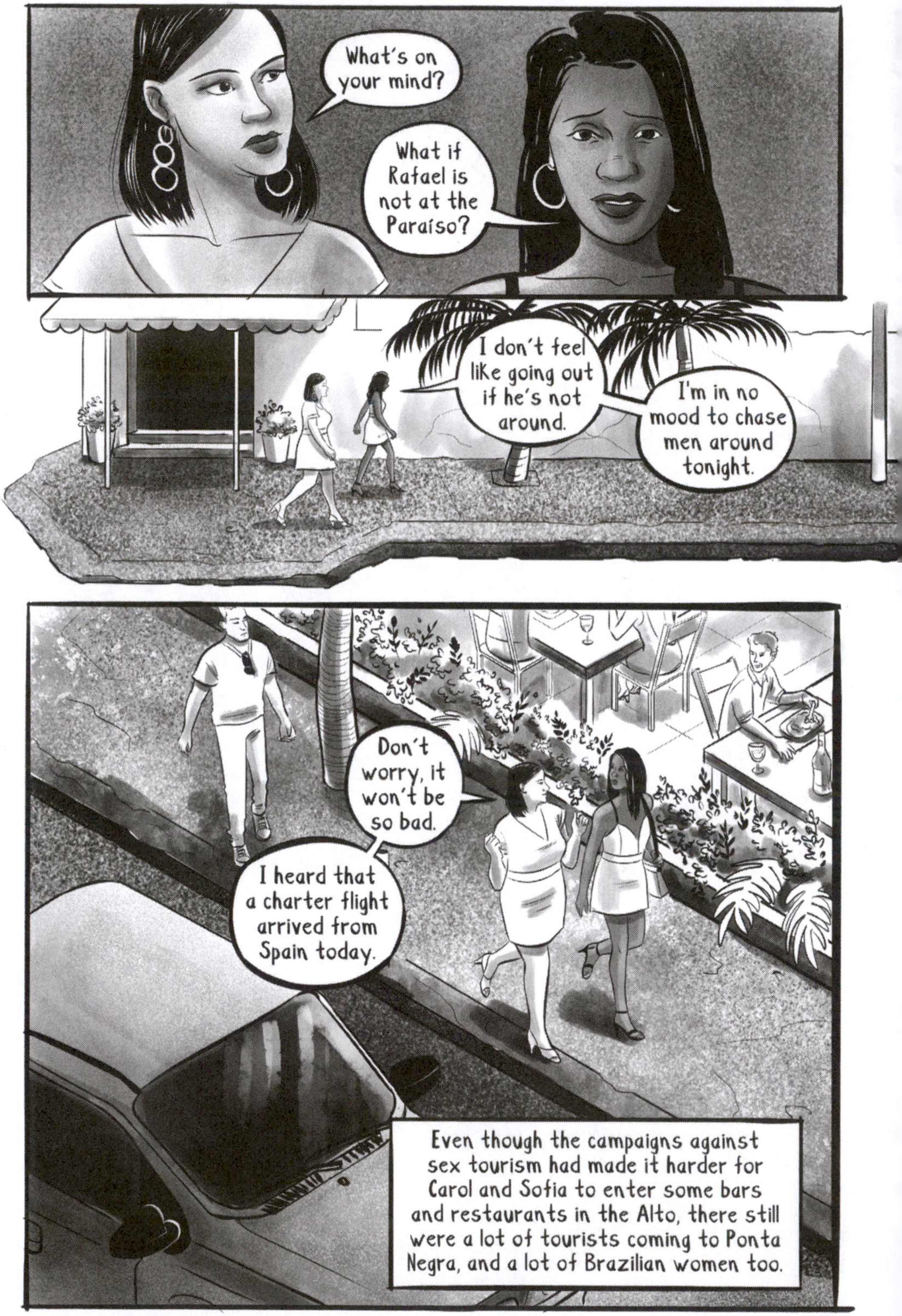
What's on your mind?
What if Rafael is not at the Paraíso?
I don't feel like going out if he's not around.
I'm in no mood to chase men around tonight.
Don't worry, it won't be so bad.
I heard that a charter flight arrived from Spain today.
Even though the campaigns against sex tourism had made it harder for Carol and Sofia to enter some bars and restaurants in the Alto, there still were a lot of tourists coming to Ponta Negra, and a lot of Brazilian women too.

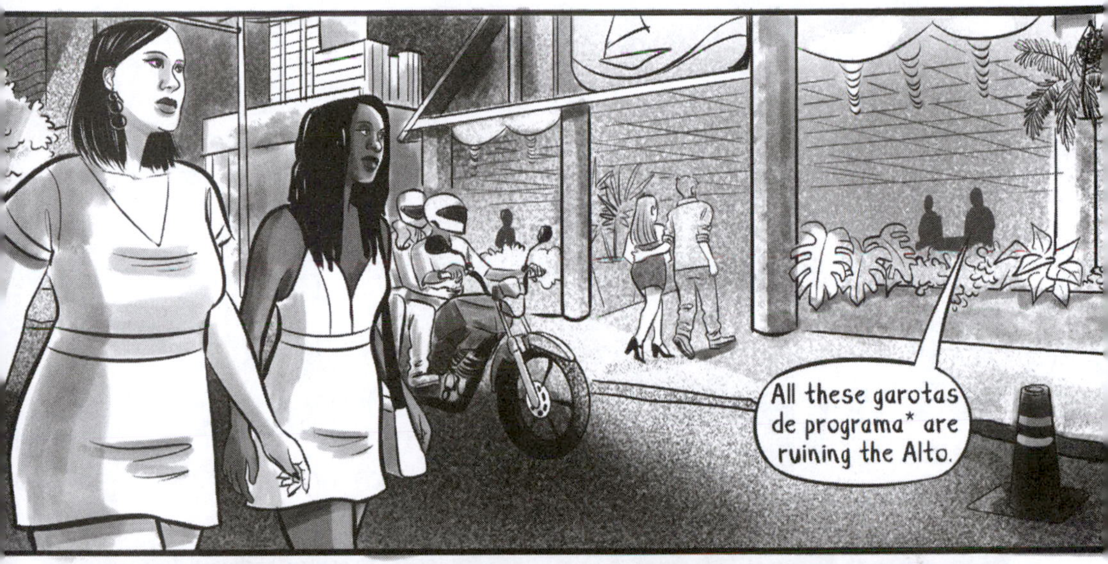
All these garotas de programa* are ruining the Alto.

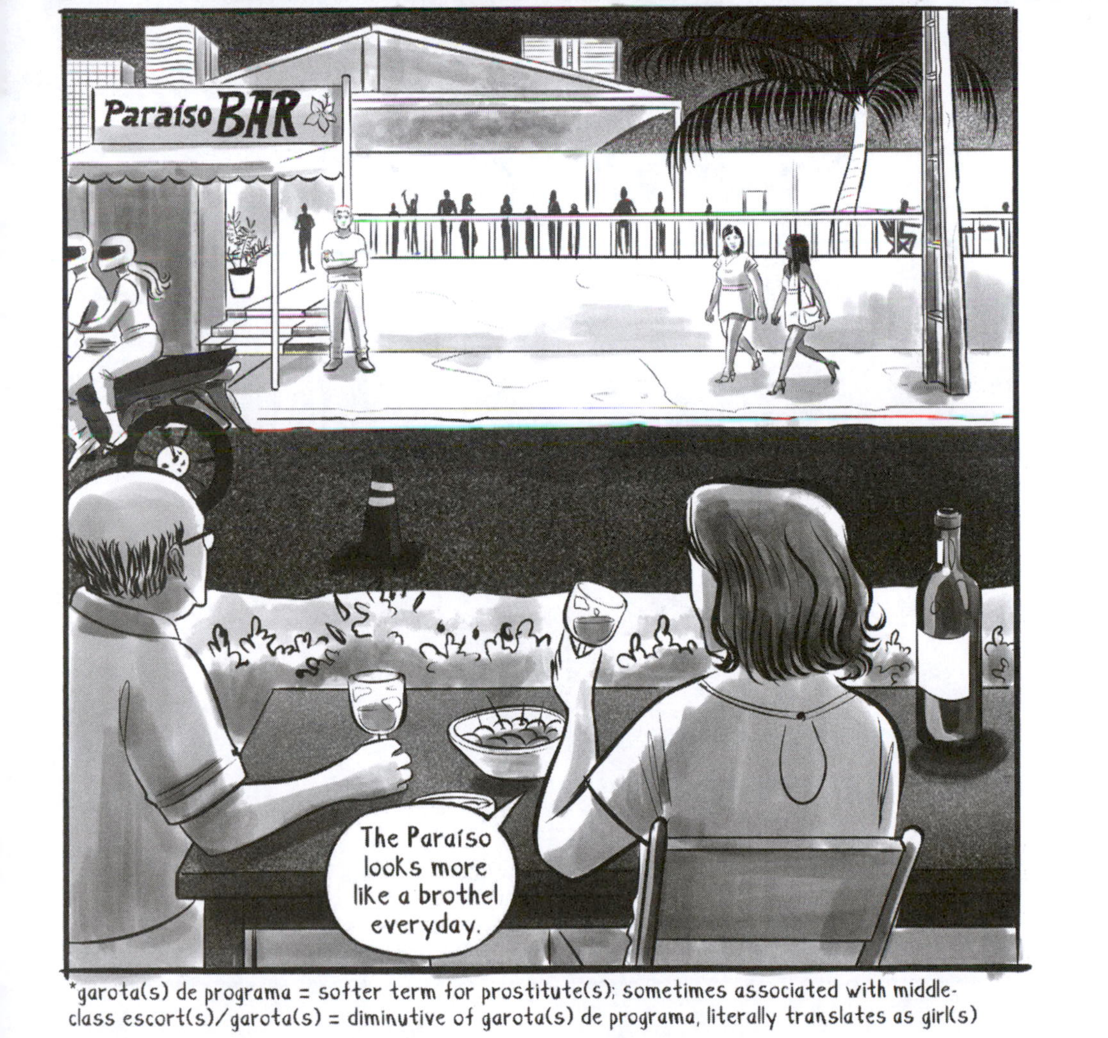
Paraíso BAR
The Paraíso looks more like a brothel everyday.

*garota(s) de programa = softer term for prostitute(s); sometimes associated with middle-class escort(s)/garota(s) = diminutive of garota(s) de programa, literally translates as girl(s)

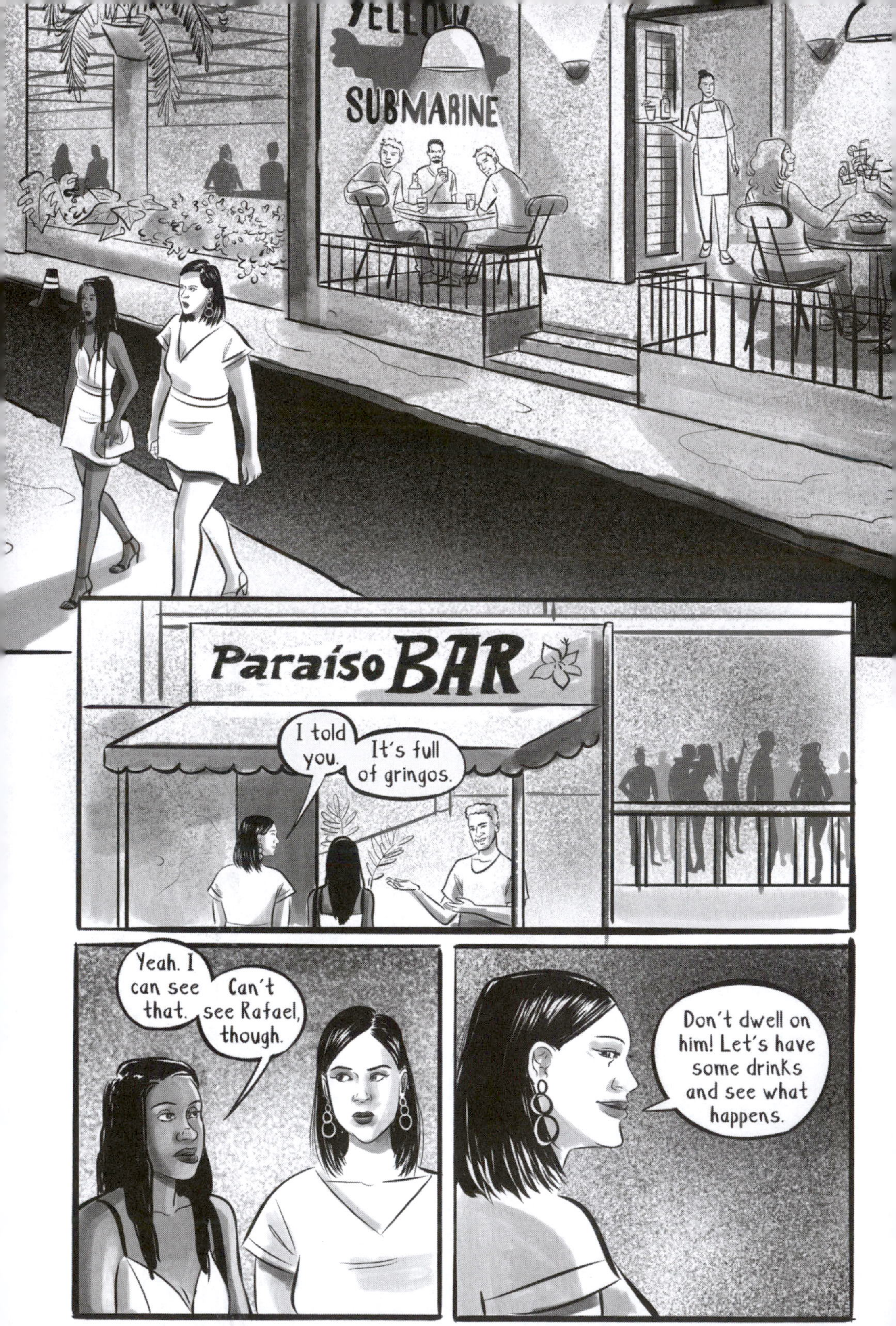
SUBMARINE
Paraíso BAR
I told you.
It's full of gringos.
Yeah. I can see that.
Can't see Rafael, though.
Don't dwell on him! Let's have some drinks and see what happens.

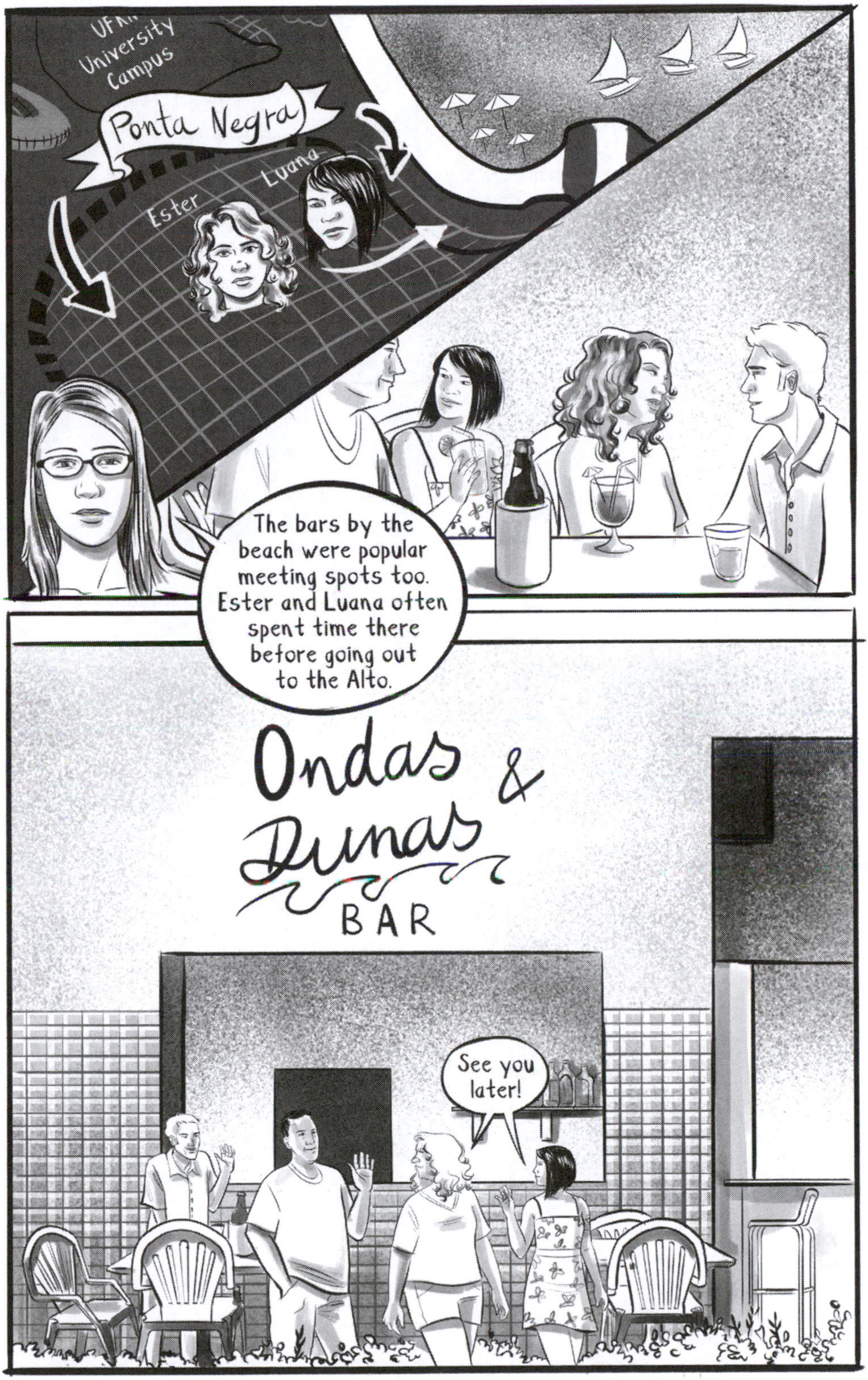
UFRN University Campus
Ponta Negra
Luana
Ester
The bars by the beach were popular meeting spots too. Ester and Luana often spent time there before going out to the Alto.
Ondas & Dunas BAR
See you later!

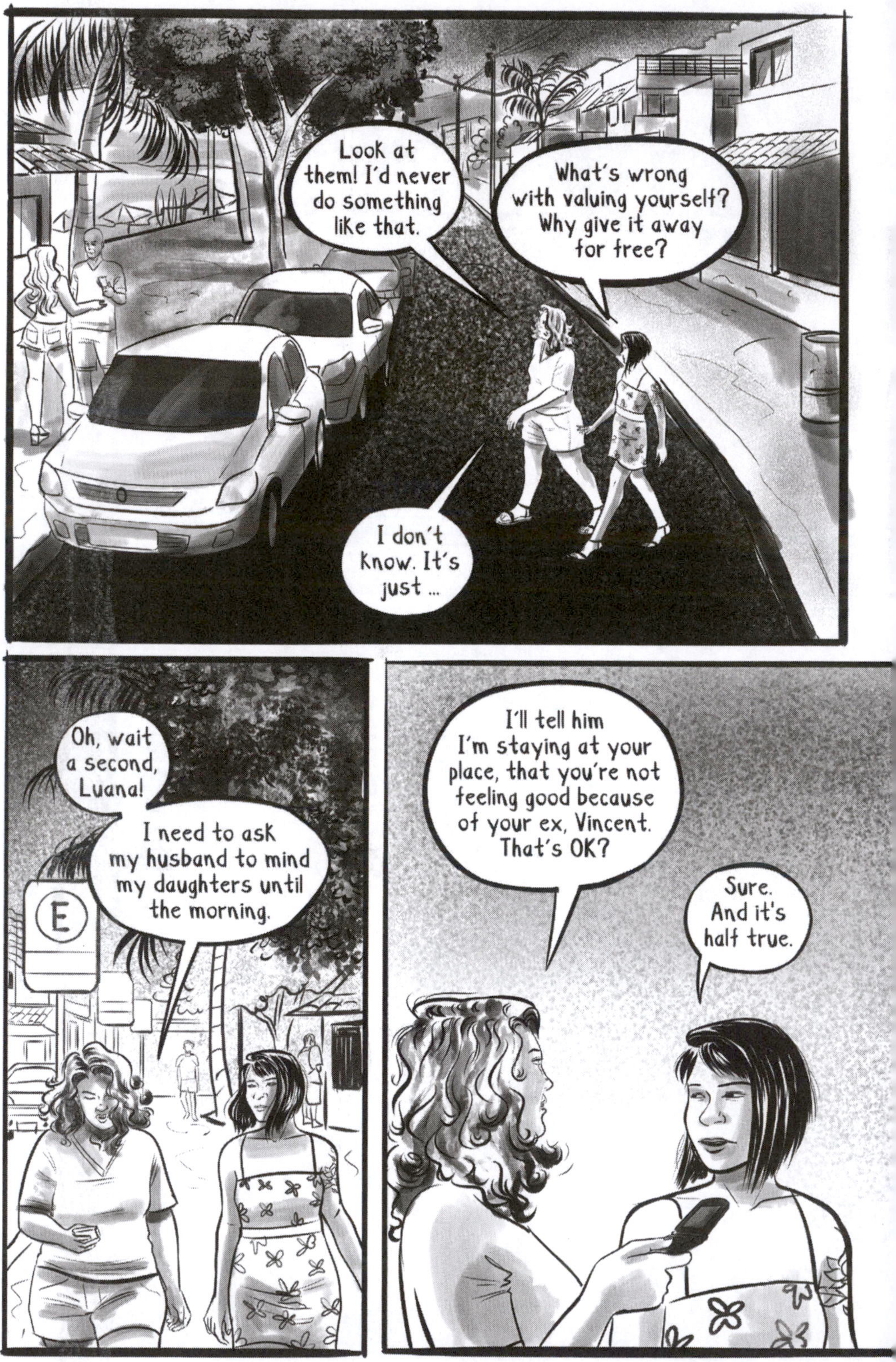

Look at them! I'd never do something like that.
What's wrong with valuing yourself? Why give it away for free?
I don't know. It's just ...
Oh, wait a second, Luana!
I need to ask my husband to mind my daughters until the morning.
E
I'll tell him I'm staying at your place, that you're not feeling good because of your ex, Vincent. That's OK?
Sure. And it's half true.

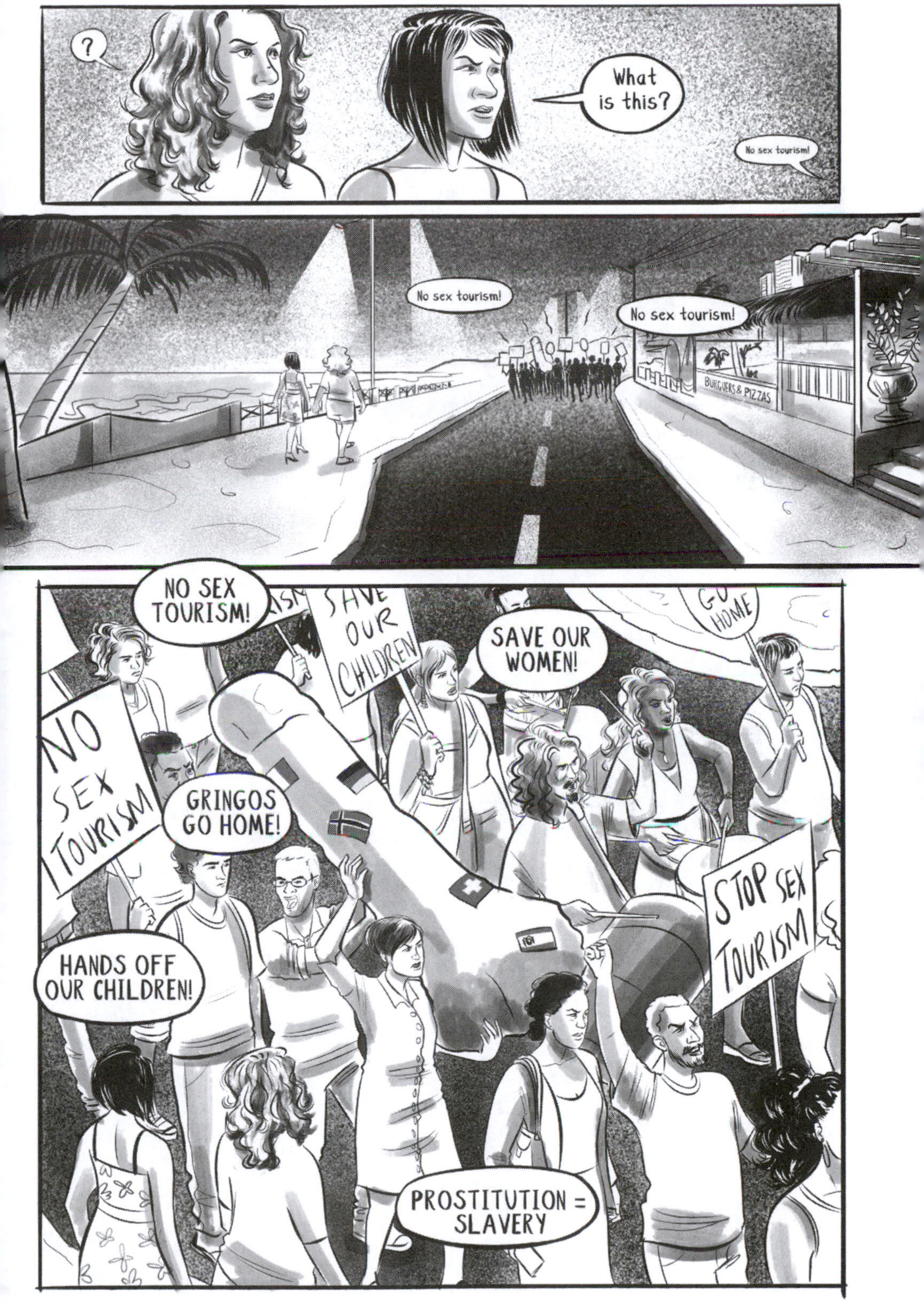
?
What is this?
No sex tourism!
No sex tourism!
No sex tourism!
NO SEX TOURISM!
SAVE OUR CHILDREN
SAVE OUR WOMEN!
GO HOME
NO SEX TOURISM
GRINGOS GO HOME!
STOP SEX TOURISM
HANDS OFF OUR CHILDREN!
PROSTITUTION = SLAVERY
BURGUERS & PIZZAS

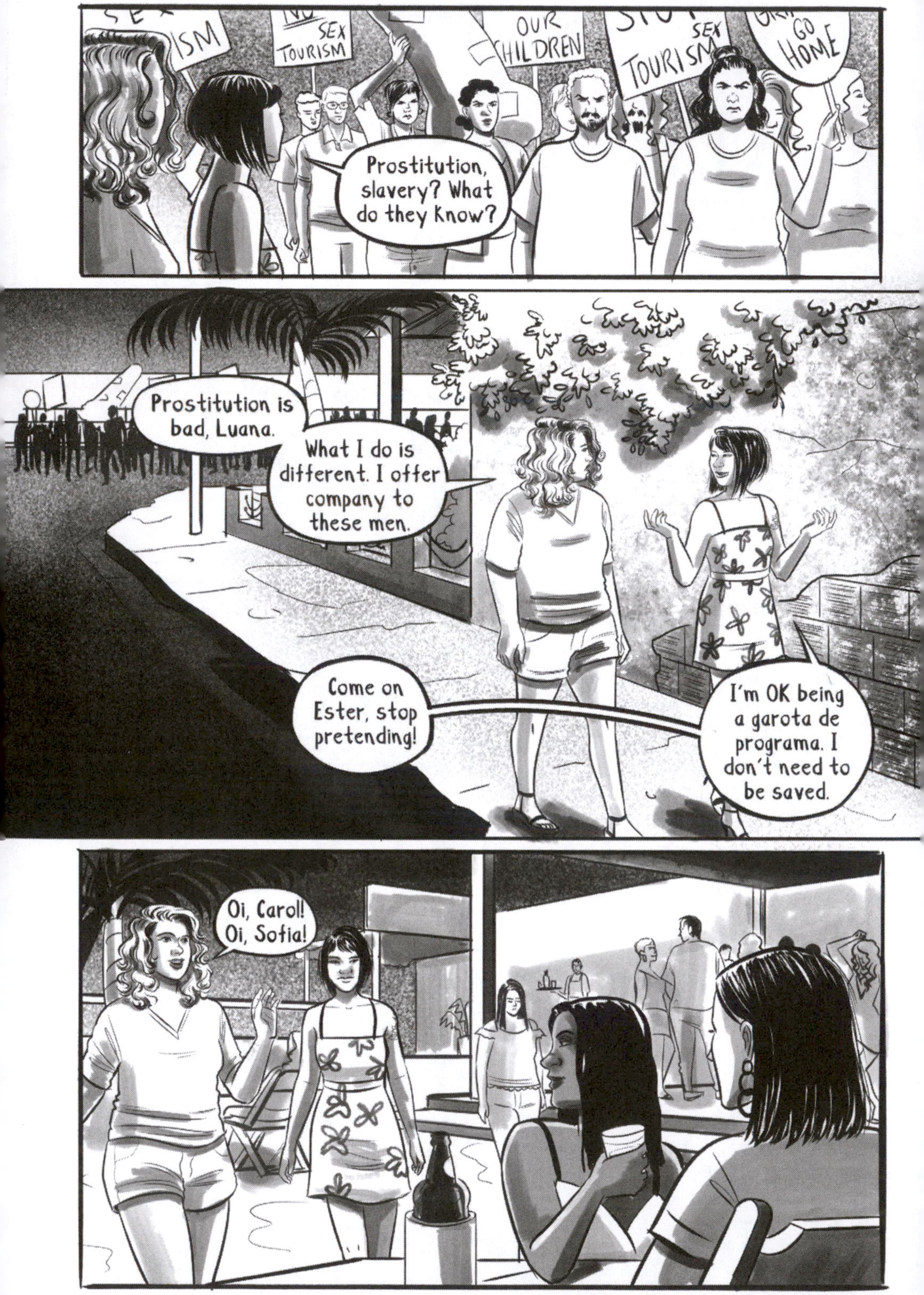
NO SEX TOURISM
OUR CHILDREN
SEX TOURISM
GO HOME
Prostitution, slavery? What do they know?
Prostitution is bad, Luana.
What I do is different. I offer company to these men.
Come on Ester, stop pretending!
I'm OK being a garota de programa. I don't need to be saved.
Oi, Carol! Oi, Sofia!

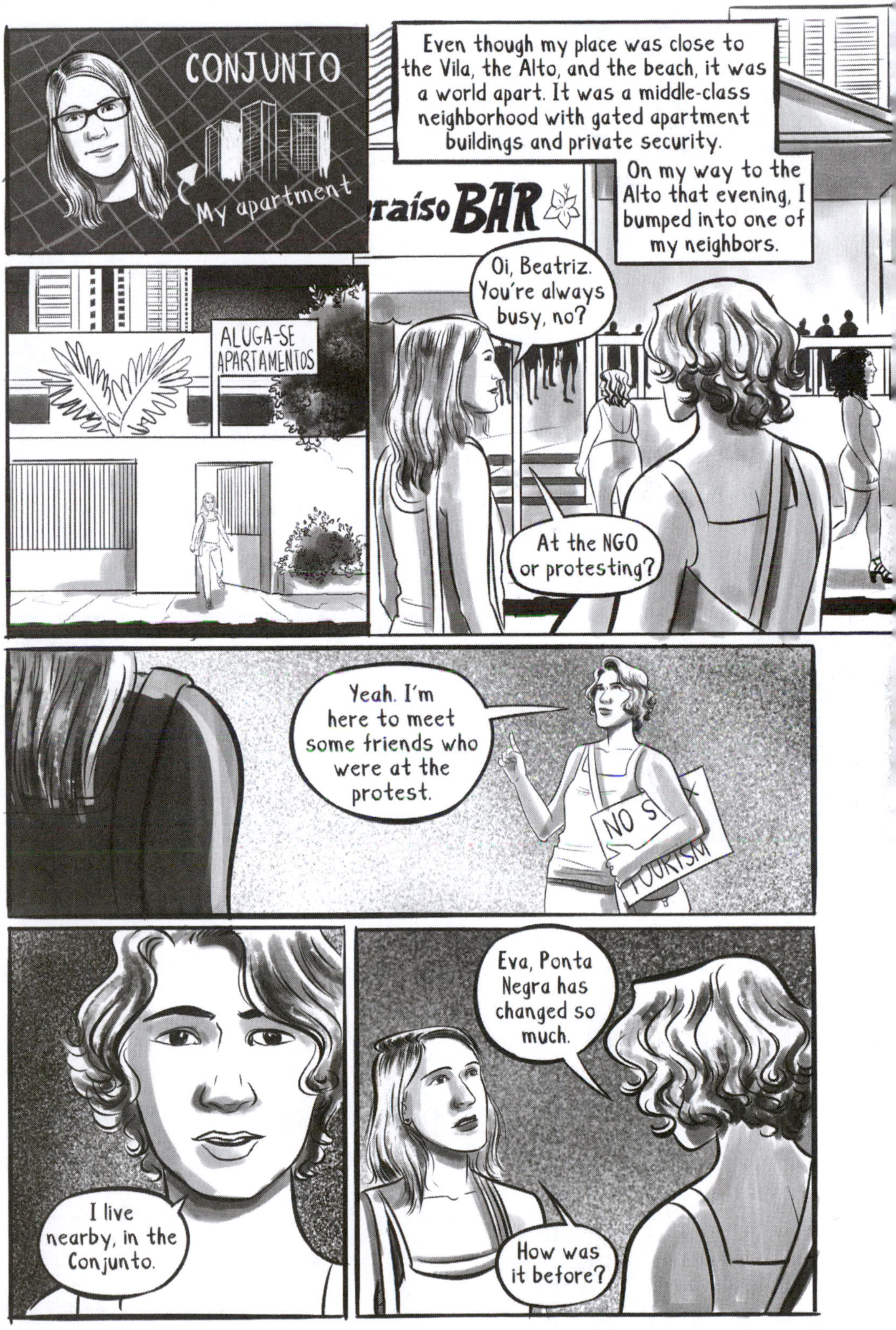
CONJUNTO
My apartment
Even though my place was close to the Vila, the Alto, and the beach, it was a world apart. It was a middle-class neighborhood with gated apartment buildings and private security.
raíso BAR
On my way to the Alto that evening, I bumped into one of my neighbors.
ALUGA-SE APARTAMENTOS
Oi, Beatriz. You're always busy, no?
At the NGO or protesting?
Yeah. I'm here to meet some friends who were at the protest.
TOURISM
I live nearby, in the Conjunto.
Eva, Ponta Negra has changed so much.
How was it before?

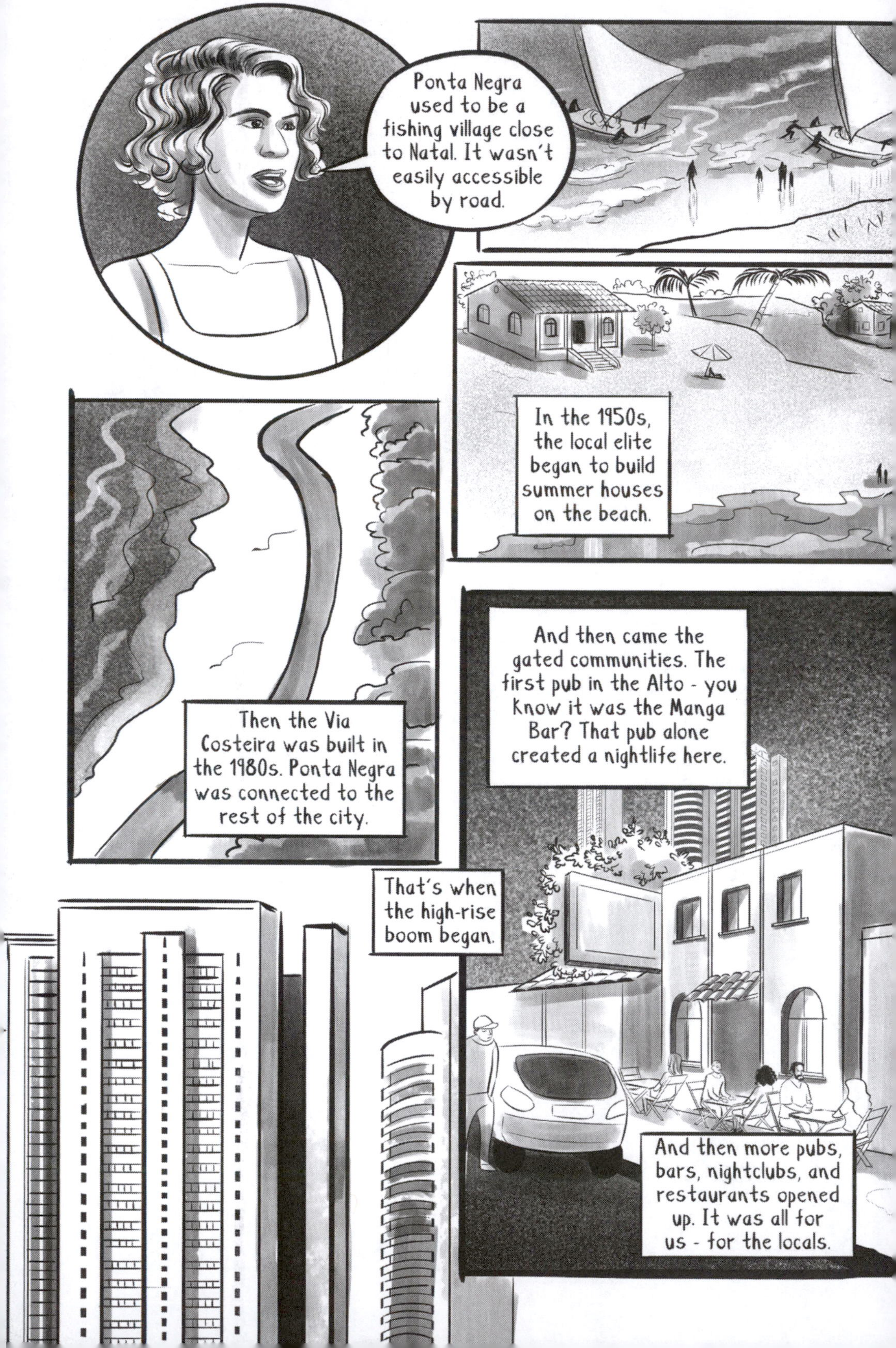
Ponta Negra used to be a fishing village close to Natal. It wasn't easily accessible by road.
In the 1950s, the local elite began to build summer houses on the beach.
Then the Via Costeira was built in the 1980s. Ponta Negra was connected to the rest of the city.
And then came the gated communities. The first pub in the Alto - you know it was the Manga Bar? That pub alone created a nightlife here.
That's when the high-rise boom began.
And then more pubs, bars, nightclubs, and restaurants opened up. It was all for us - for the locals.

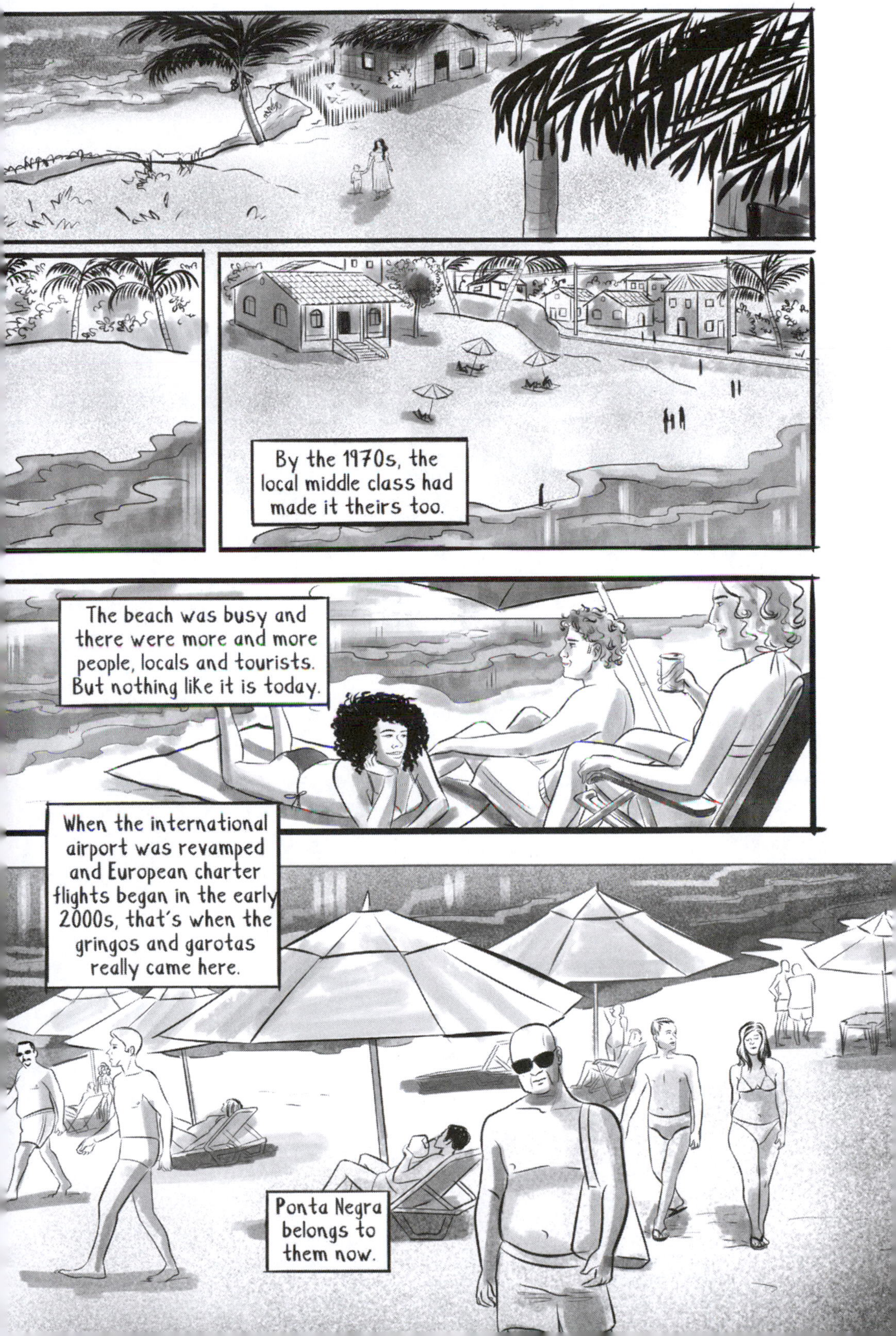
By the 1970s, the local middle class had made it theirs too.
The beach was busy and there were more and more people, locals and tourists. But nothing like it is today.
When the international airport was revamped and European charter flights began in the early 2000s, that's when the gringos and garotas really came here.
Ponta Negra belongs to them now.

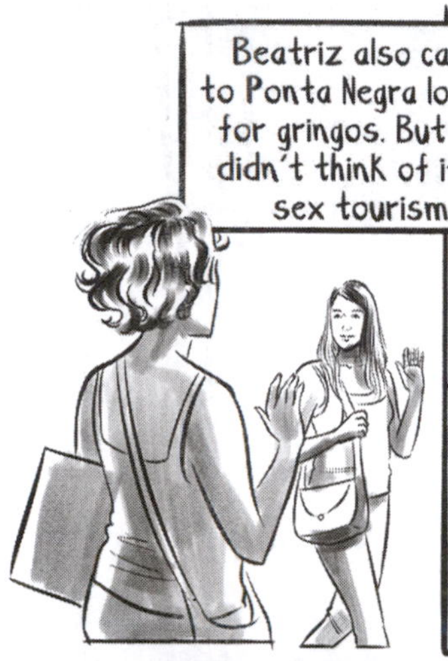
Beatriz also came to Ponta Negra looking for gringos. But she didn't think of it as sex tourism.

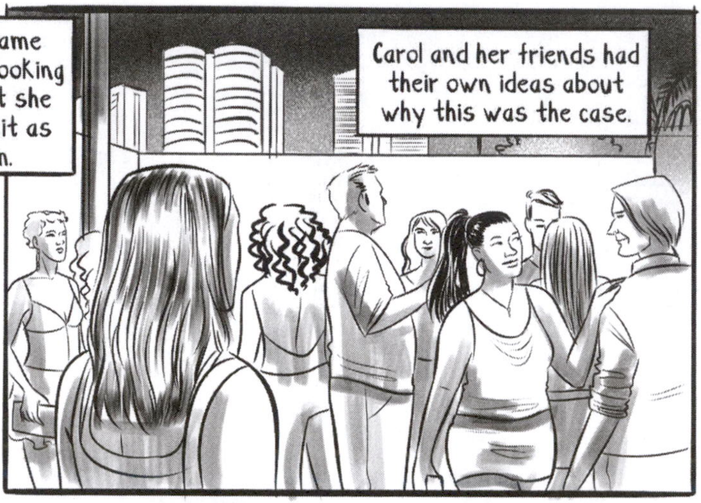
Carol and her friends had their own ideas about why this was the case.

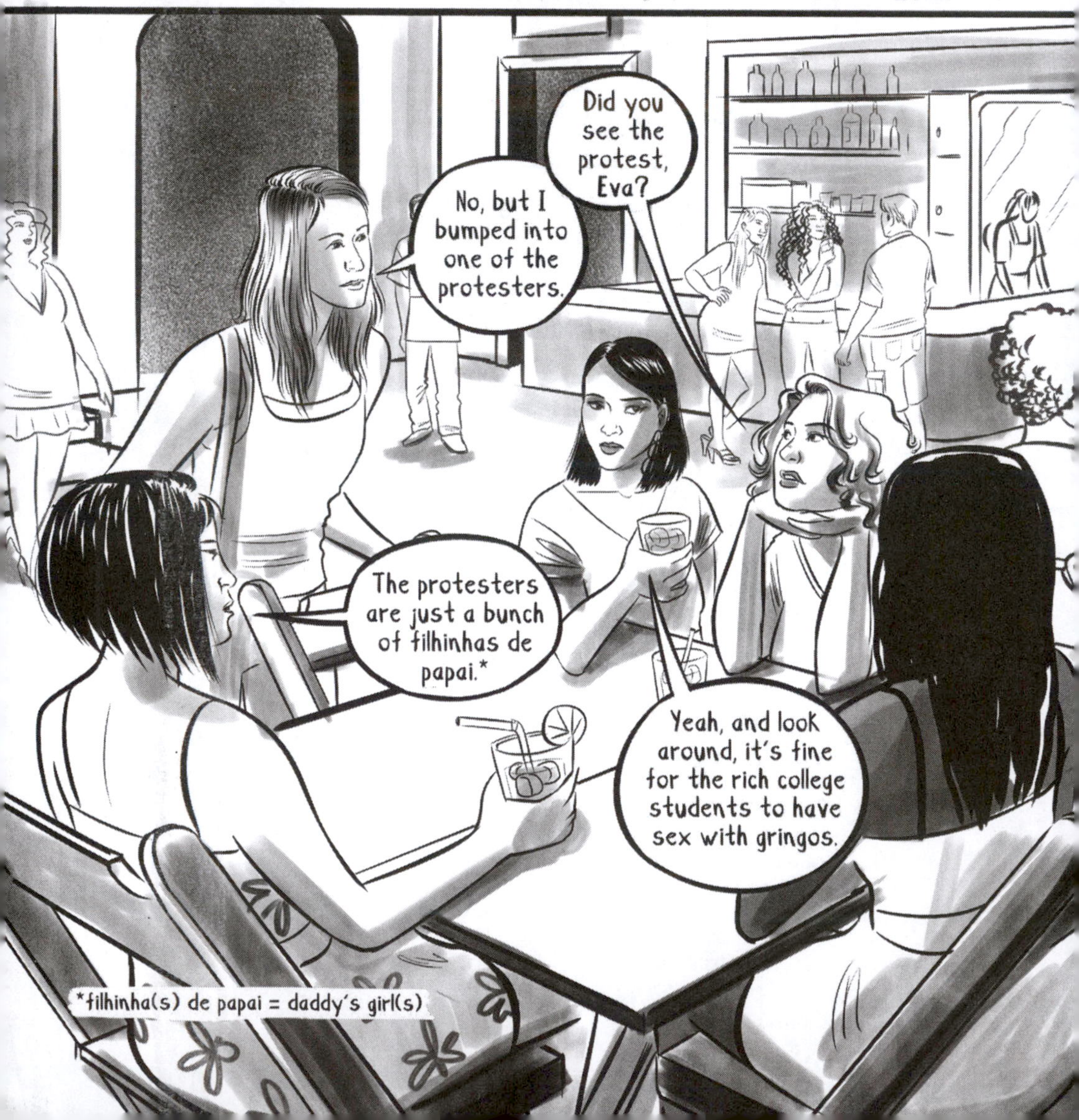
Did you see the protest, Eva?
No, but I bumped into one of the protesters.
The protesters are just a bunch of filhinhas de papai.*
Yeah, and look around, it's fine for the rich college students to have sex with gringos.
*filhinha(s) de papai = daddy's girl(s)

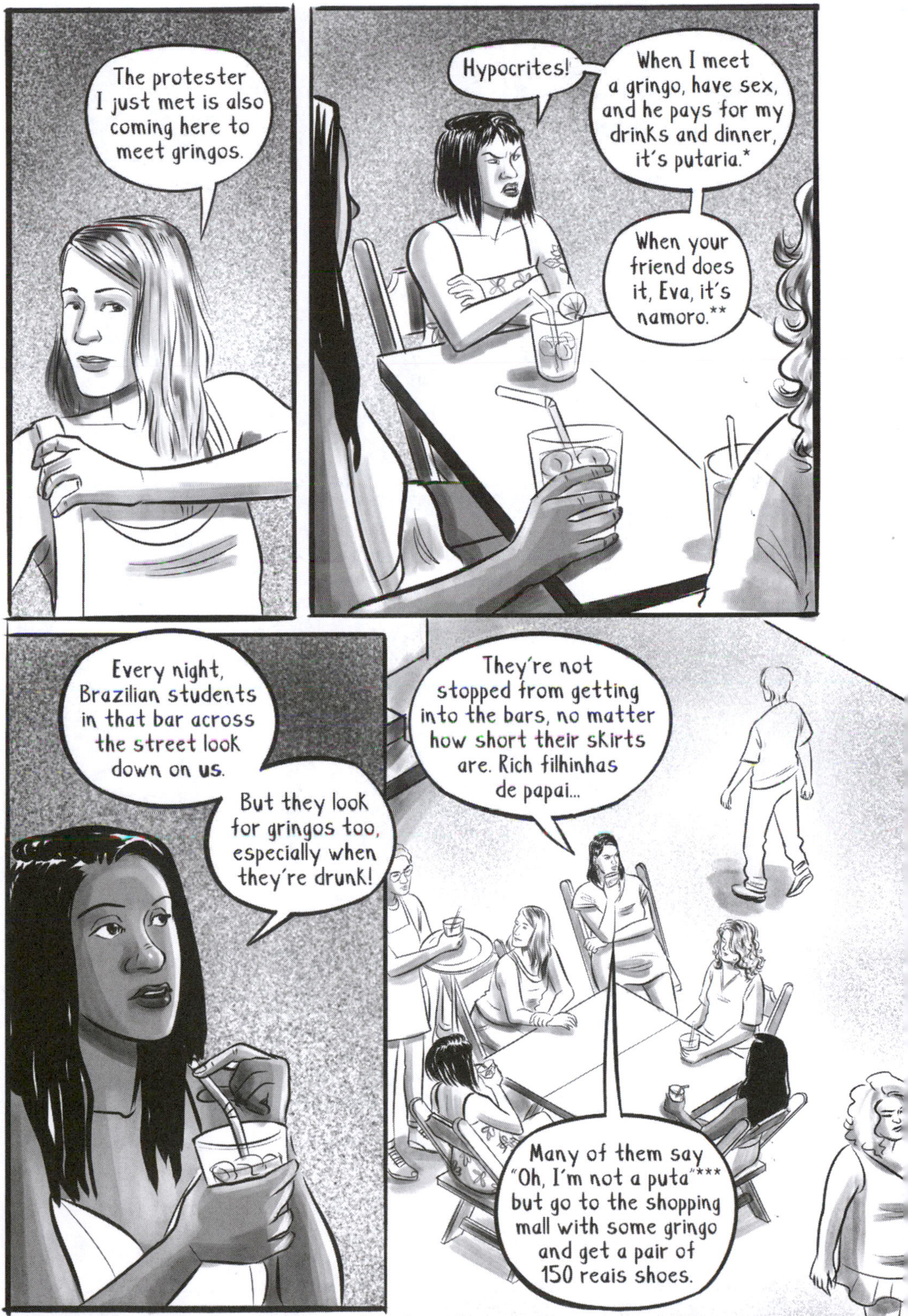
The protester I just met is also coming here to meet gringos.
Hypocrites!
When I meet a gringo, have sex, and he pays for my drinks and dinner, it's putaria.*
When your friend does it, Eva, it's namoro.**
Every night, Brazilian students in that bar across the street look down on us.
But they look for gringos too, especially when they're drunk!
They're not stopped from getting into the bars, no matter how short their skirts are. Rich filhinhas de papai...
Many of them say "Oh, I'm not a puta"*** but go to the shopping mall with some gringo and get a pair of 150 reais shoes.

*putaria = whoring, whoring around

**namoro = dating, courtship

***puta = whore

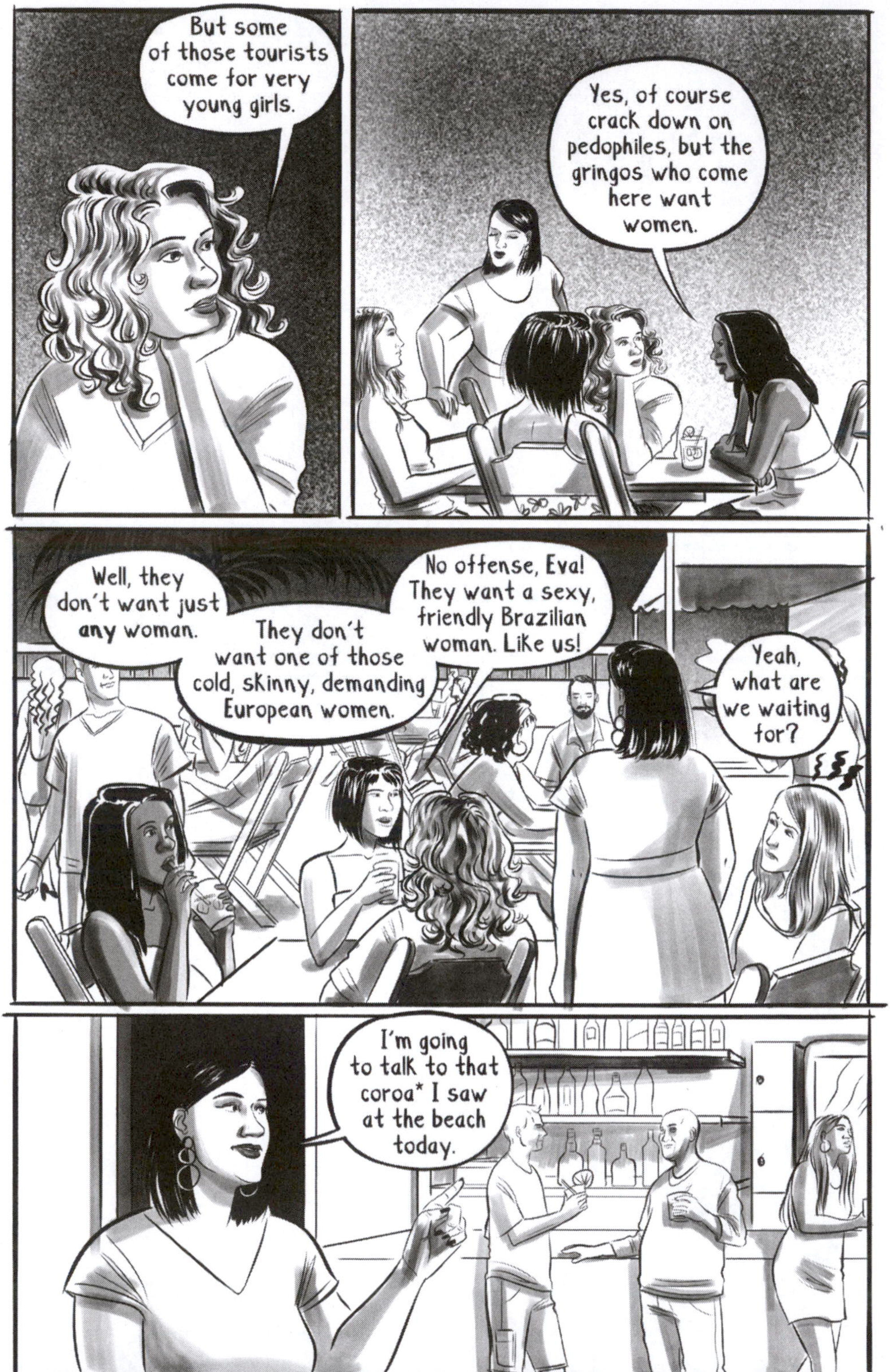
But some of those tourists come for very young girls.
Yes, of course crack down on pedophiles, but the gringos who come here want women.
Well, they don't want just any woman.
They don't want one of those cold, skinny, demanding European women.
No offense, Eva! They want a sexy, friendly Brazilian woman. Like us!
Yeah, what are we waiting for?
I'm going to talk to that coroa* I saw at the beach today.

*coroa = literally translates as crown; colloquially used to refer to an older, richer, whiter man. Close to a "sugar daddy."

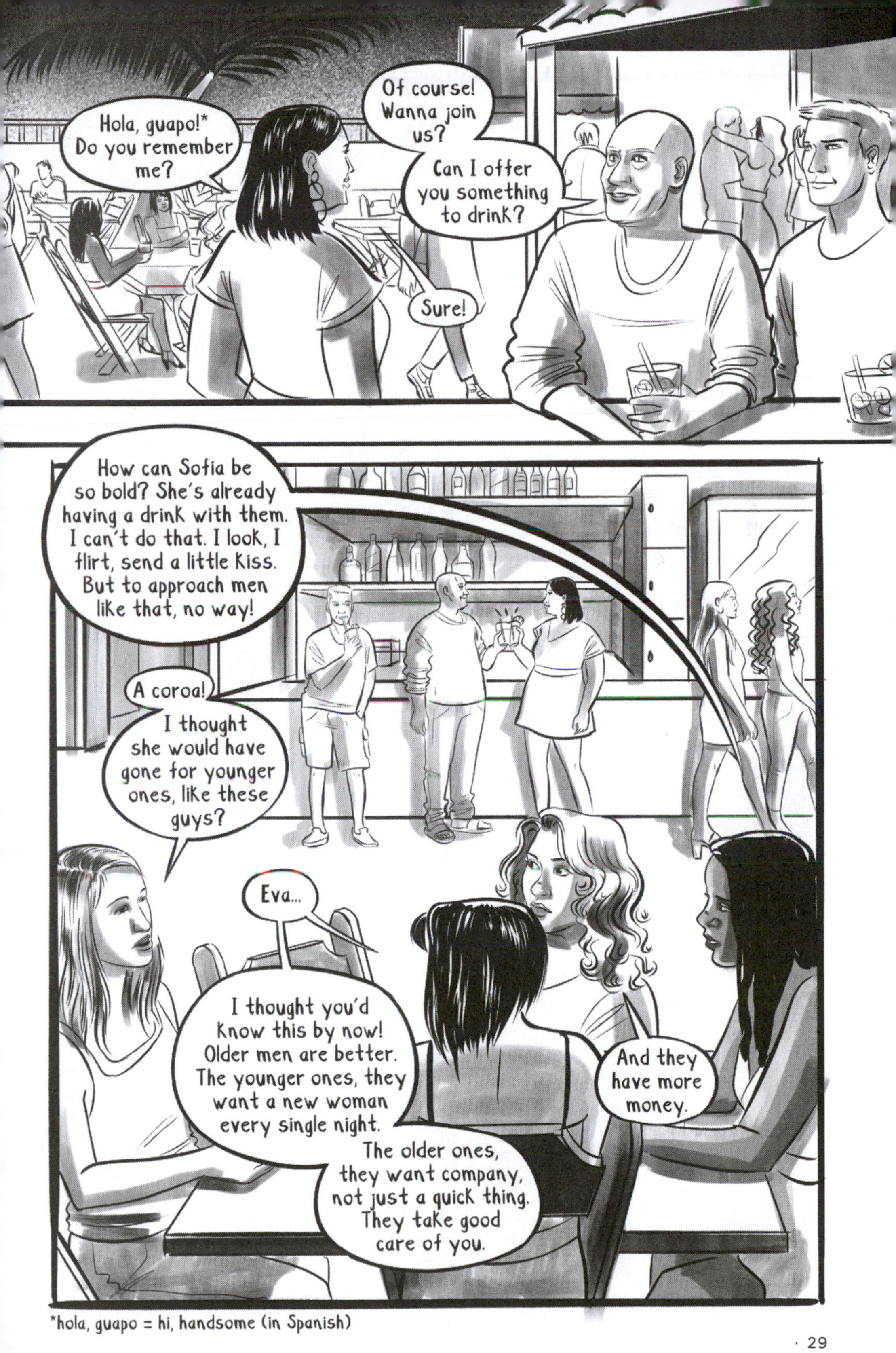

Hola, guapo!* Do you remember me?
Of course! Wanna join us?
Can I offer you something to drink?
Sure!
How can Sofia be so bold? She's already having a drink with them. I can't do that. I look, I flirt, send a little kiss. But to approach men like that, no way!
A coroa!
I thought she would have gone for younger ones, like these guys?
Eva...
I thought you'd know this by now! Older men are better. The younger ones, they want a new woman every single night.
The older ones, they want company, not just a quick thing. They take good care of you.
And they have more money.

*hola, guapo = hi, handsome (in Spanish)

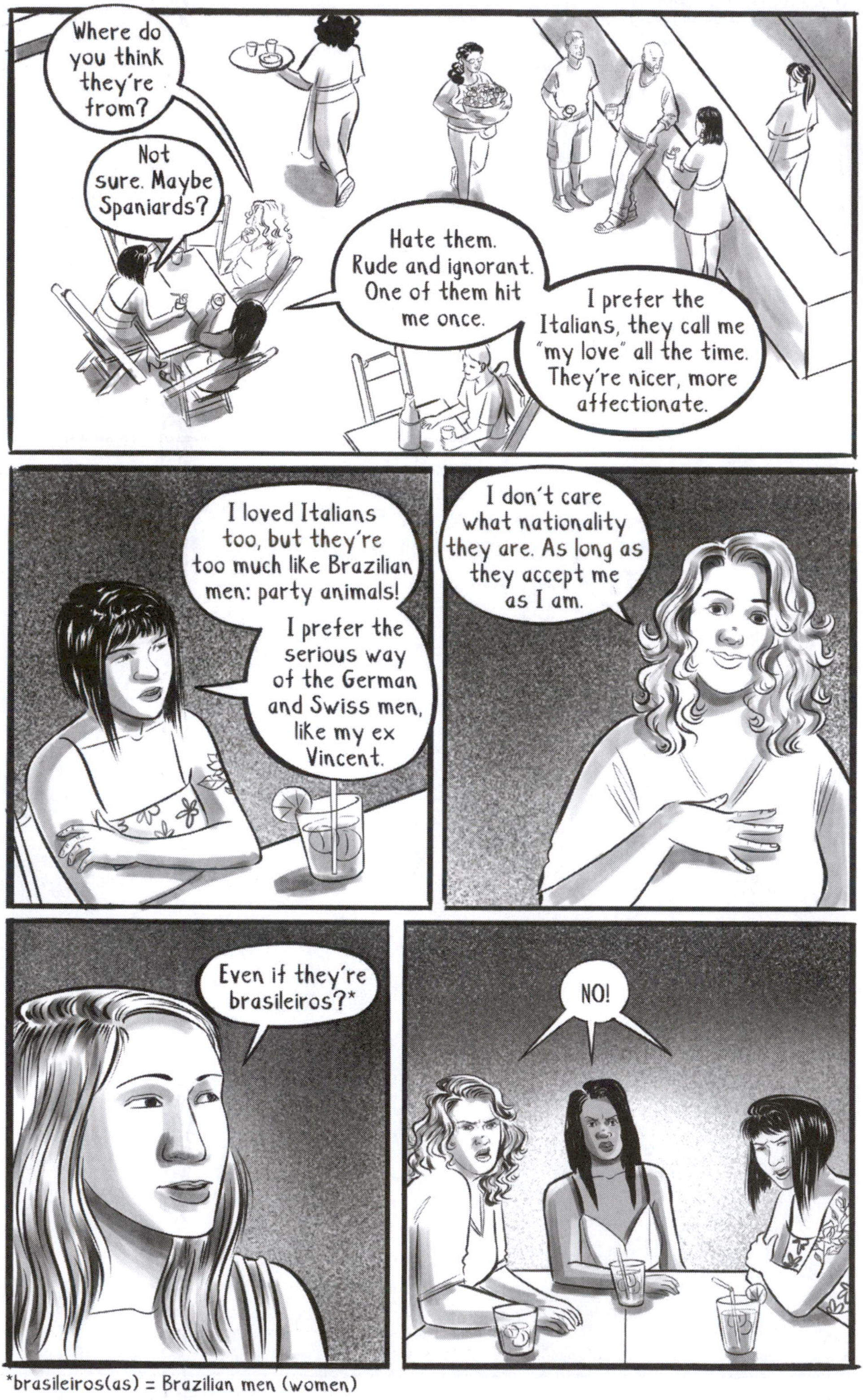
Where do you think they're from?
Not sure. Maybe Spaniards?
Hate them. Rude and ignorant. One of them hit me once.
I prefer the Italians, they call me "my love" all the time. They're nicer, more affectionate.
I loved Italians too, but they're too much like Brazilian men: party animals!
I prefer the serious way of the German and Swiss men, like my ex Vincent.
I don't care what nationality they are. As long as they accept me as I am.
Even if they're brasileiros?*
NO!

*brasileiros(as) = Brazilian men (women)

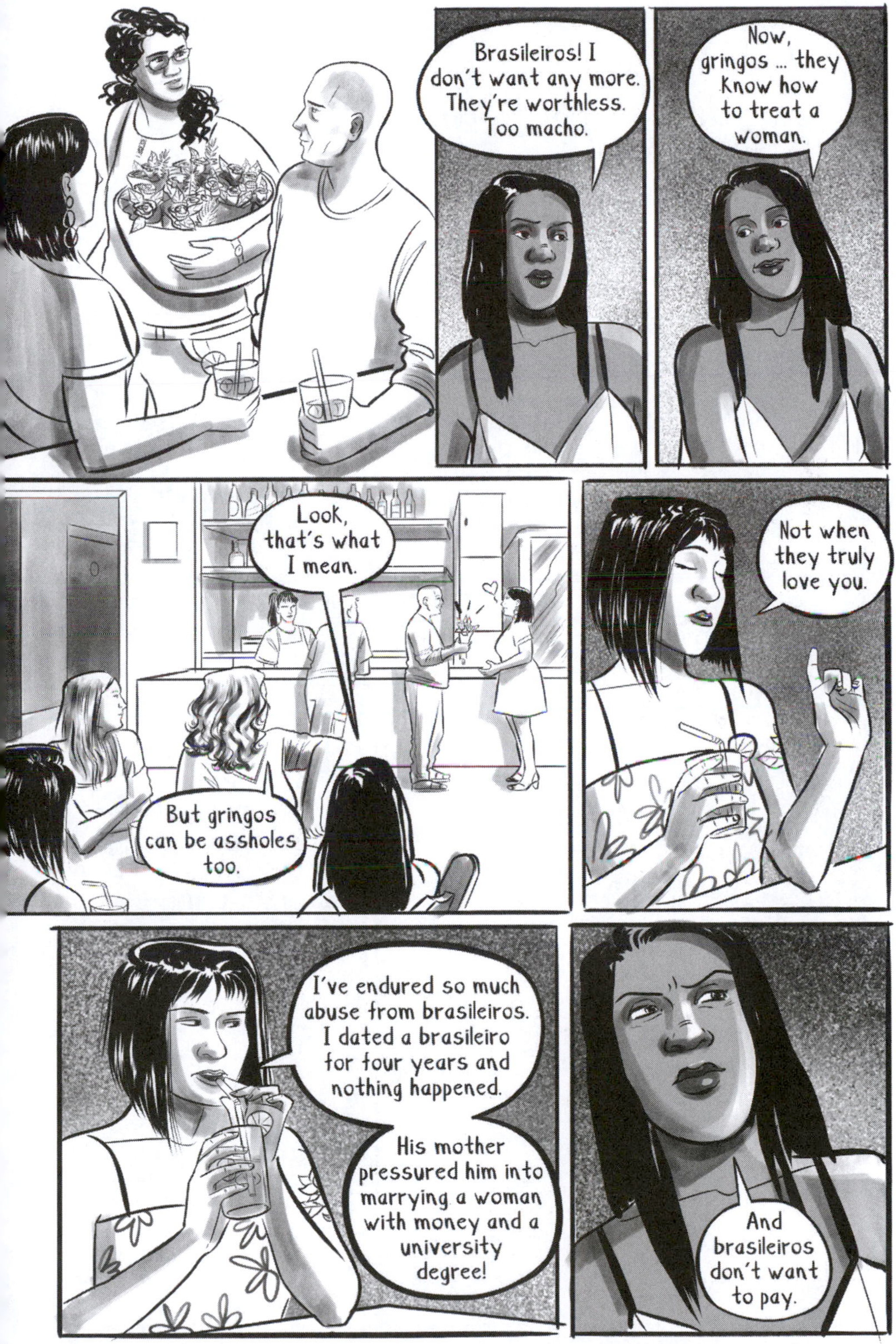
Brasileiros! I don't want any more. They're worthless. Too macho.
Now, gringos ... they know how to treat a woman.
Look, that's what I mean.
But gringos can be assholes too.
Not when they truly love you.
I've endured so much abuse from brasileiros. I dated a brasileiro for four years and nothing happened.
His mother pressured him into marrying a woman with money and a university degree!
And brasileiros don't want to pay.

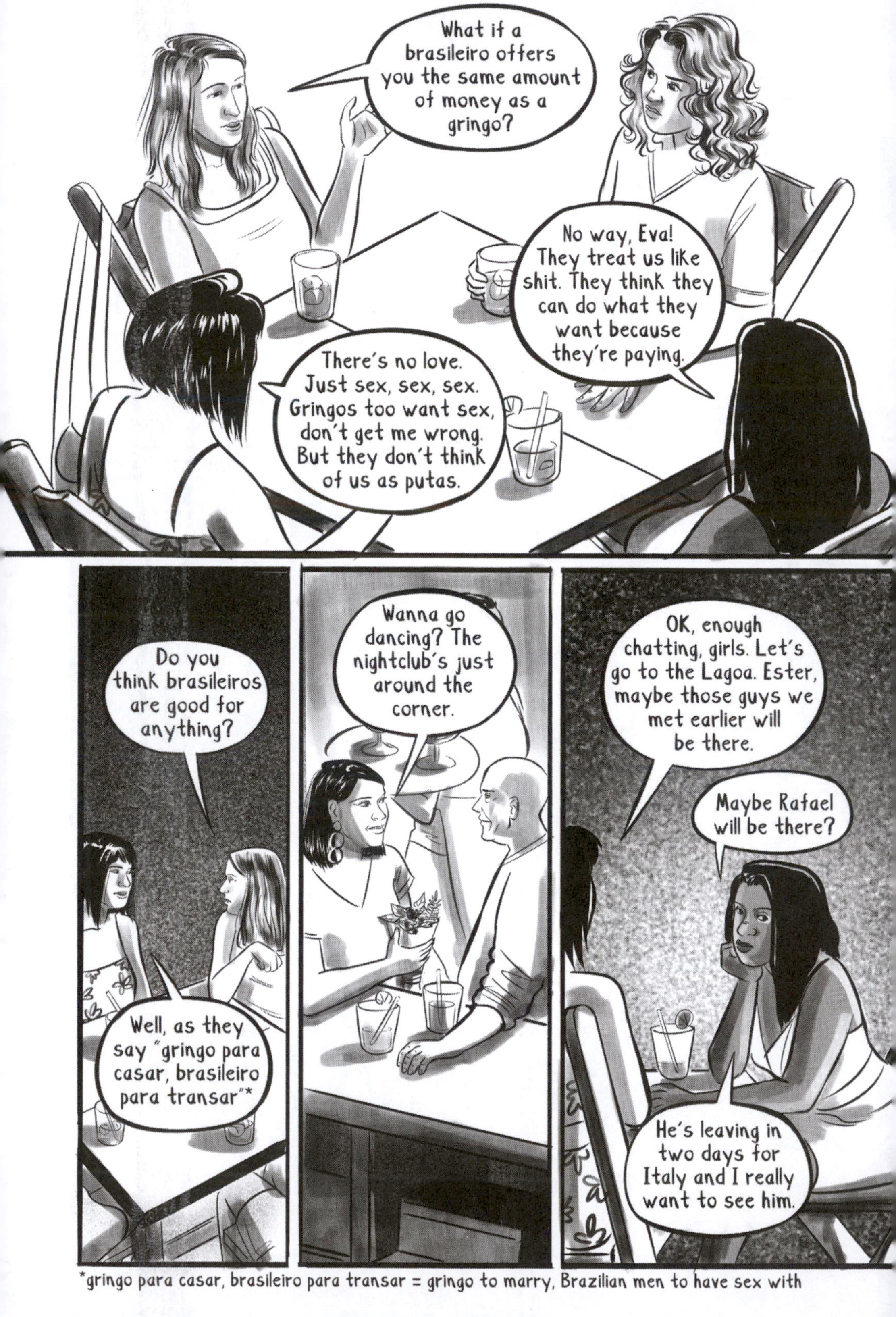
What if a brasileiro offers you the same amount of money as a gringo?
No way, Eva! They treat us like shit. They think they can do what they want because they're paying.
There's no love. Just sex, sex, sex. Gringos too want sex, don't get me wrong. But they don't think of us as putas.
Do you think brasileiros are good for anything?
Well, as they say "gringo para casar, brasileiro para transar"*
Wanna go dancing? The nightclub's just around the corner.
OK, enough chatting, girls. Let's go to the Lagoa. Ester, maybe those guys we met earlier will be there.
Maybe Rafael will be there?
He's leaving in two days for Italy and I really want to see him.

*gringo para casar, brasileiro para transar = gringo to marry, Brazilian men to have sex with

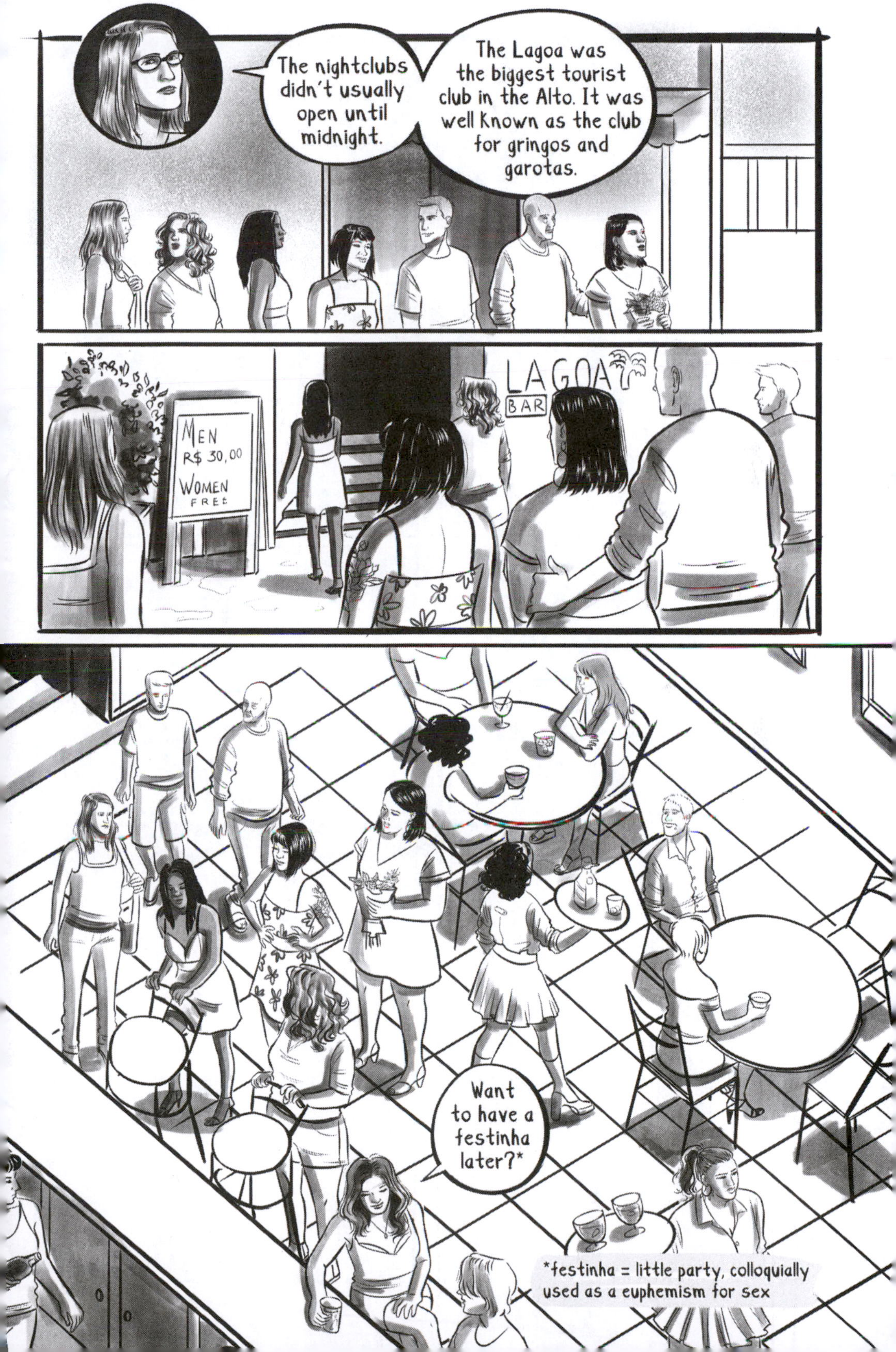
The nightclubs didn't usually open until midnight.
The Lagoa was the biggest tourist club in the Alto. It was well known as the club for gringos and garotas.
MEN R$ 30,00
WOMEN FREE
LAGOA
BAR
Want to have a festinha later?*
*festinha = little party, colloquially used as a euphemism for sex

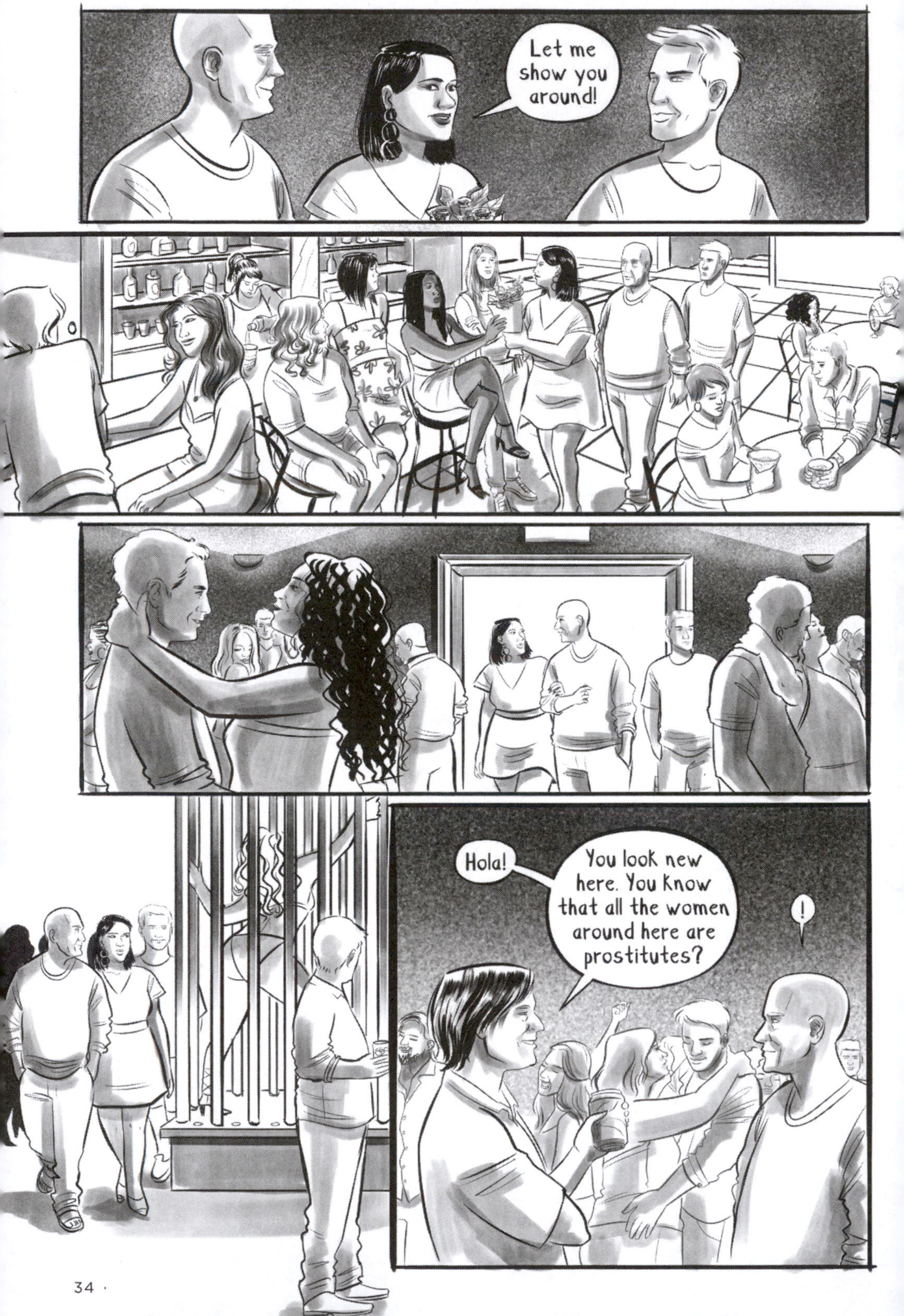
Let me show you around!
Hola!
You look new here. You know that all the women around here are prostitutes?
!

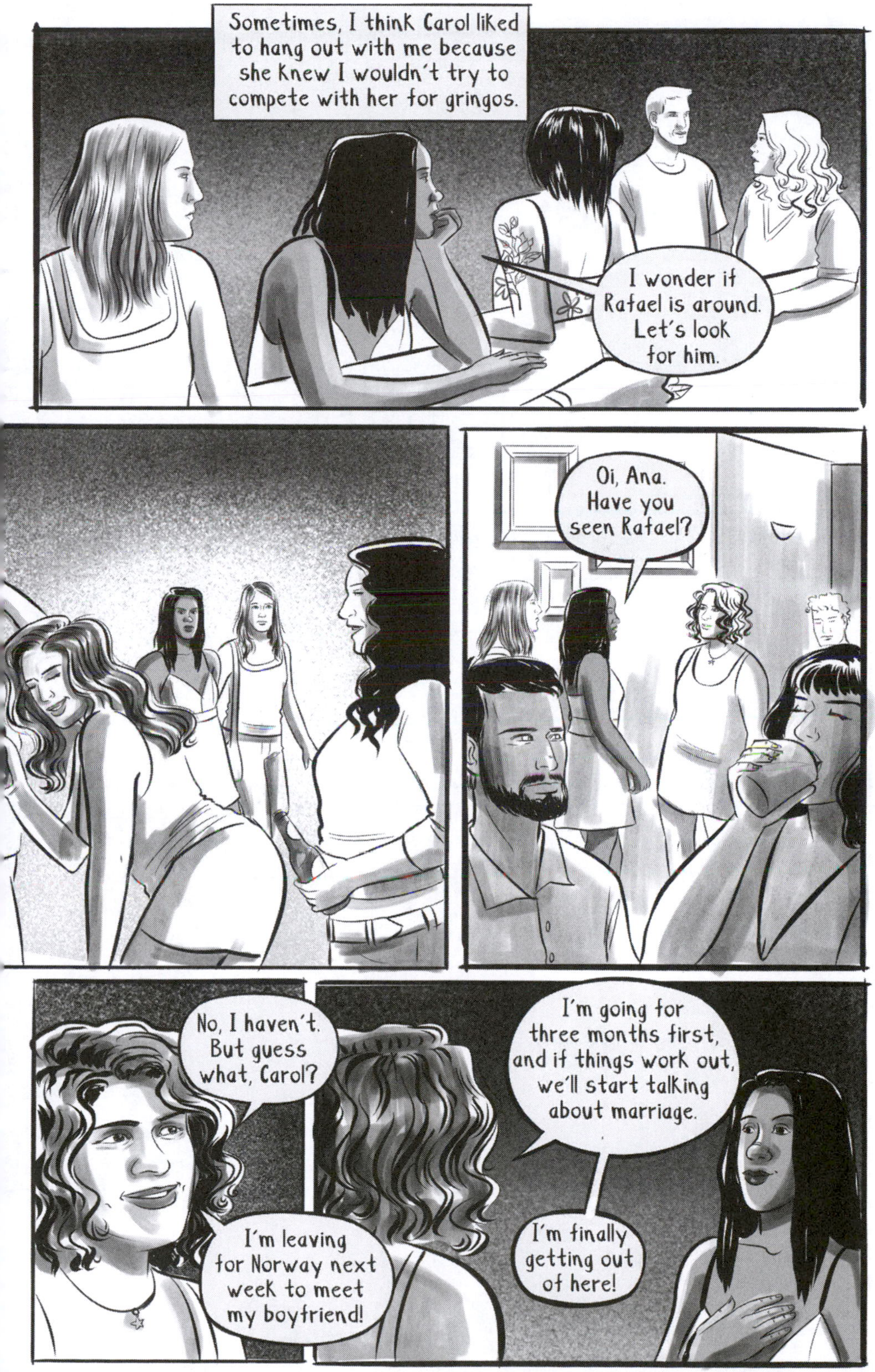
Sometimes, I think Carol liked to hang out with me because she knew I wouldn't try to compete with her for gringos.
I wonder if Rafael is around. Let's look for him.
Oi, Ana. Have you seen Rafael?
No, I haven't. But guess what, Carol?
I'm leaving for Norway next week to meet my boyfriend!
I'm going for three months first, and if things work out, we'll start talking about marriage.
I'm finally getting out of here!

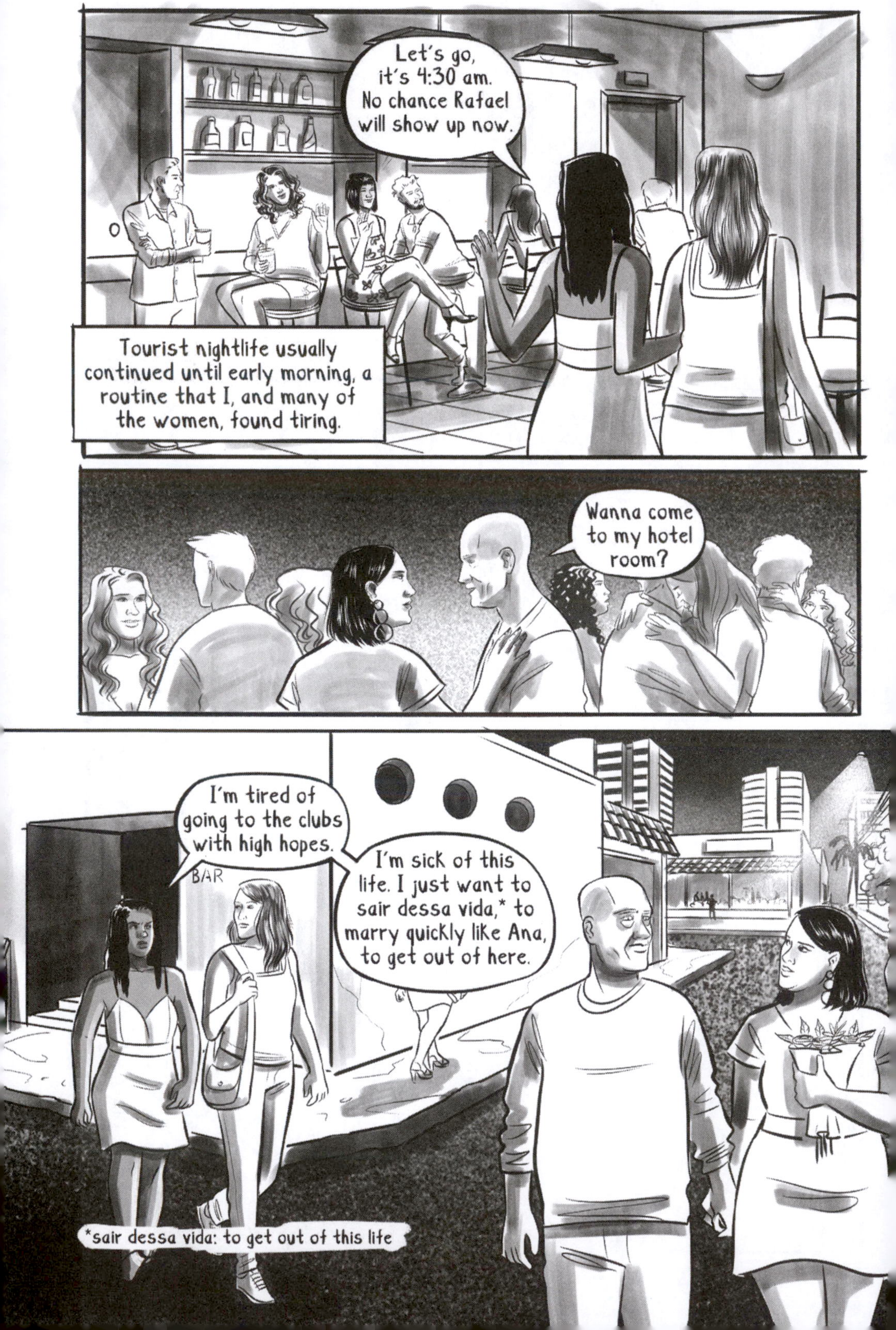
Let's go, it's 4:30 am. No chance Rafael will show up now.
Tourist nightlife usually continued until early morning, a routine that I, and many of the women, found tiring.
Wanna come to my hotel room?
I'm tired of going to the clubs with high hopes.
BAR
I'm sick of this life. I just want to sair dessa vida,* to marry quickly like Ana, to get out of here.
*sair dessa vida: to get out of this life

Fieldnotes

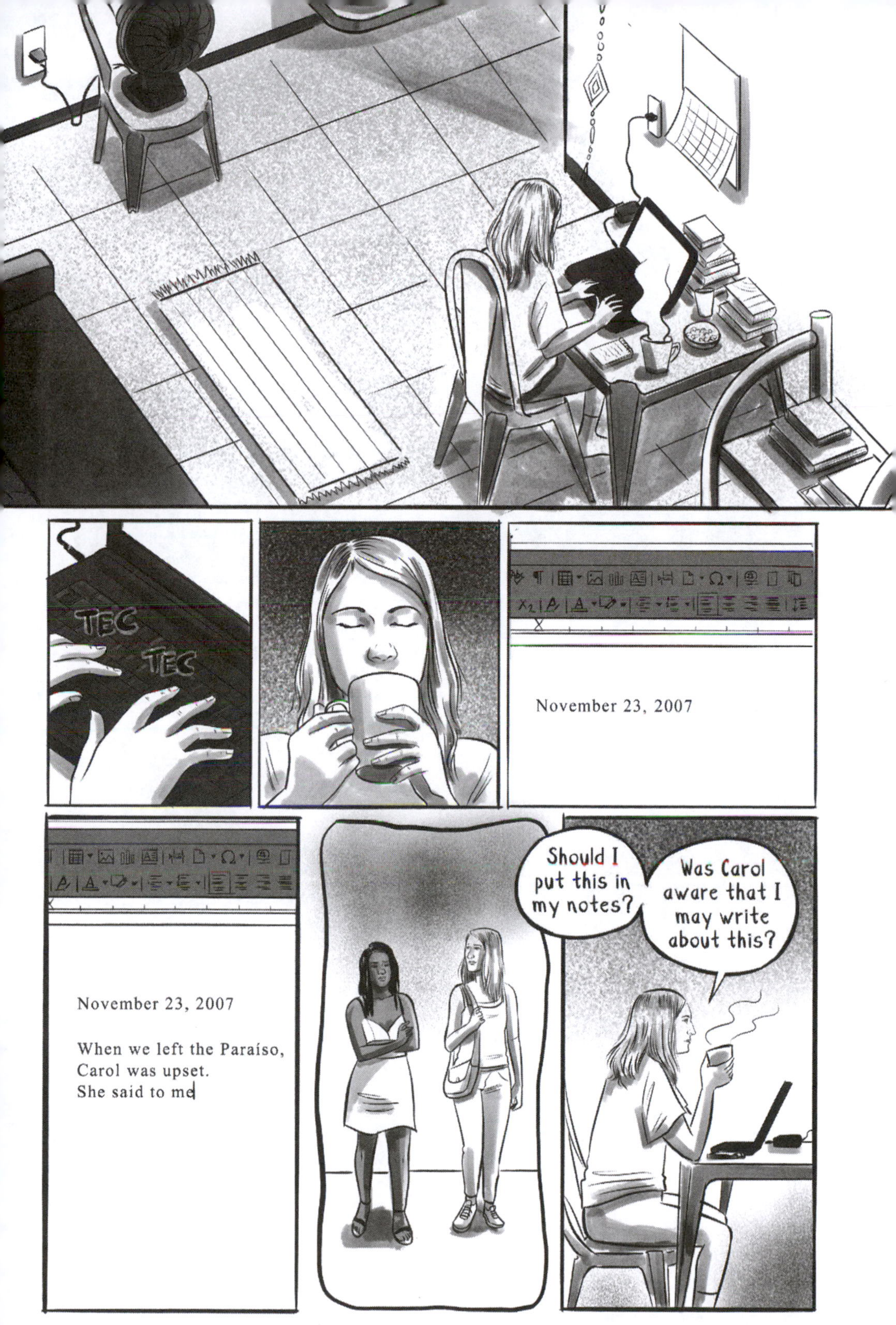

TEC
TEC
November 23, 2007
November 23, 2007
When we left the Paraíso,
Carol was upset.
She said to me
Should I put this in my notes?
Was Carol aware that I may write about this?

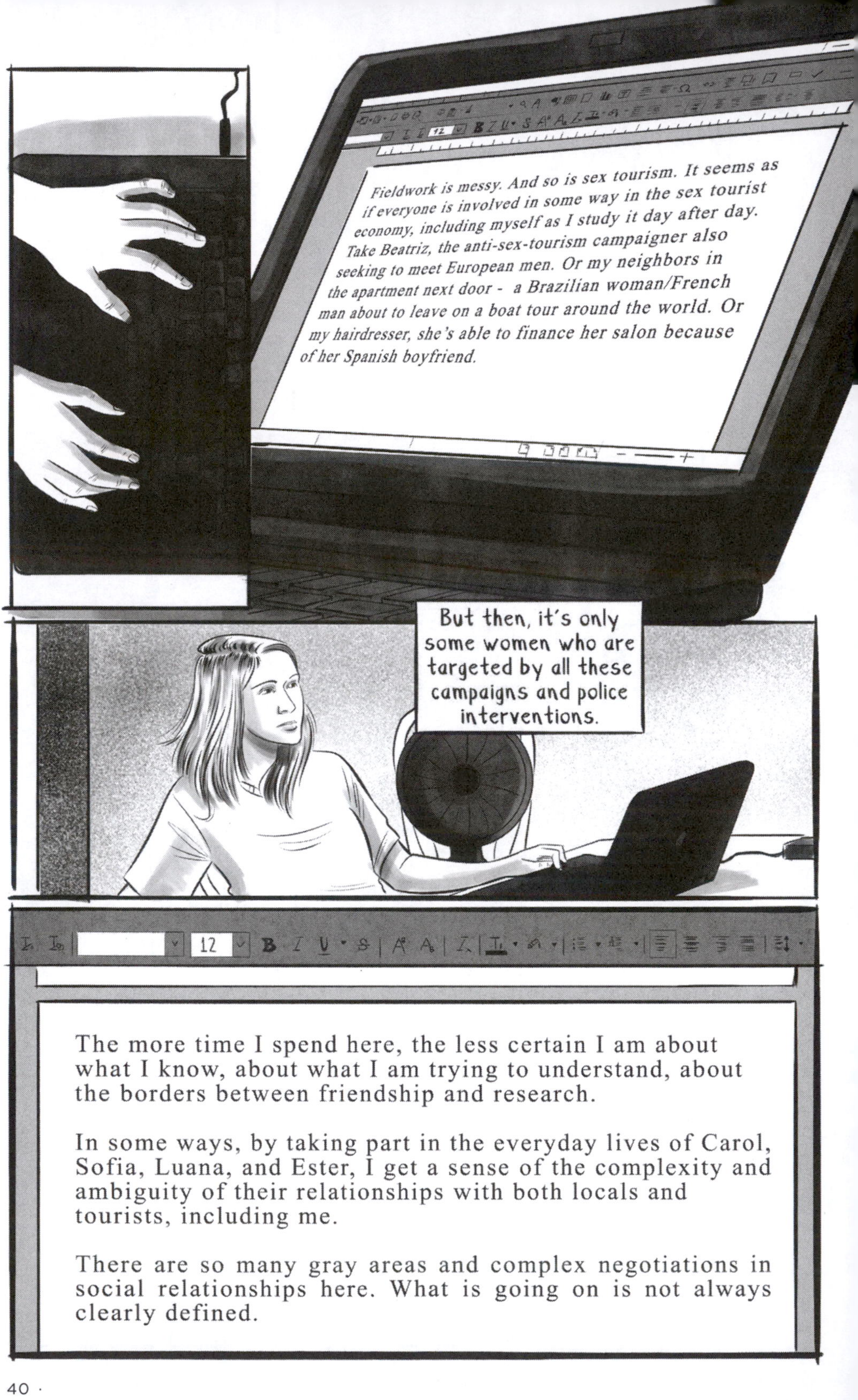
Fieldwork is messy. And so is sex tourism. It seems as if everyone is involved in some way in the sex tourist economy, including myself as I study it day after day. Take Beatriz, the anti-sex-tourism campaigner also seeking to meet European men. Or my neighbors in the apartment next door - a Brazilian woman/French man about to leave on a boat tour around the world. Or my hairdresser, she's able to finance her salon because of her Spanish boyfriend.
But then, it's only some women who are targeted by all these campaigns and police interventions.

The more time I spend here, the less certain I am about what I know, about what I am trying to understand, about the borders between friendship and research.

In some ways, by taking part in the everyday lives of Carol, Sofia, Luana, and Ester, I get a sense of the complexity and ambiguity of their relationships with both locals and tourists, including me.

There are so many gray areas and complex negotiations in social relationships here. What is going on is not always clearly defined.

PART 2: GRINGO LOVE?

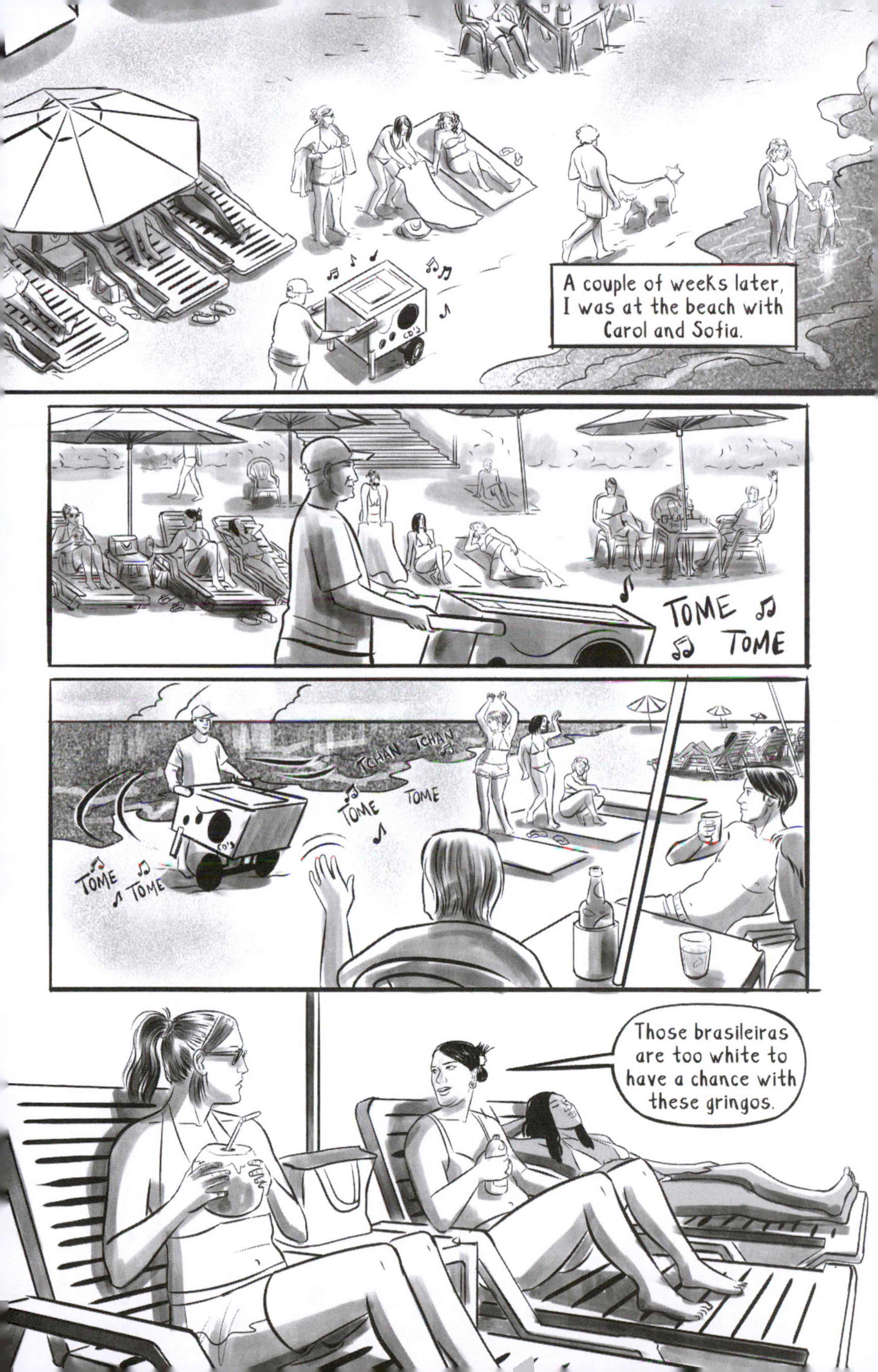
A couple of weeks later, I was at the beach with Carol and Sofia.
CD'S
TOME TOME
TCHAN TCHAN
TOME TOME
TOME TOME
CD'S
Those brasileiras are too white to have a chance with these gringos.

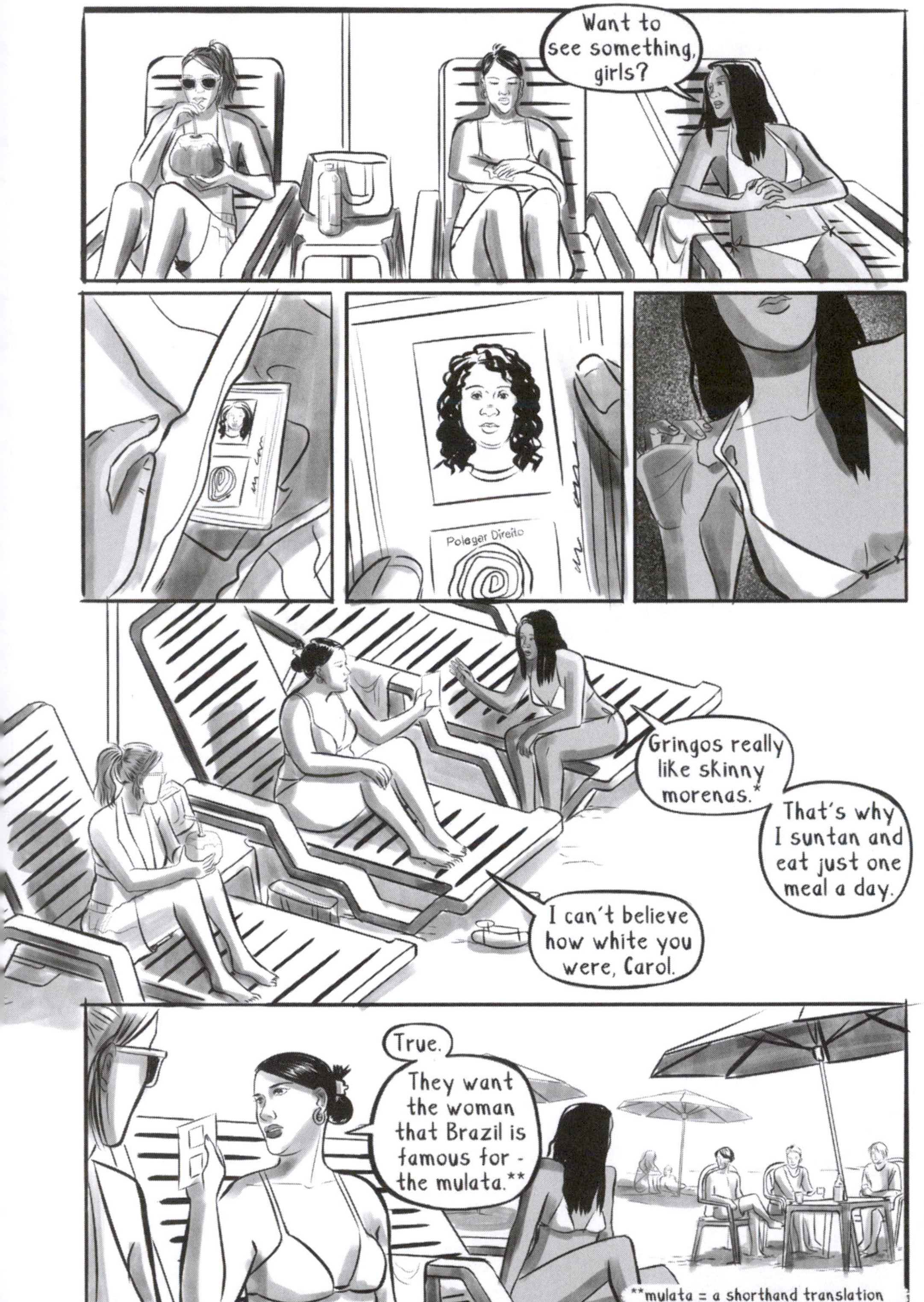
Want to see something, girls?
Polegar Direito
Gringos really like skinny morenas.*
That's why I suntan and eat just one meal a day.
I can't believe how white you were, Carol.
True.
They want the woman that Brazil is famous for - the mulata.**

*morena(s) = literally translates here as brown woman (women); a context-dependent category that may refer to a brunette, Indigenous woman, or mixed-race woman.

**mulata = a shorthand translation would be mixed-race woman; it has a sexual connotation, too. More on the multiple meanings of these words in the appendices.

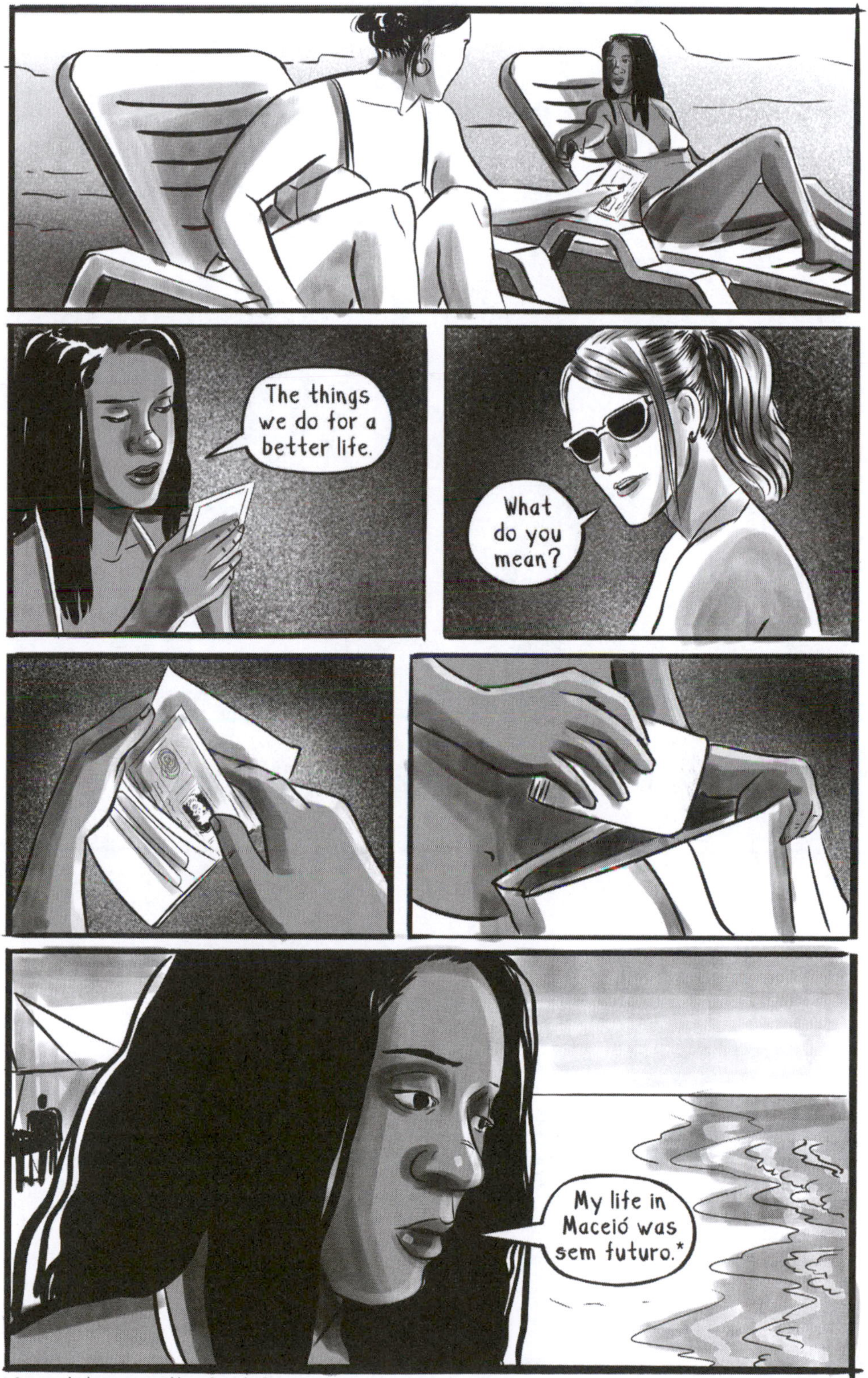
The things we do for a better life.
What do you mean?
My life in Maceió was sem futuro.*

*sem futuro = without a future

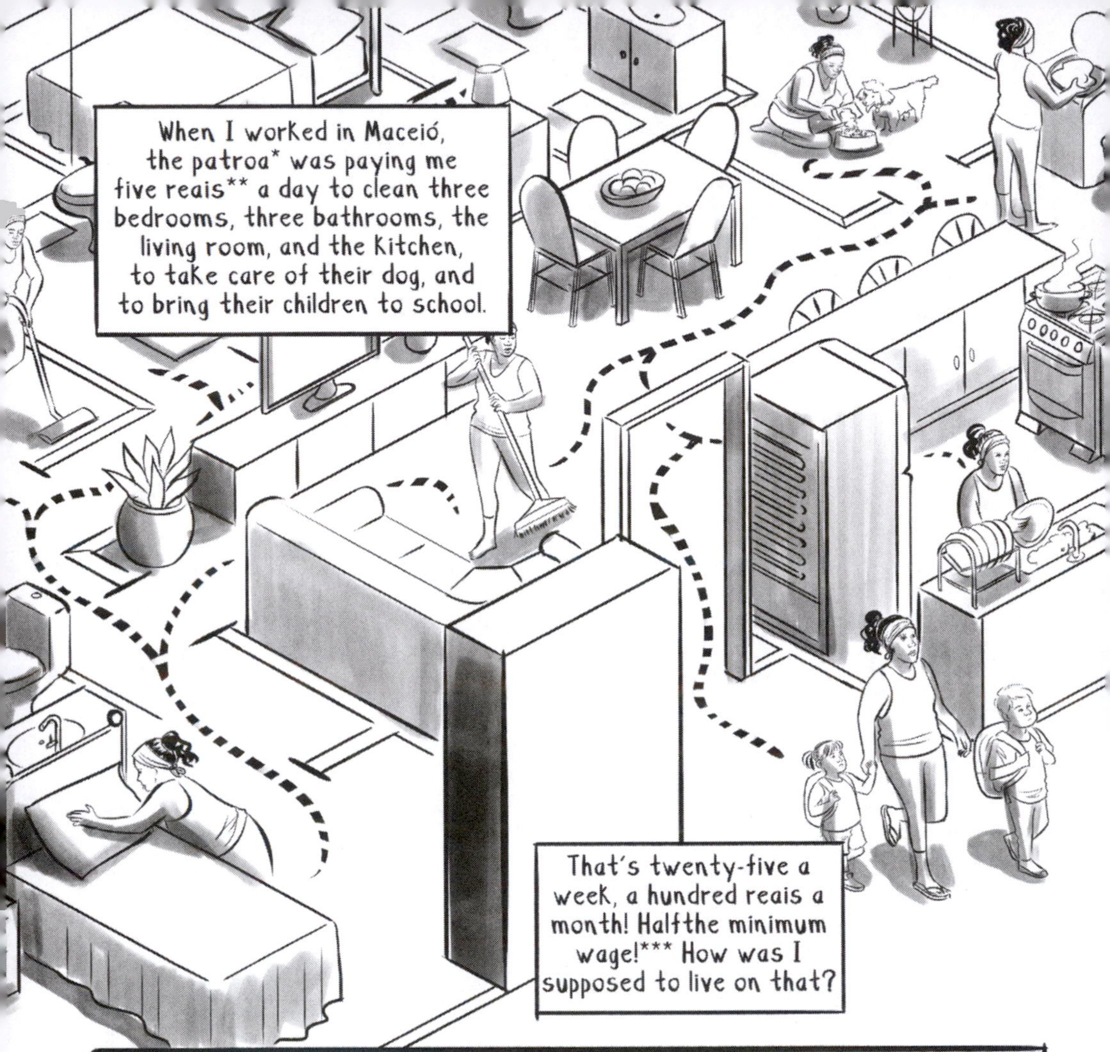
When I worked in Maceió, the patroa* was paying me five reais** a day to clean three bedrooms, three bathrooms, the living room, and the Kitchen, to take care of their dog, and to bring their children to school.
That's twenty-five a week, a hundred reais a month! Halfthe minimum wage!*** How was I supposed to live on that?

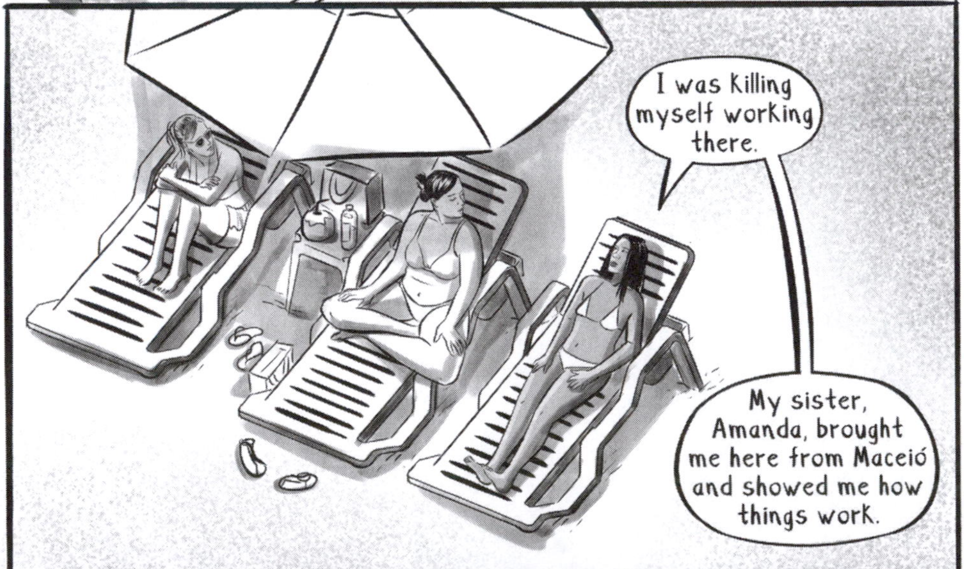
I was Killing myself working there.
My sister, Amanda, brought me here from Maceió and showed me how things work.

*patrão/patroa = male/female boss
**real/reais = Brazilian currency

***Note: While these rates may appear exaggerated, they are taken from interview excerpts.

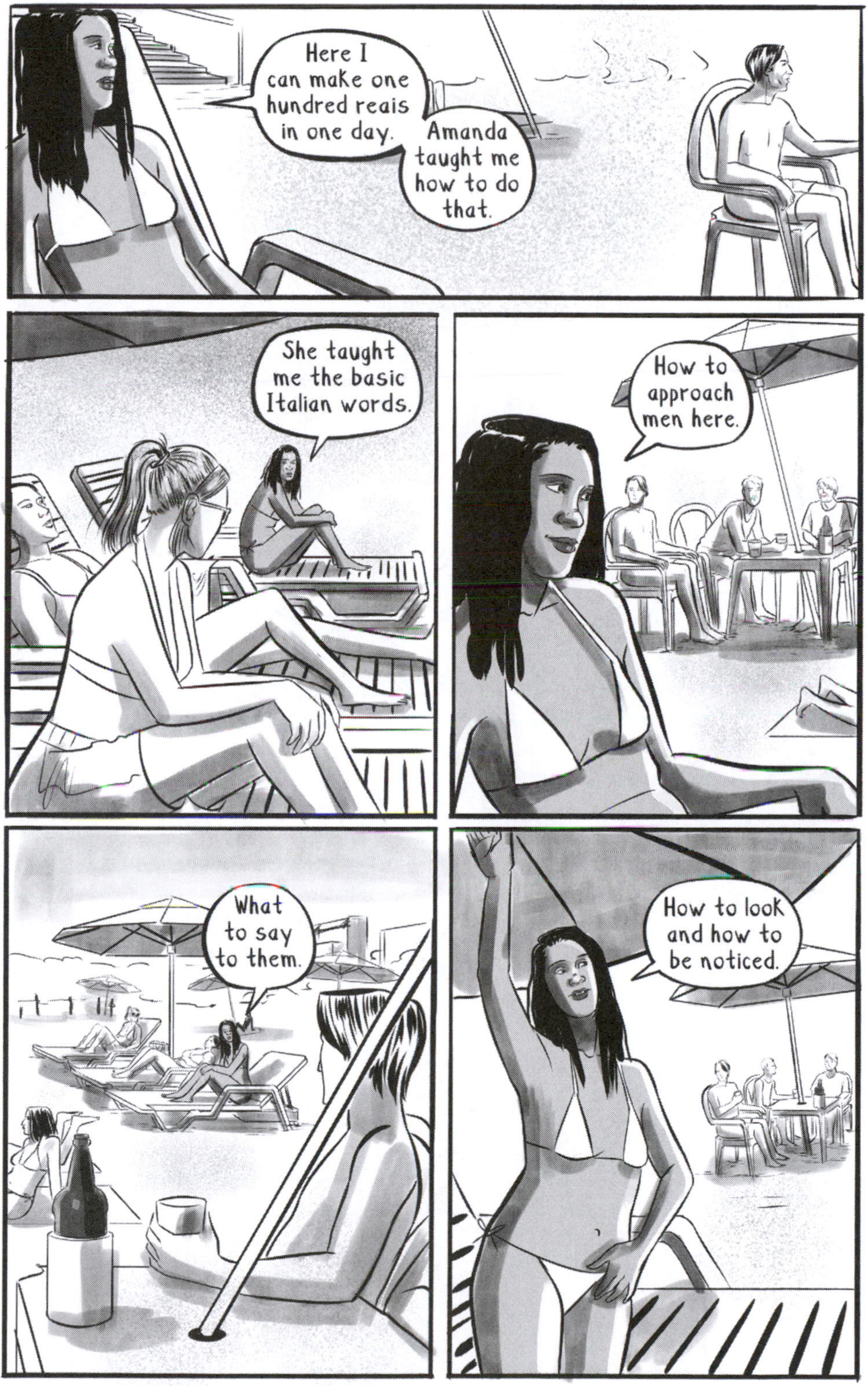
Here I can make one hundred reais in one day.
Amanda taught me how to do that.
She taught me the basic Italian words.
How to approach men here.
What to say to them.
How to look and how to be noticed.

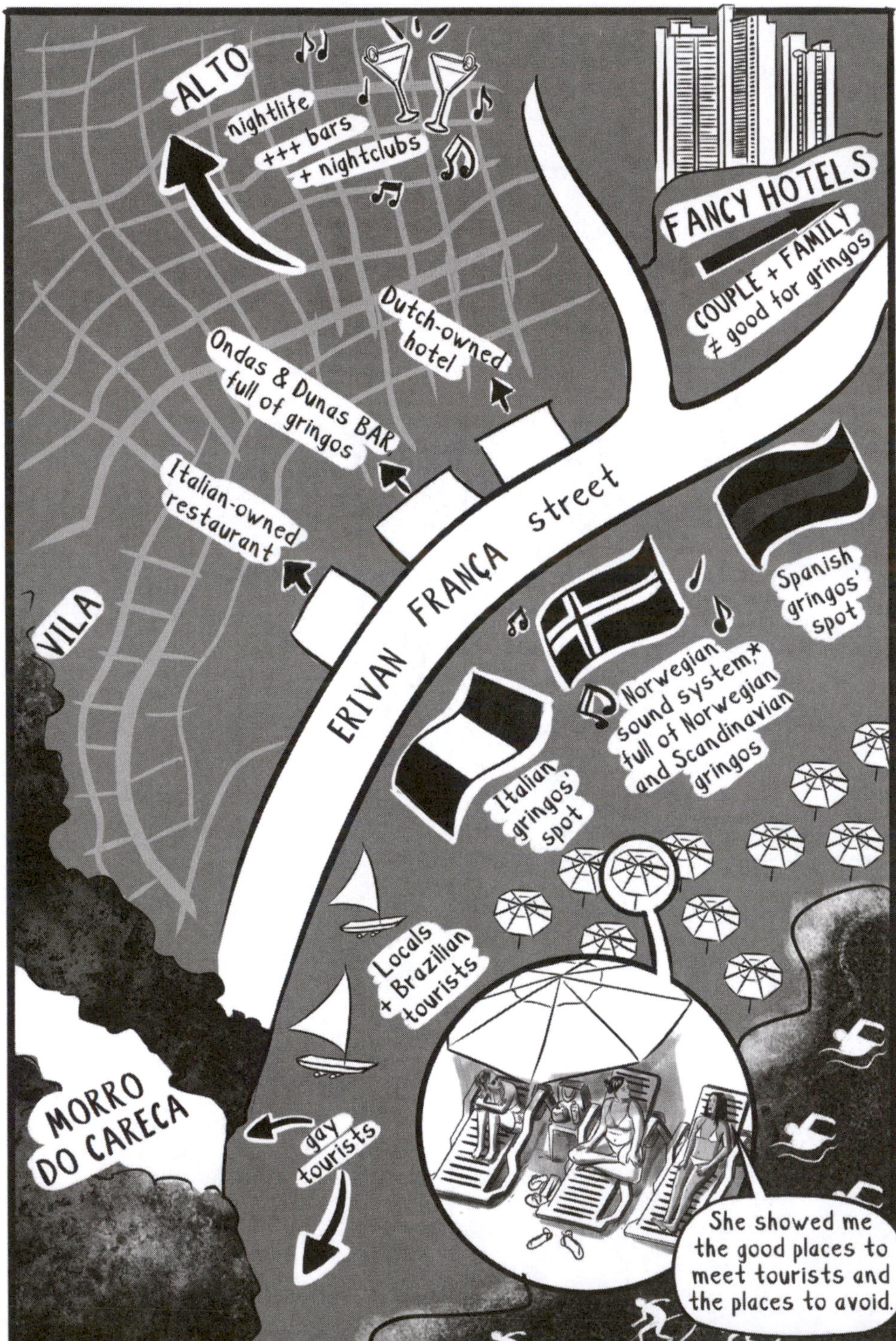
ALTO
nightlife
+++ bars
+ nightclubs
FANCY HOTELS
COUPLE + FAMILY
≠ good for gringos
Dutch-owned hotel
Ondas & Dunas BAR full of gringos
Italian-owned restaurant
ERIVAN FRANÇA street
VILA
Spanish gringos' spot
Norwegian sound system,* full of Norwegian and Scandinavian gringos
Italian gringos' spot
Locals + Brazilian tourists
MORRO DO CARECA
gay tourists
She showed me the good places to meet tourists and the places to avoid.
Atlantic Ocean

*sound system = the portable, handmade sound system playing music from CDs, as visible in the opening page to PART 2

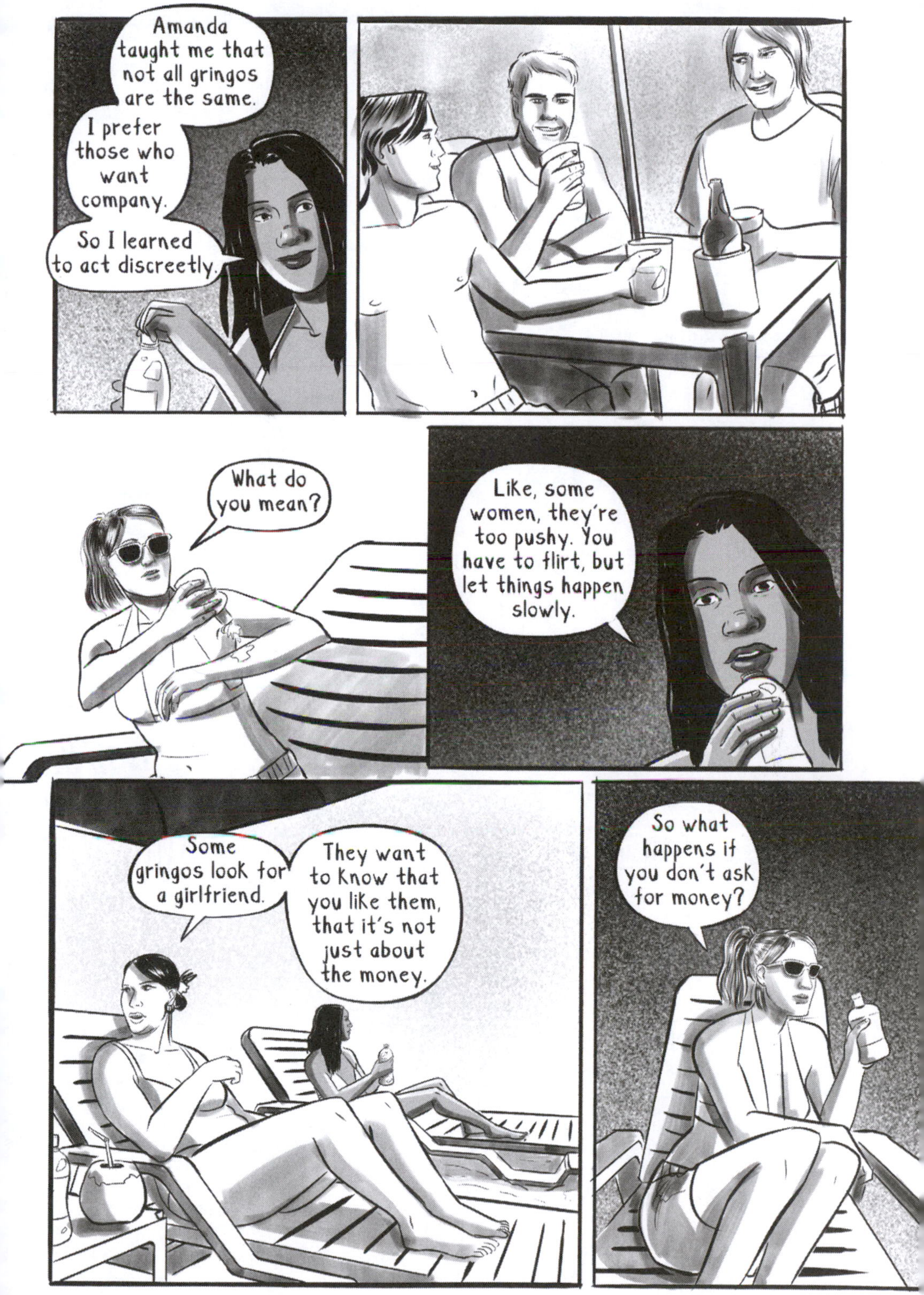
Amanda taught me that not all gringos are the same.
I prefer those who want company.
So I learned to act discreetly.
What do you mean?
Like, some women, they're too pushy. You have to flirt, but let things happen slowly.
Some gringos look for a girlfriend.
They want to know that you like them, that it's not just about the money.
So what happens if you don't ask for money?

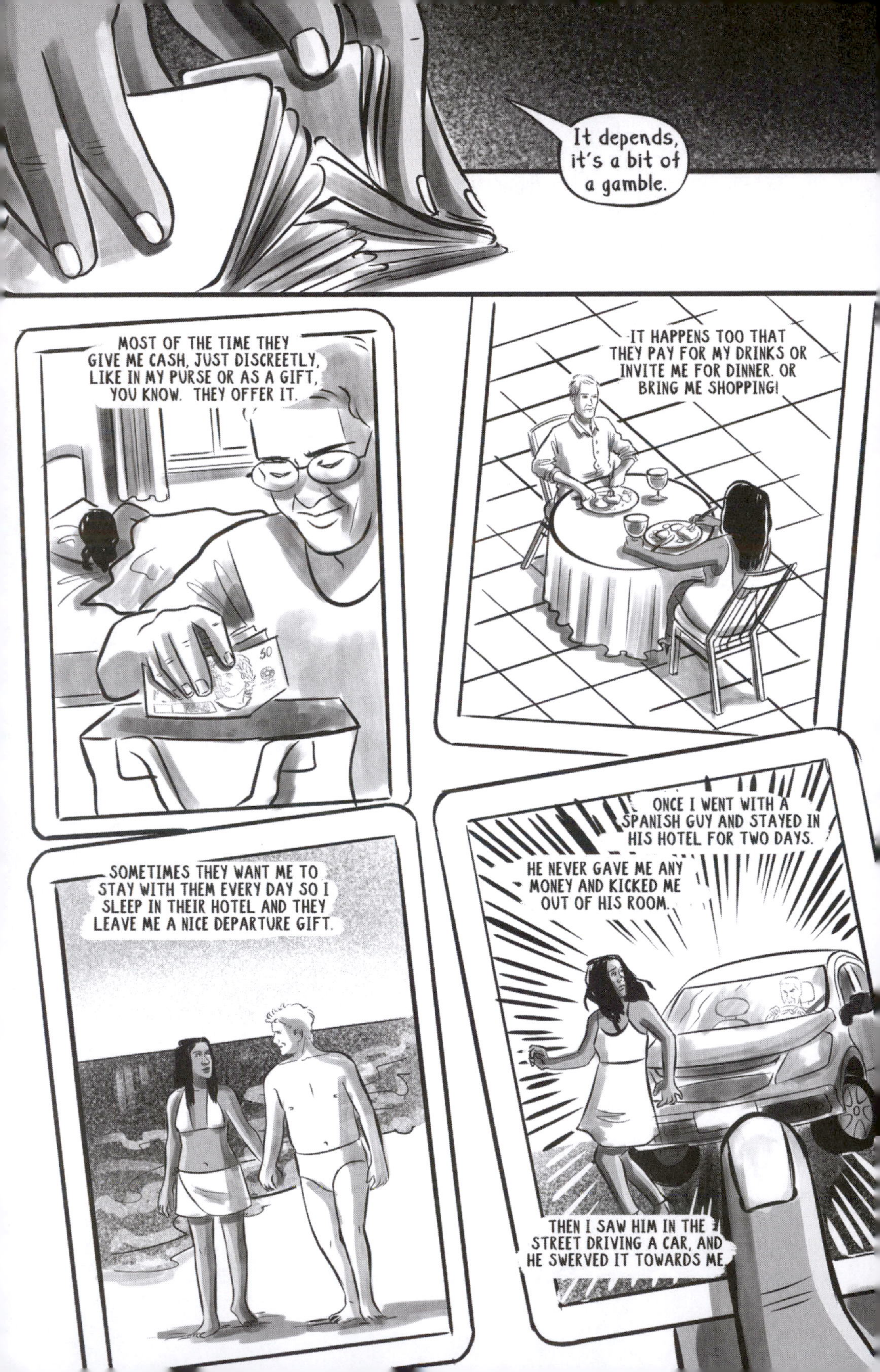
It depends, it's a bit of a gamble.
MOST OF THE TIME THEY GIVE ME CASH, JUST DISCREETLY, LIKE IN MY PURSE OR AS A GIFT, YOU KNOW. THEY OFFER IT.
IT HAPPENS TOO THAT THEY PAY FOR MY DRINKS OR INVITE ME FOR DINNER. OR BRING ME SHOPPING!
SOMETIMES THEY WANT ME TO STAY WITH THEM EVERY DAY SO I SLEEP IN THEIR HOTEL AND THEY LEAVE ME A NICE DEPARTURE GIFT.
ONCE I WENT WITH A SPANISH GUY AND STAYED IN HIS HOTEL FOR TWO DAYS.
HE NEVER GAVE ME ANY MONEY AND KICKED ME OUT OF HIS ROOM.
THEN I SAW HIM IN THE STREET DRIVING A CAR, AND HE SWERVED IT TOWARDS ME.

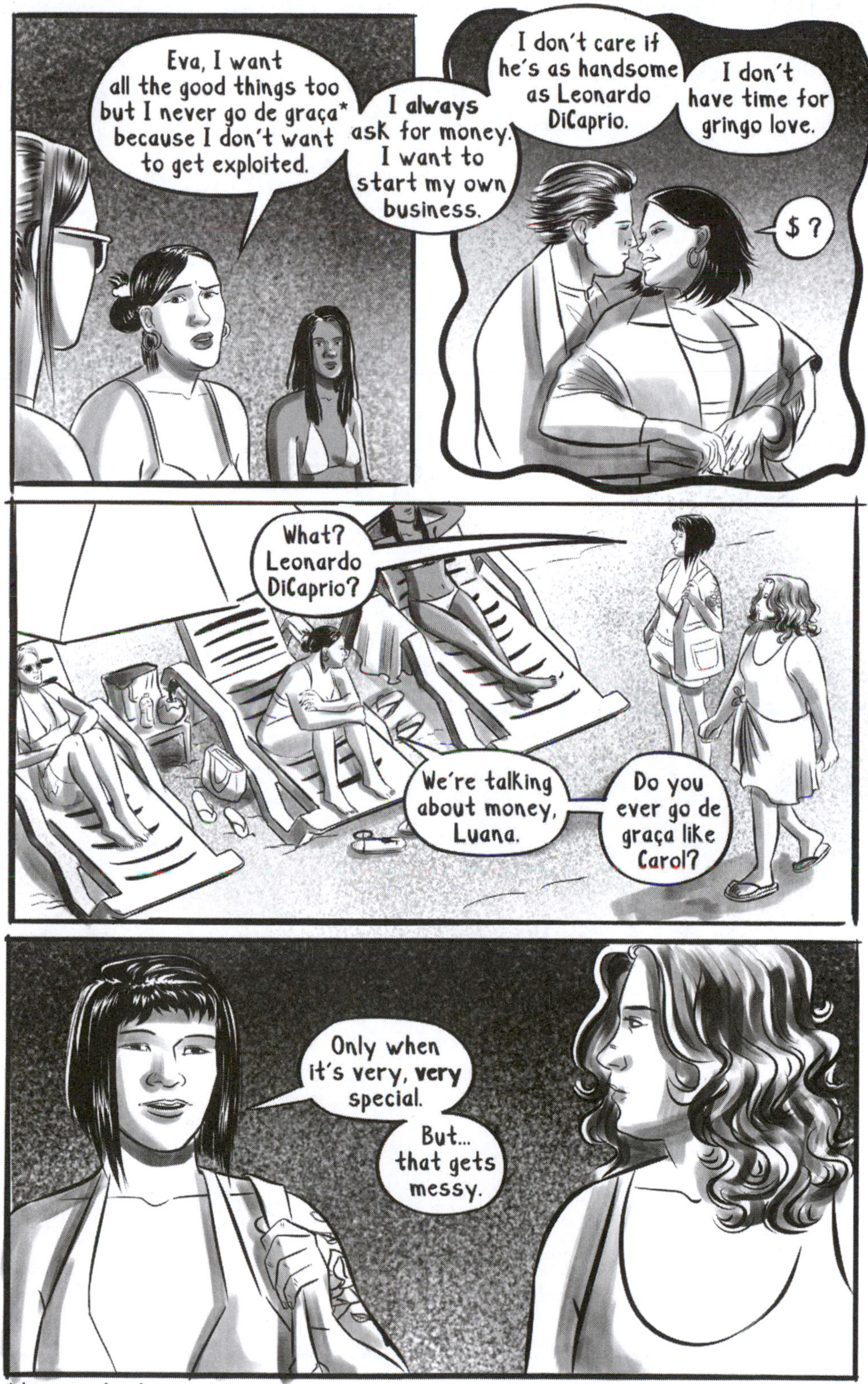
Eva, I want all the good things too but I never go de graça* because I don't want to get exploited.
I always ask for money. I want to start my own business.
I don't care if he's as handsome as Leonardo DiCaprio.
I don't have time for gringo love.
$?
What? Leonardo DiCaprio?
We're talking about money, Luana.
Do you ever go de graça like Carol?
Only when it's very, very special.
But... that gets messy.

*de graça: for free

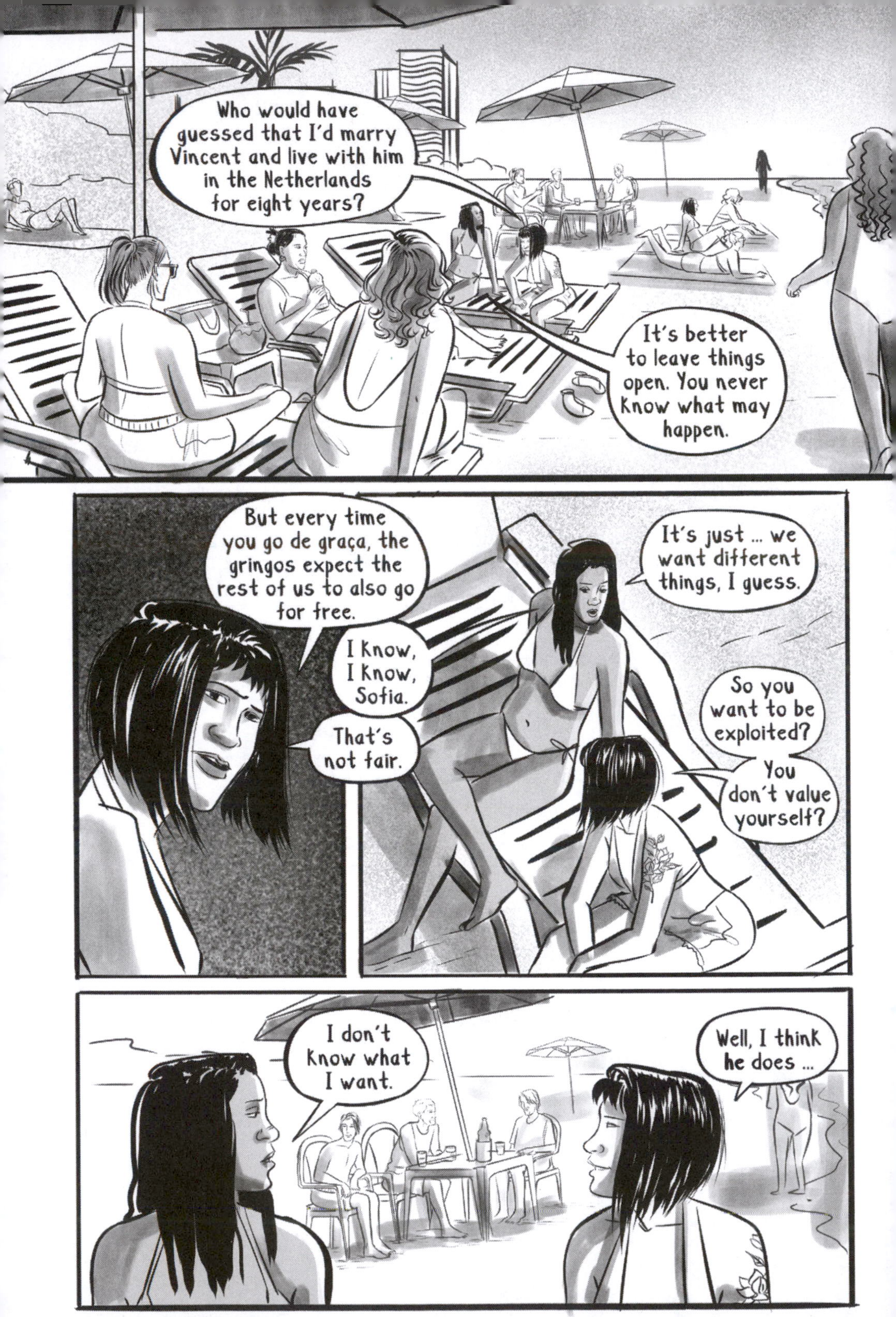
Who would have guessed that I'd marry Vincent and live with him in the Netherlands for eight years?
It's better to leave things open. You never know what may happen.
But every time you go de graça, the gringos expect the rest of us to also go for free.
I know, I know, Sofia.
That's not fair.
It's just ... we want different things, I guess.
So you want to be exploited?
You don't value yourself?
I don't know what I want.
Well, I think he does ...

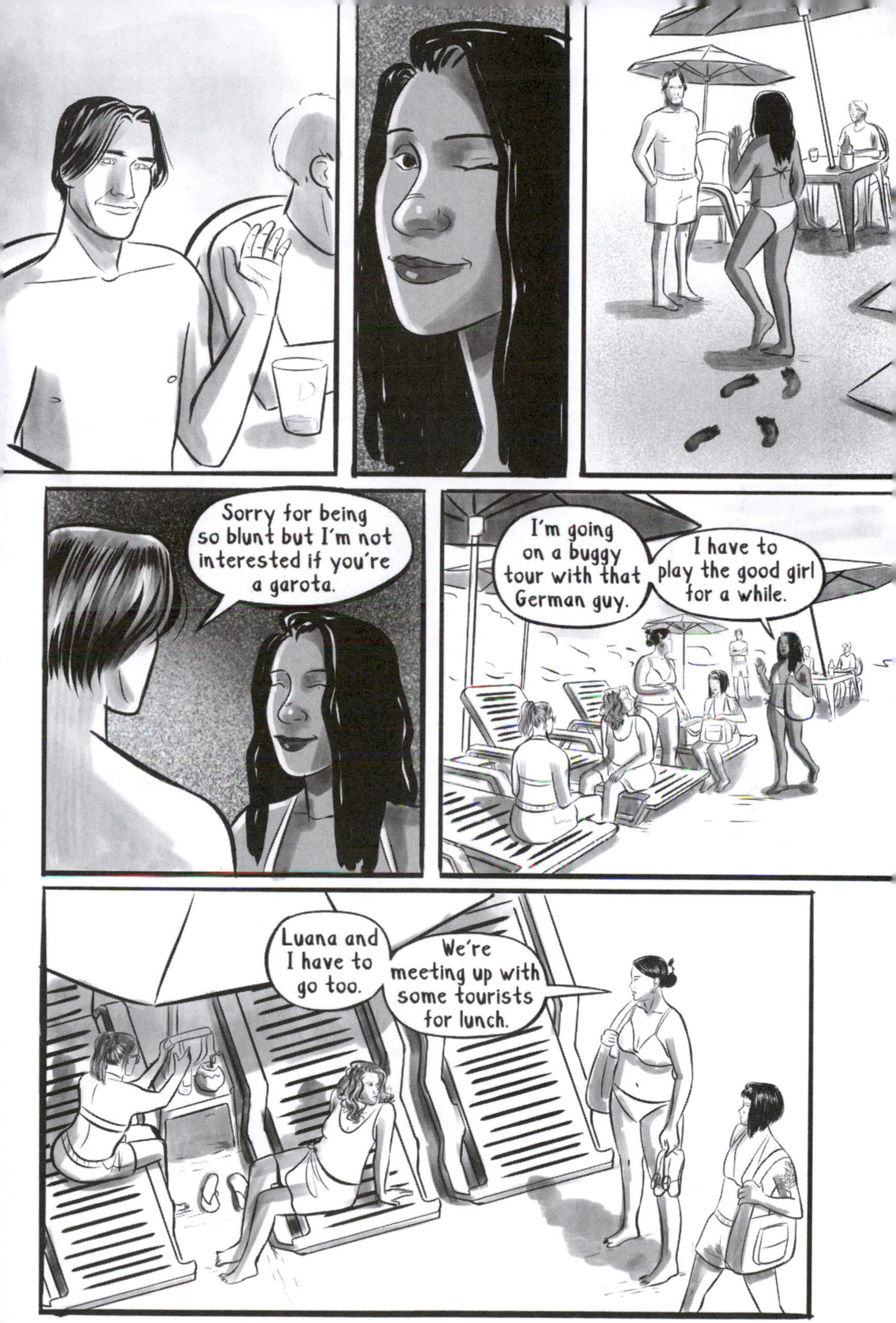
Sorry for being so blunt but I'm not interested if you're a garota.
I'm going on a buggy tour with that German guy.
I have to play the good girl for a while.
Luana and I have to go too.
We're meeting up with some tourists for lunch.

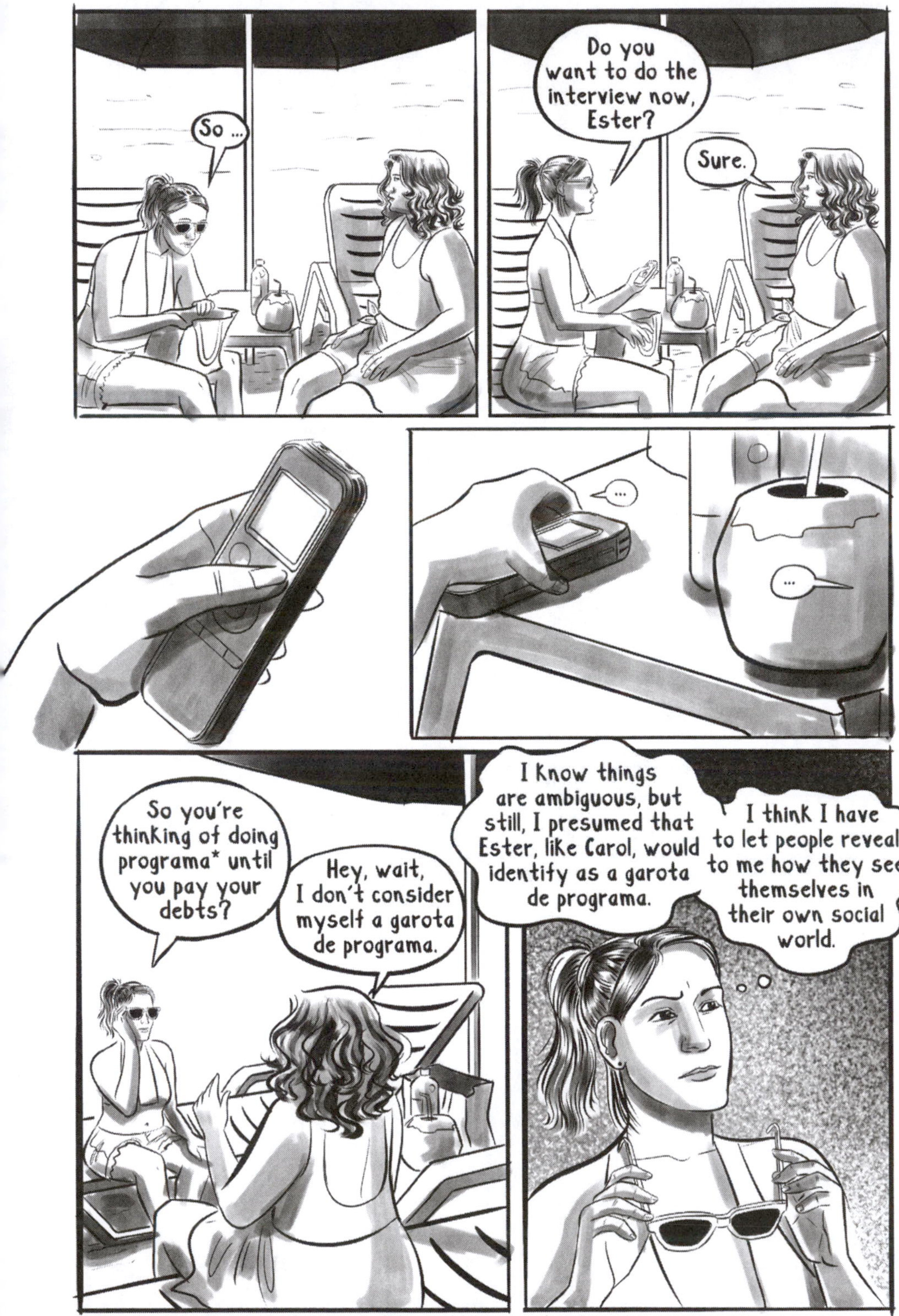
So ...
Do you want to do the interview now, Ester?
Sure.
...
...
So you're thinking of doing programa* until you pay your debts?
Hey, wait, I don't consider myself a garota de programa.
I know things are ambiguous, but still, I presumed that Ester, like Carol, would identify as a garota de programa.
I think I have to let people reveal to me how they see themselves in their own social world.

*programa = an explicit arrangement to exchange sex for money

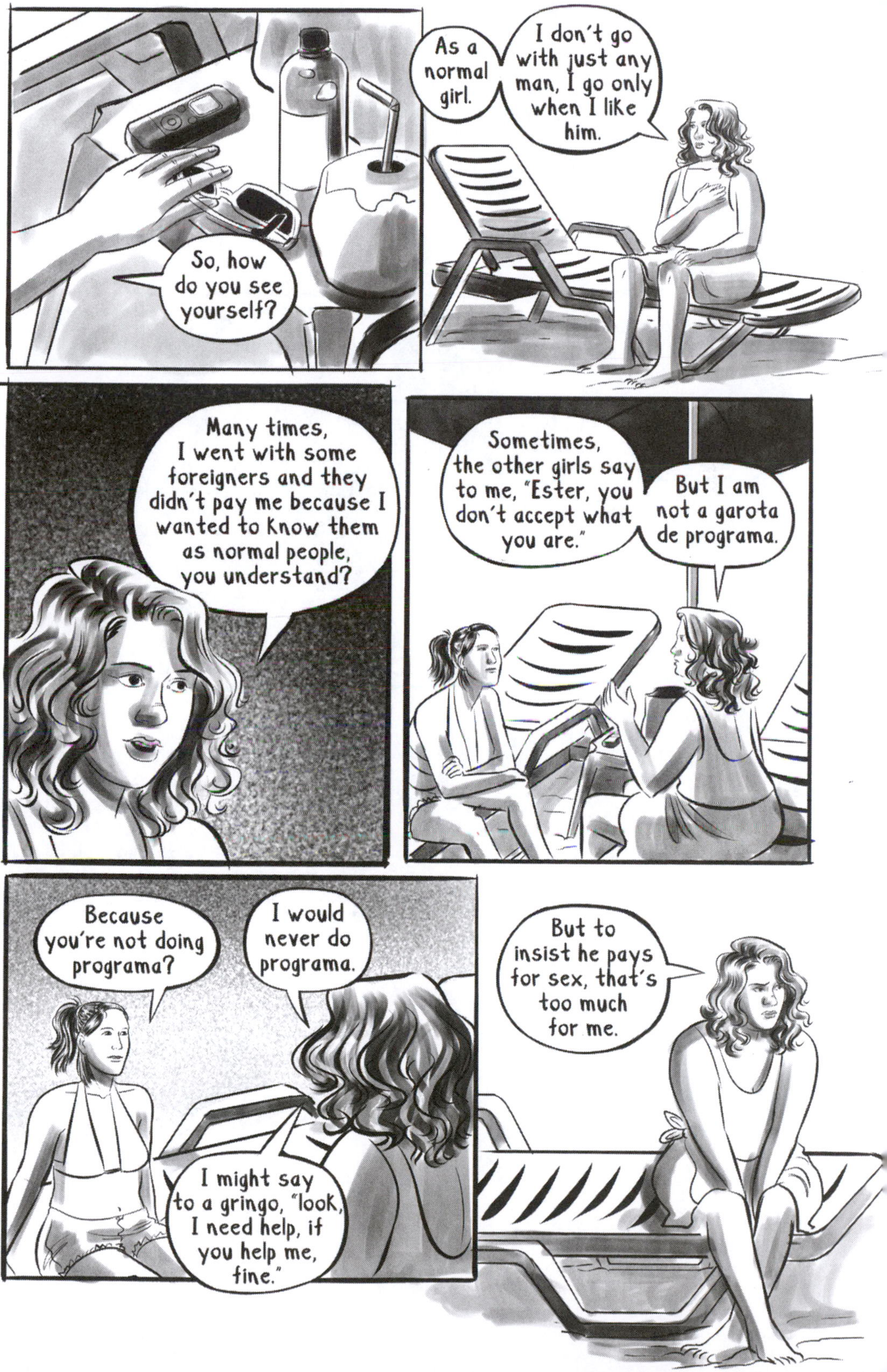
So, how do you see yourself?
As a normal girl.
I don't go with just any man, I go only when I like him.
Many times, I went with some foreigners and they didn't pay me because I wanted to know them as normal people, you understand?
Sometimes, the other girls say to me, "Ester, you don't accept what you are."
But I am not a garota de programa.
Because you're not doing programa?
I would never do programa.
I might say to a gringo, "look, I need help, if you help me, fine."
But to insist he pays for sex, that's too much for me.

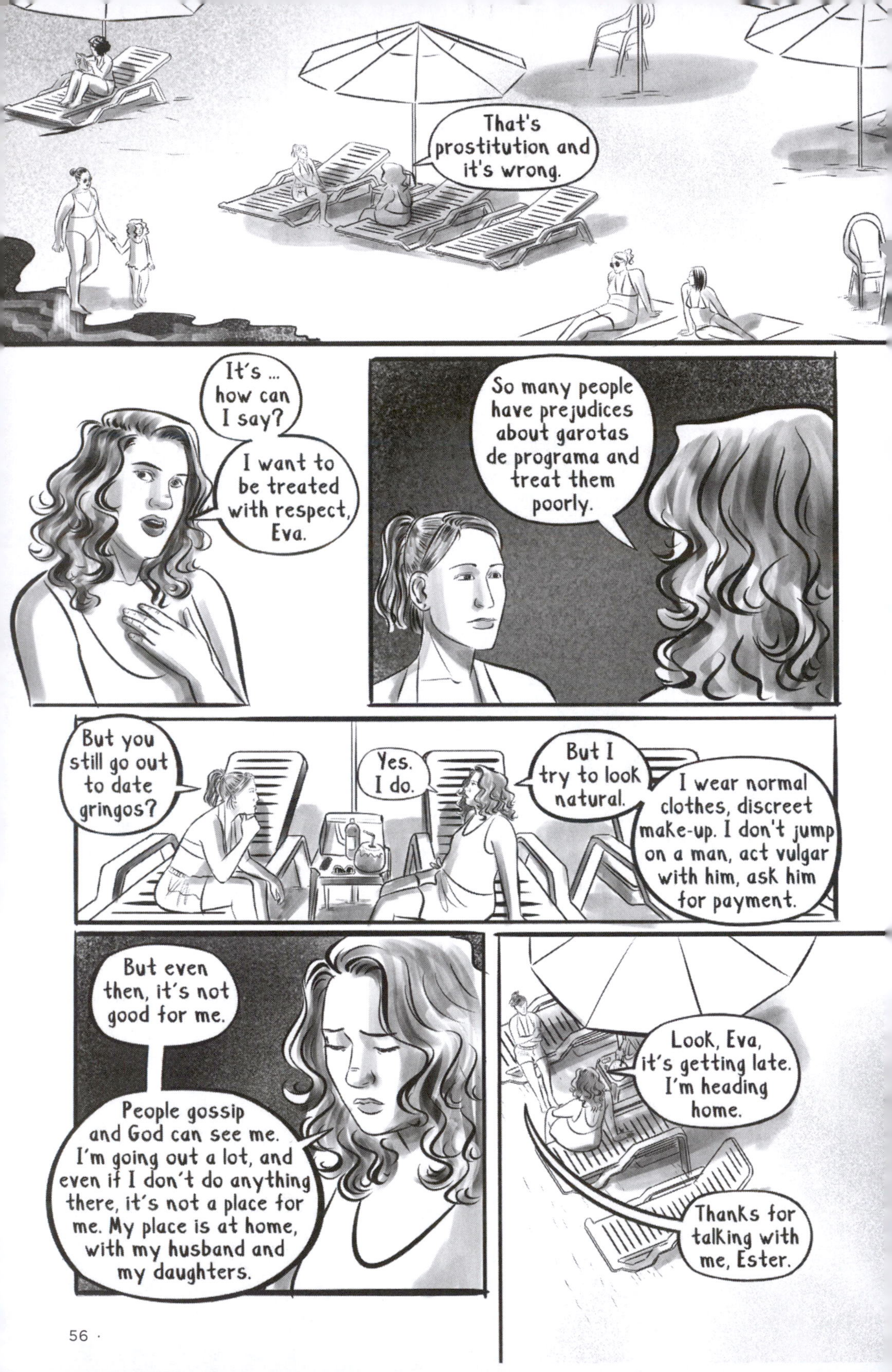
That's prostitution and it's wrong.
It's ... how can I say?
I want to be treated with respect, Eva.
So many people have prejudices about garotas de programa and treat them poorly.
But you still go out to date gringos?
Yes. I do.
But I try to look natural.
I wear normal clothes, discreet make-up. I don't jump on a man, act vulgar with him, ask him for payment.
But even then, it's not good for me.
People gossip and God can see me. I'm going out a lot, and even if I don't do anything there, it's not a place for me. My place is at home, with my husband and my daughters.
Look, Eva, it's getting late. I'm heading home.
Thanks for talking with me, Ester.

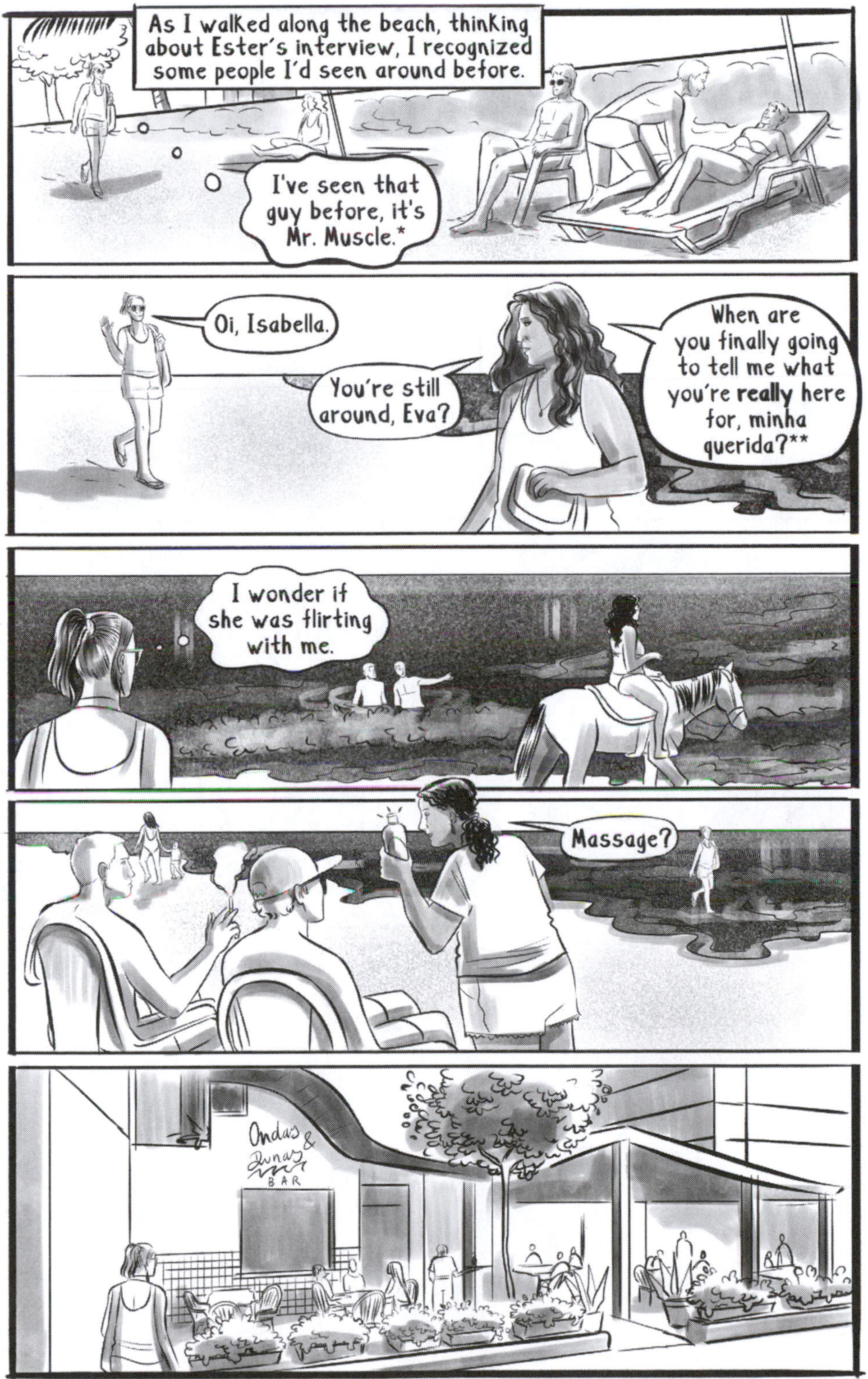
As I walked along the beach, thinking about Ester's interview, I recognized some people I'd seen around before.
I've seen that guy before, it's Mr. Muscle.*
Oi, Isabella.
You're still around, Eva?
When are you finally going to tell me what you're **really** here for, minha querida?**
I wonder if she was flirting with me.
Massage?
Ondas & Dunas
BAR

*Note: I sometimes used nicknames for people I wrote about in my fieldnotes.

**minha querida = my dear

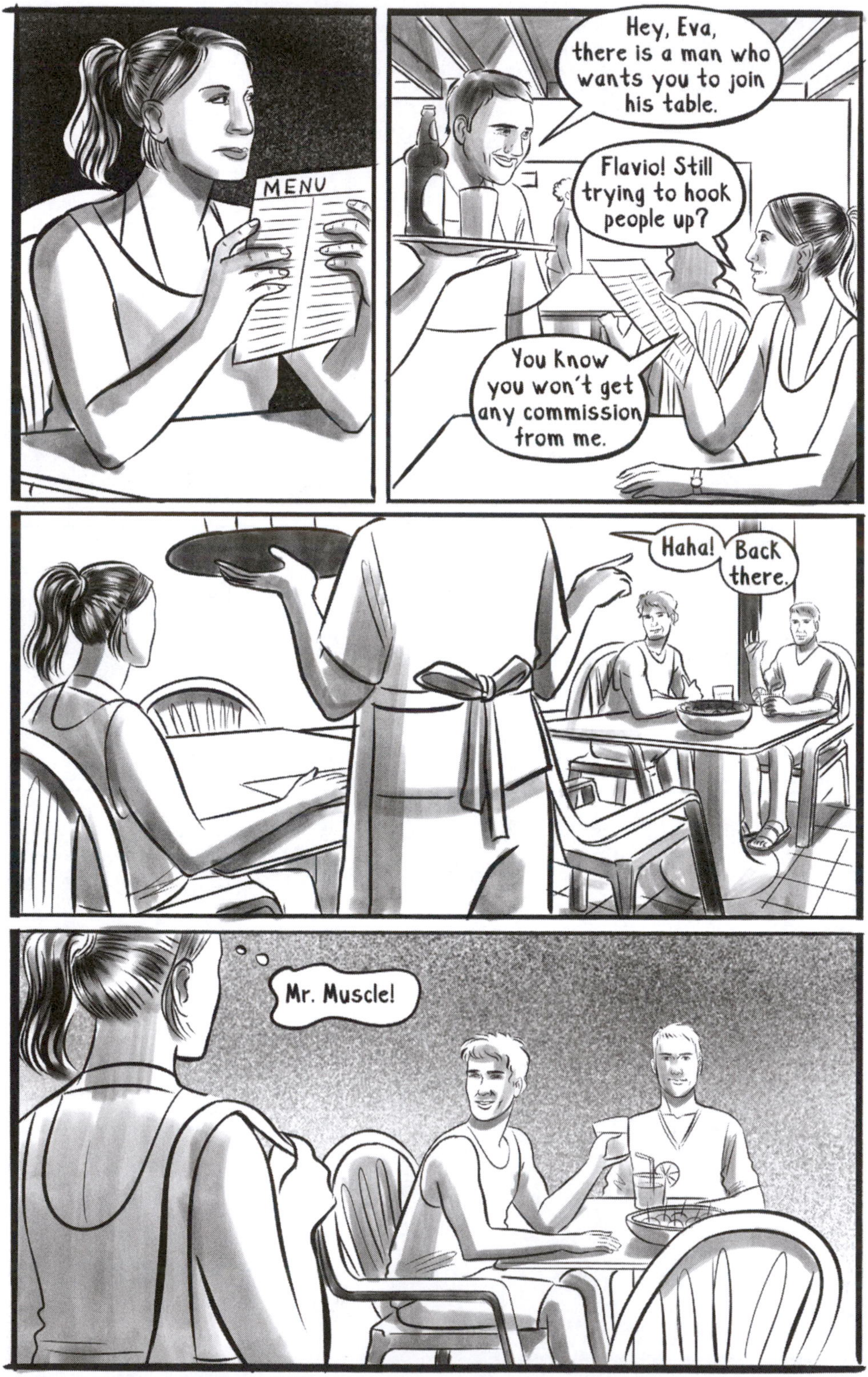
MENU
Hey, Eva, there is a man who wants you to join his table.
Flavio! Still trying to hook people up?
You know you won't get any commission from me.
Haha!
Back there.
Mr. Muscle!

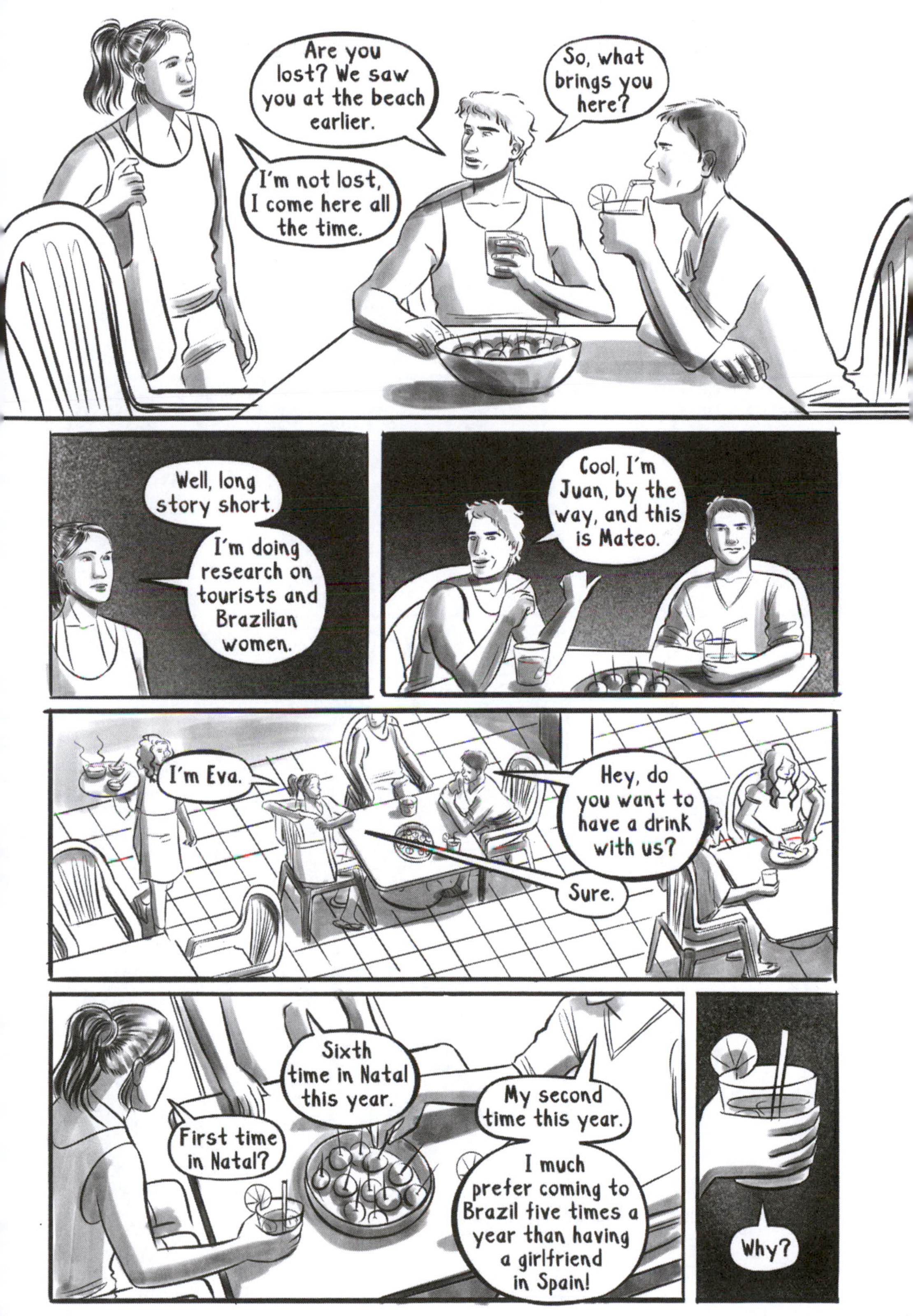
Are you lost? We saw you at the beach earlier.
So, what brings you here?
I'm not lost, I come here all the time.
Well, long story short.
I'm doing research on tourists and Brazilian women.
Cool, I'm Juan, by the way, and this is Mateo.
I'm Eva.
Hey, do you want to have a drink with us?
Sure.
First time in Natal?
Sixth time in Natal this year.
My second time this year.
I much prefer coming to Brazil five times a year than having a girlfriend in Spain!
Why?

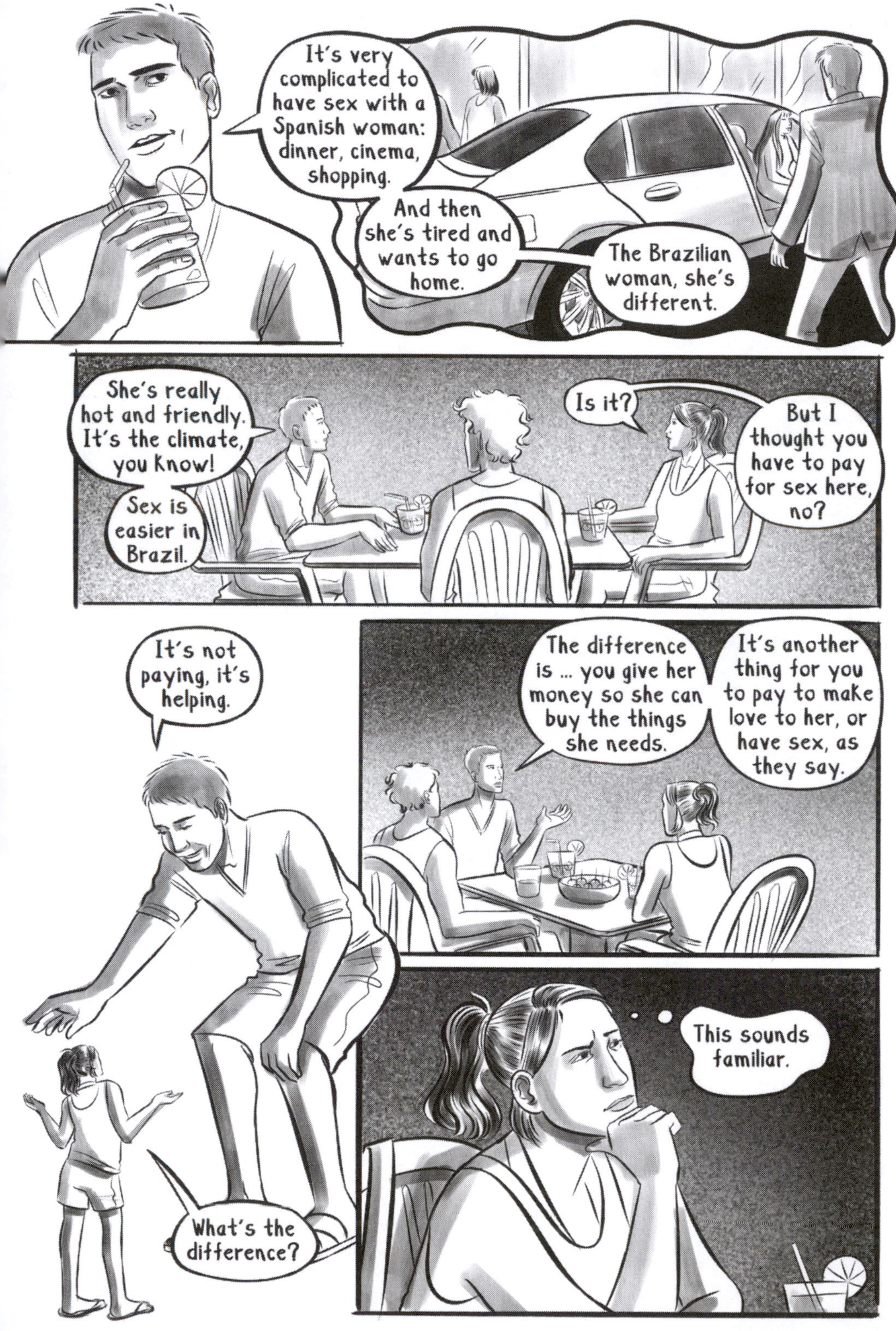
It's very complicated to have sex with a Spanish woman: dinner, cinema, shopping.
And then she's tired and wants to go home.
The Brazilian woman, she's different.
She's really hot and friendly. It's the climate, you know!
Sex is easier in Brazil.
Is it?
But I thought you have to pay for sex here, no?
It's not paying, it's helping.
What's the difference?
The difference is ... you give her money so she can buy the things she needs.
It's another thing for you to pay to make love to her, or have sex, as they say.
This sounds familiar.

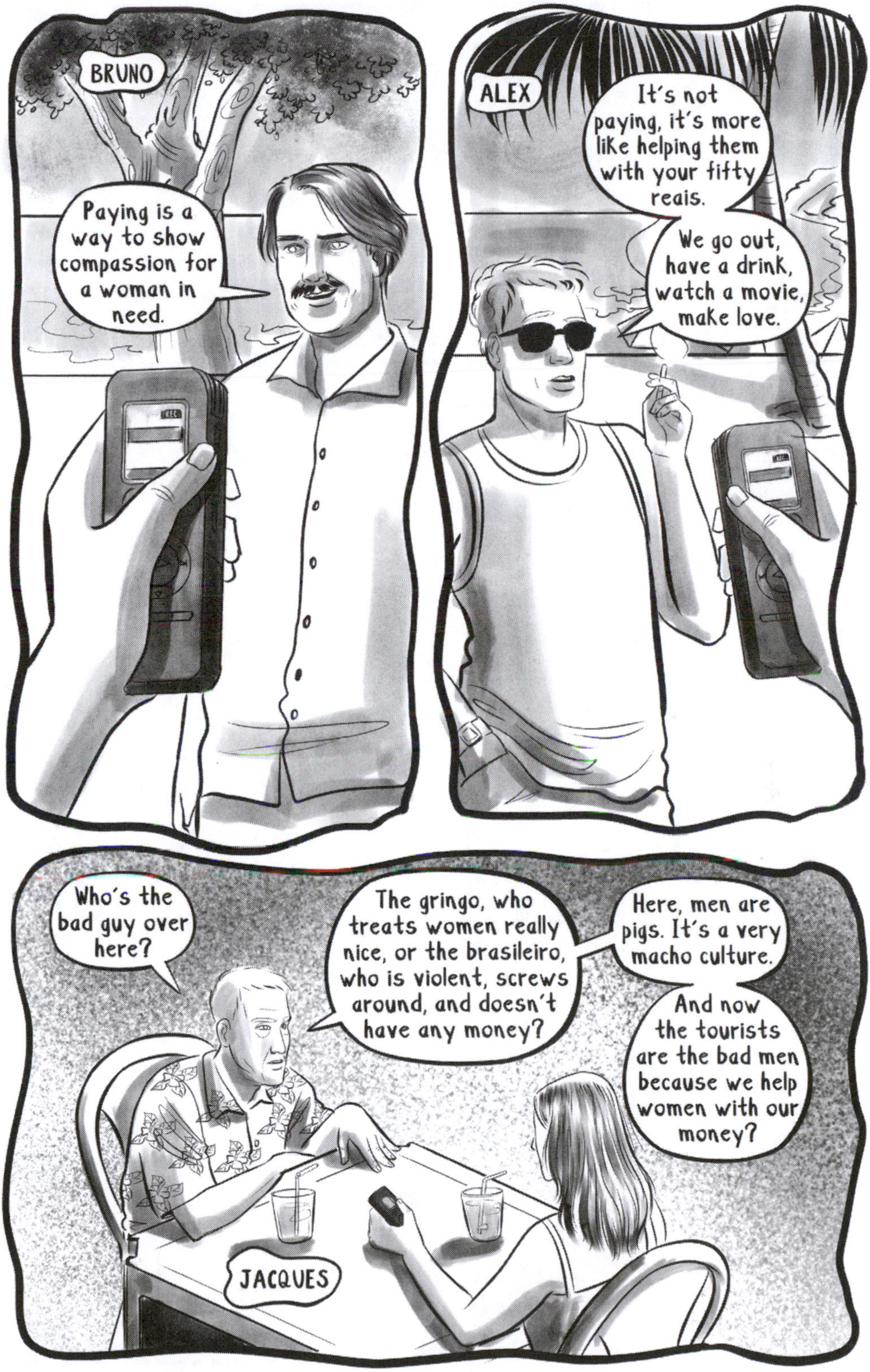
BRUNO
Paying is a way to show compassion for a woman in need.
ALEX
It's not paying, it's more like helping them with your fifty reais.
We go out, have a drink, watch a movie, make love.
Who's the bad guy over here?
The gringo, who treats women really nice, or the brasileiro, who is violent, screws around, and doesn't have any money?
Here, men are pigs. It's a very macho culture.
And now the tourists are the bad men because we help women with our money?
JACQUES

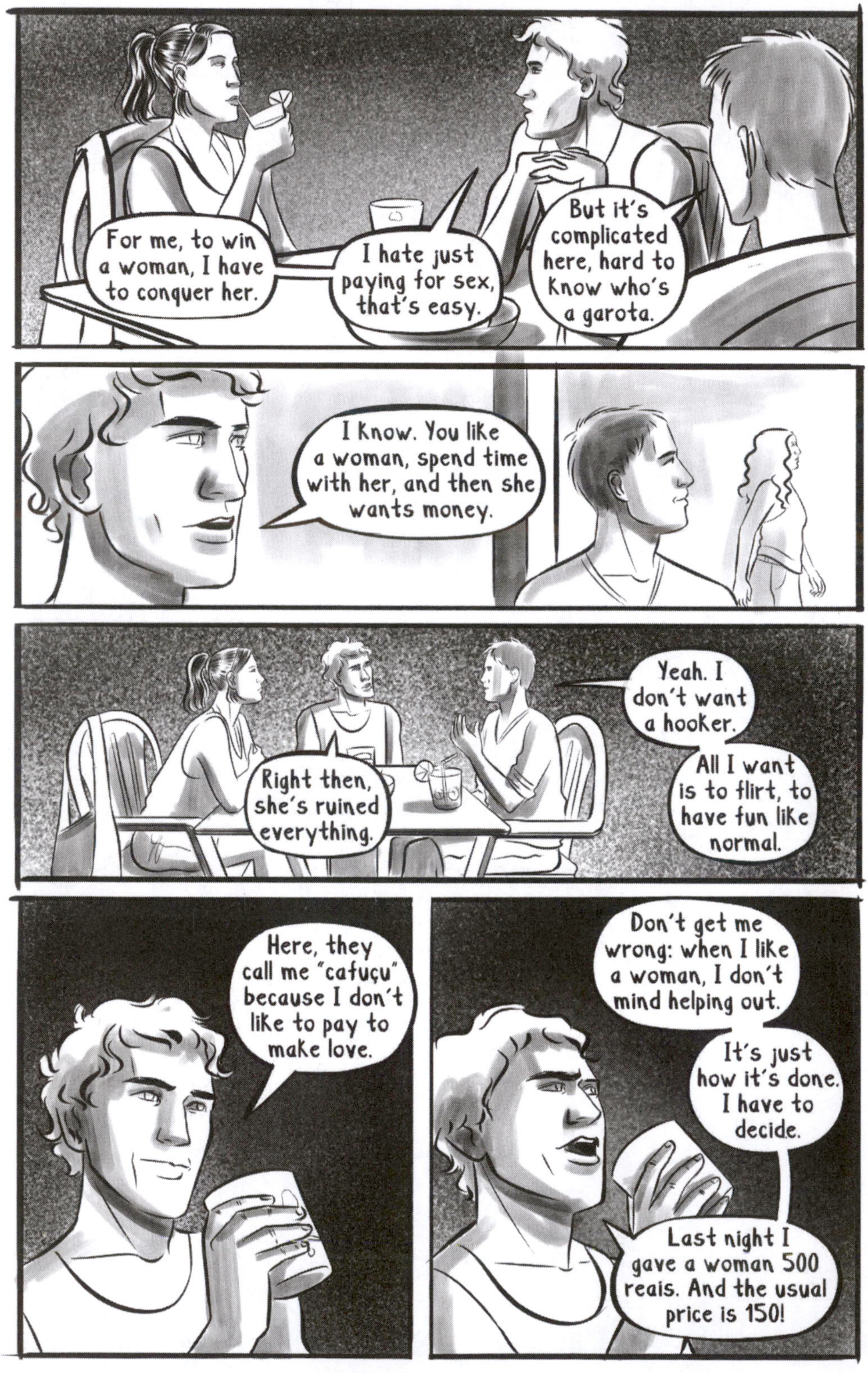
For me, to win a woman, I have to conquer her.
I hate just paying for sex, that's easy.
But it's complicated here, hard to know who's a garota.
I know. You like a woman, spend time with her, and then she wants money.
Yeah. I don't want a hooker.
All I want is to flirt, to have fun like normal.
Right then, she's ruined everything.
Here, they call me "cafuçu" because I don't like to pay to make love.
Don't get me wrong: when I like a woman, I don't mind helping out.
It's just how it's done. I have to decide.
Last night I gave a woman 500 reais. And the usual price is 150!

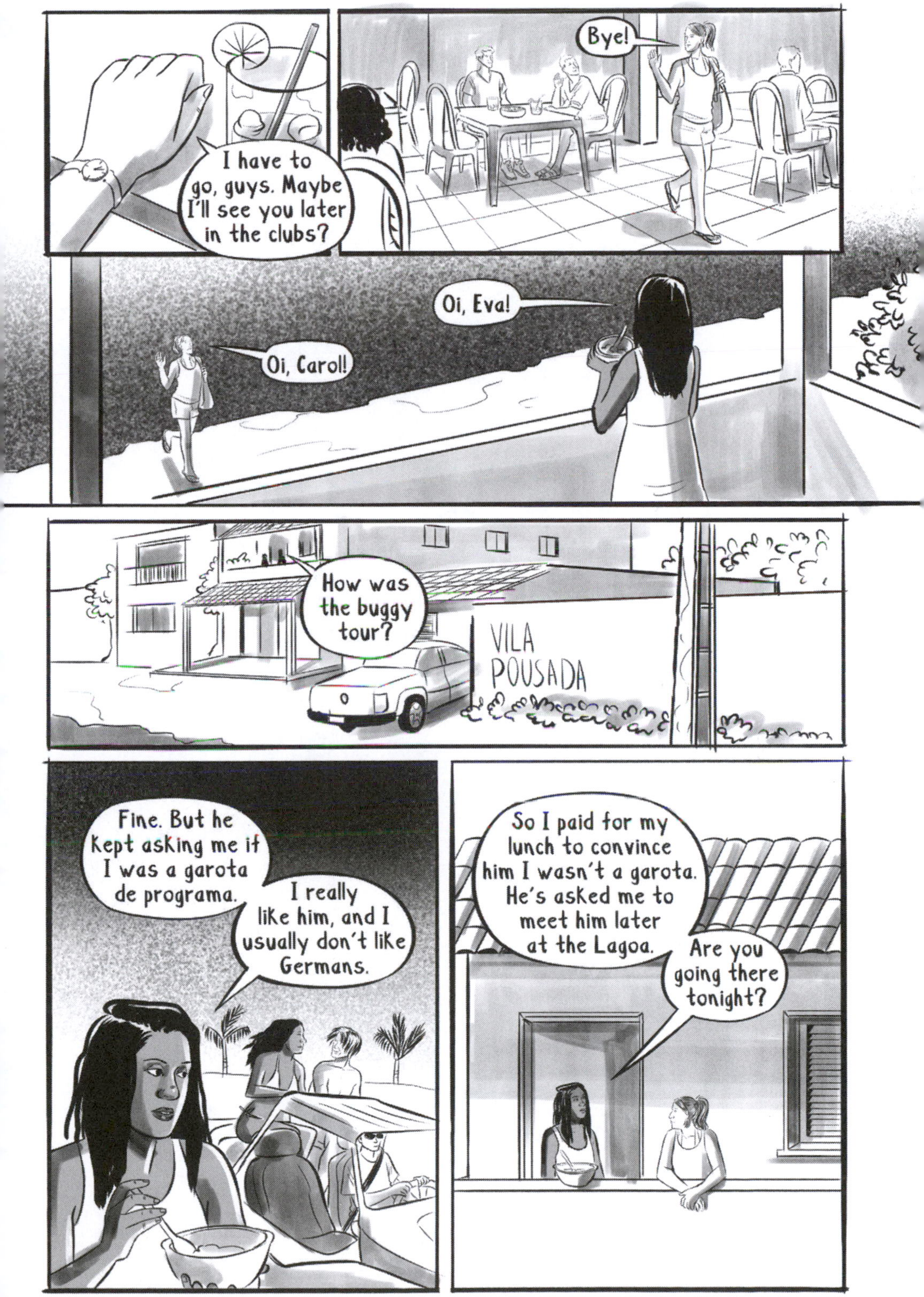
I have to go, guys. Maybe I'll see you later in the clubs?
Bye!
Oi, Eva!
Oi, Carol!
How was the buggy tour?
VILA POUSADA
Fine. But he kept asking me if I was a garota de programa.
I really like him, and I usually don't like Germans.
So I paid for my lunch to convince him I wasn't a garota. He's asked me to meet him later at the Lagoa.
Are you going there tonight?

Fieldnotes

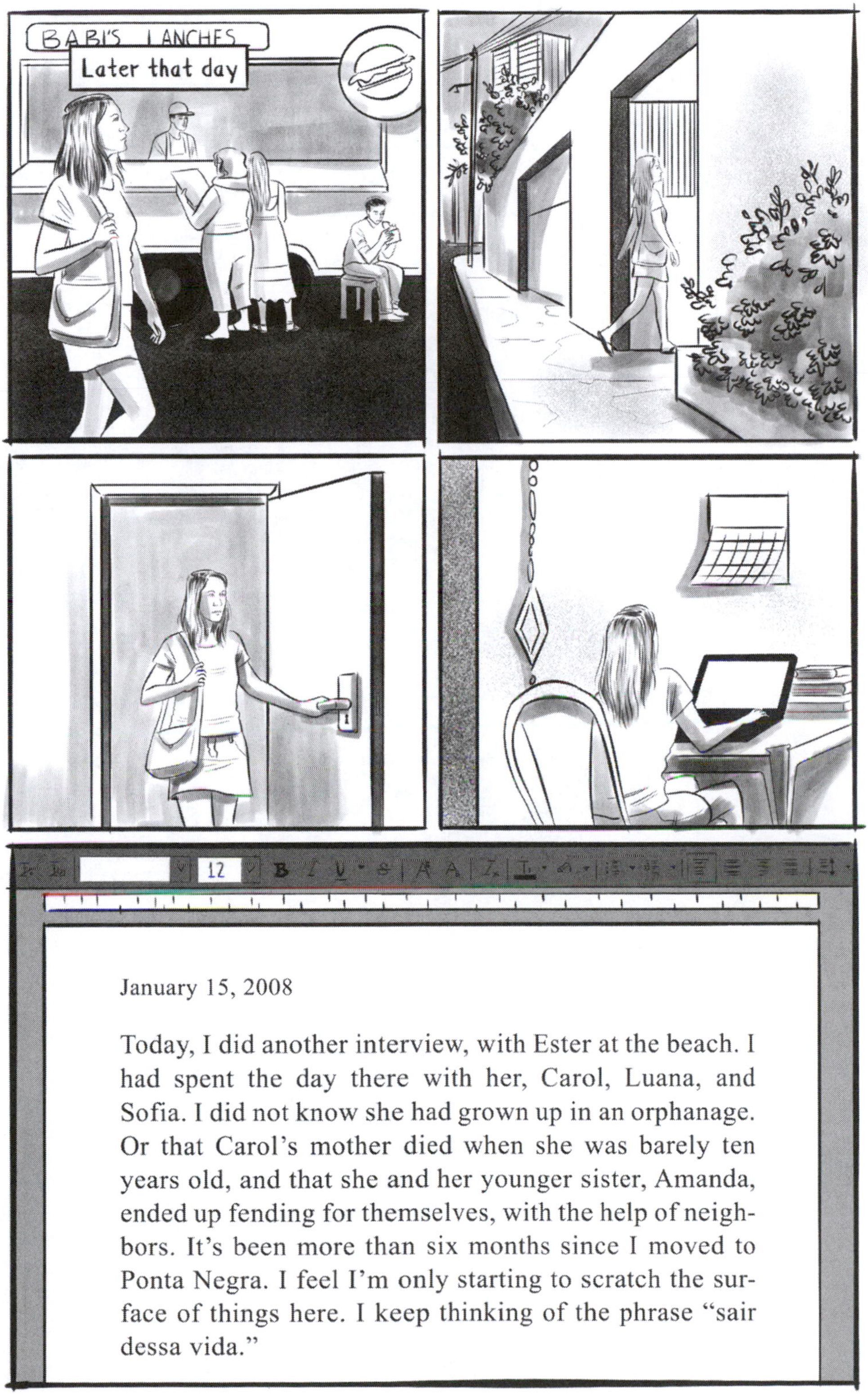
BABI'S LANCHES
Later that day
12
January 15, 2008
Today, I did another interview, with Ester at the beach. I had spent the day there with her, Carol, Luana, and Sofia. I did not know she had grown up in an orphanage. Or that Carol's mother died when she was barely ten years old, and that she and her younger sister, Amanda, ended up fending for themselves, with the help of neighbors. It's been more than six months since I moved to Ponta Negra. I feel I'm only starting to scratch the surface of things here. I keep thinking of the phrase "sair dessa vida."

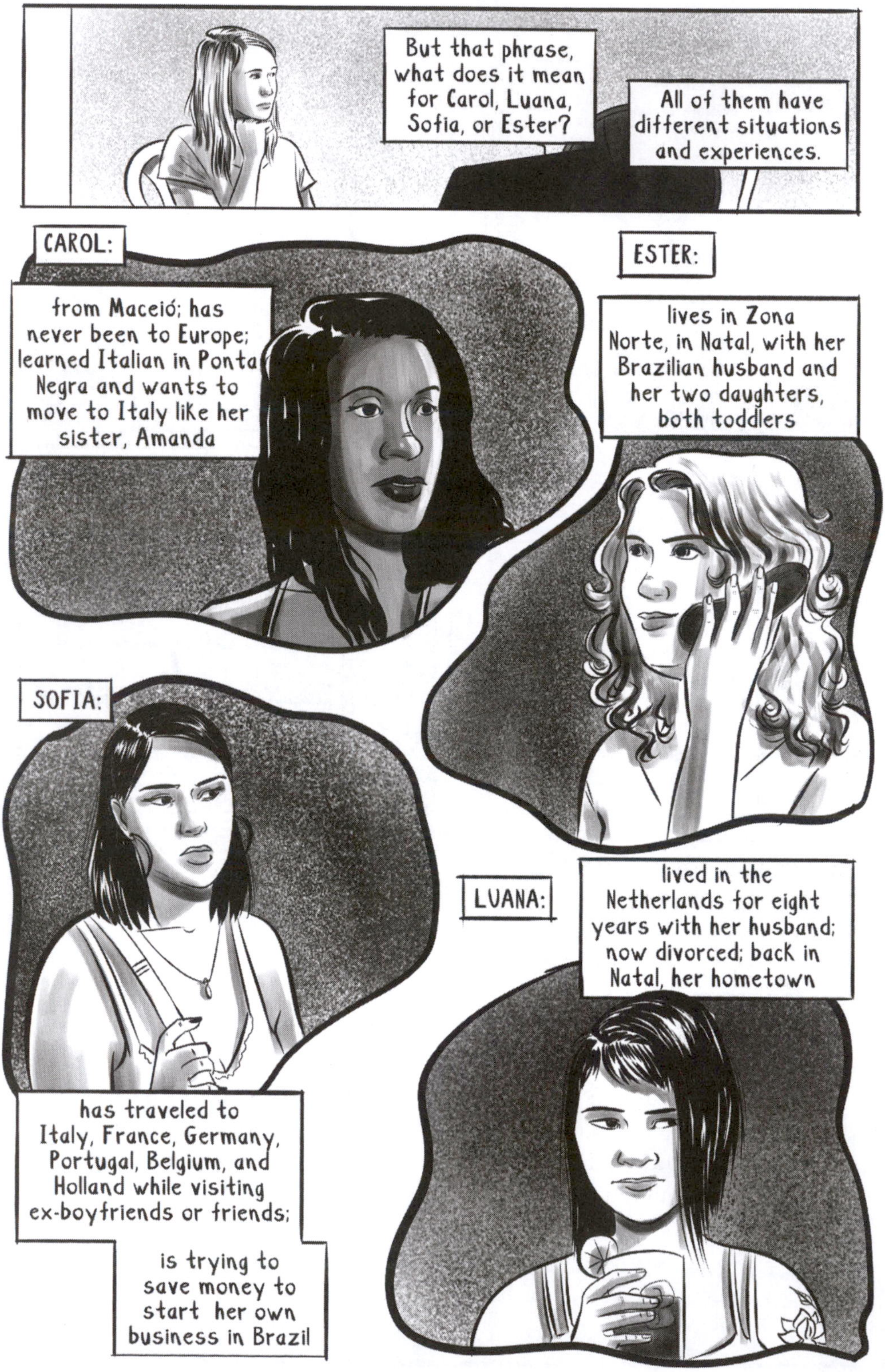
But that phrase, what does it mean for Carol, Luana, Sofia, or Ester?
All of them have different situations and experiences.
CAROL:
from Maceió; has never been to Europe; learned Italian in Ponta Negra and wants to move to Italy like her sister, Amanda
ESTER:
lives in Zona Norte, in Natal, with her Brazilian husband and her two daughters, both toddlers
SOFIA:
has traveled to Italy, France, Germany, Portugal, Belgium, and Holland while visiting ex-boyfriends or friends;
is trying to save money to start her own business in Brazil
LUANA:
lived in the Netherlands for eight years with her husband; now divorced; back in Natal, her hometown

PART 3: SAIR DESSA VIDA

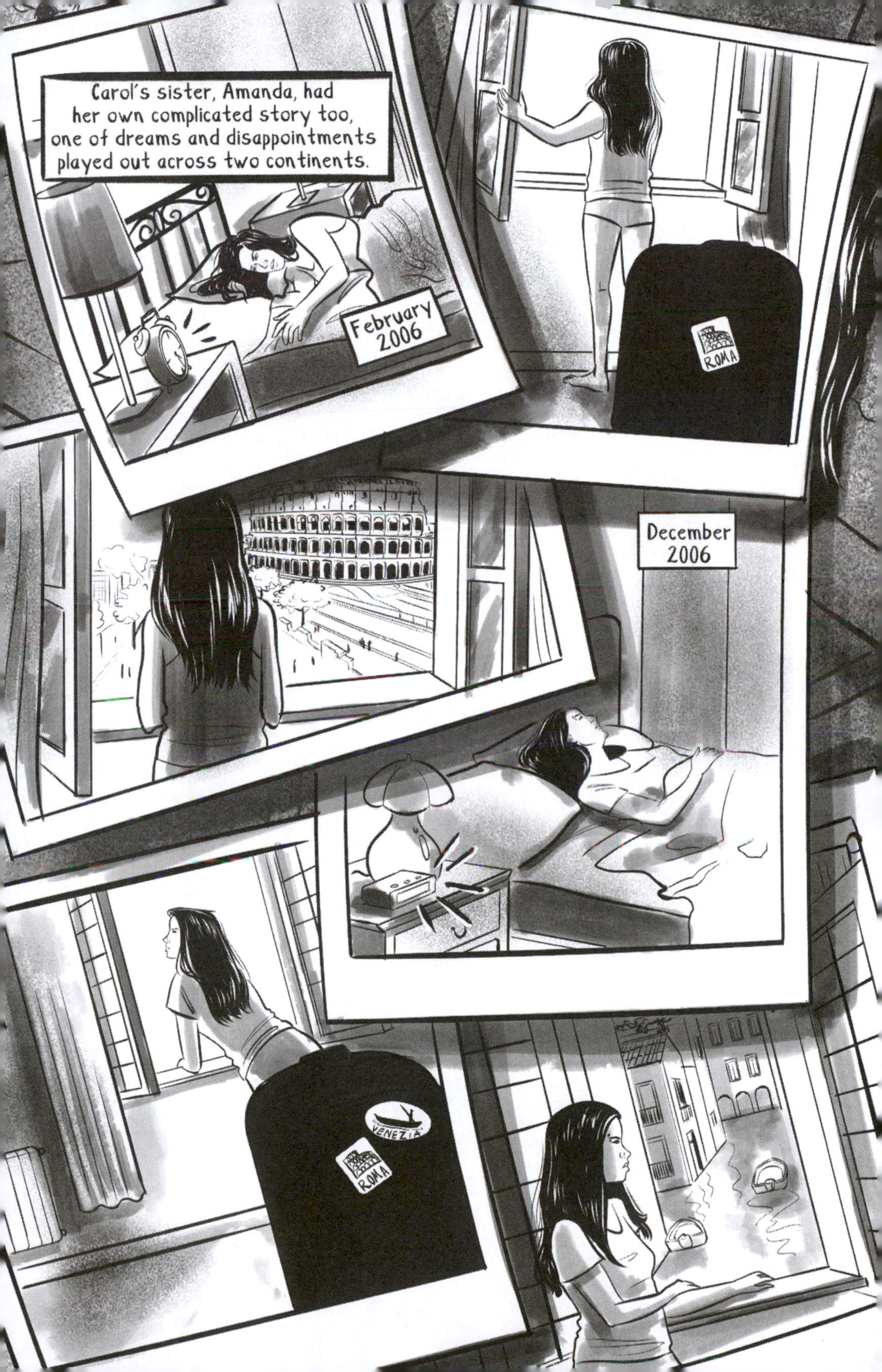
Carol's sister, Amanda, had her own complicated story too, one of dreams and disappointments played out across two continents.
February 2006
ROMA
December 2006
VENEZIA
ROMA

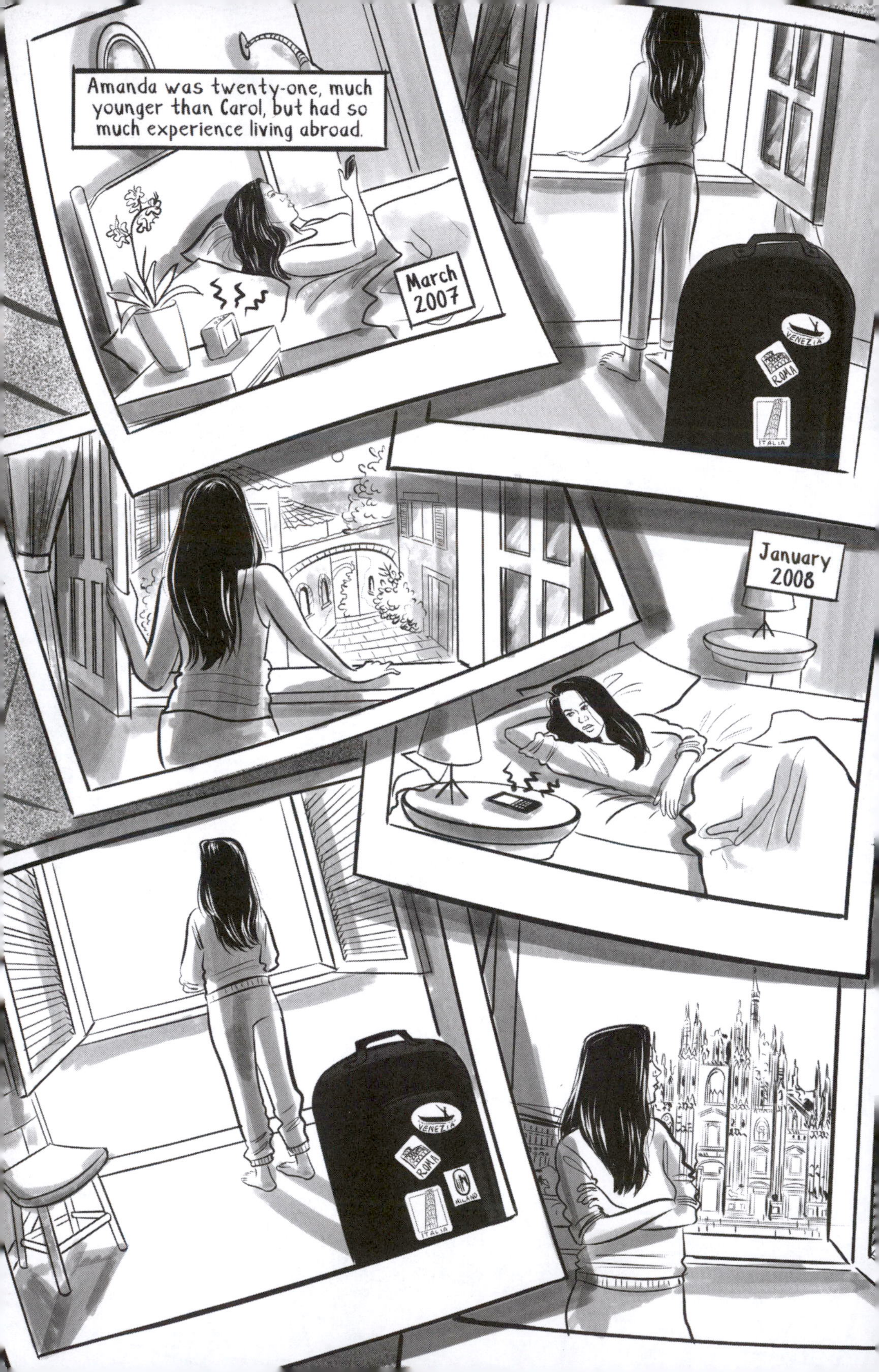

Amanda was twenty-one, much younger than Carol, but had so much experience living abroad.
March 2007
VENEZIA
ROMA
ITALIA
January 2008
VENEZIA
ROMA
MILANO
ITALIA

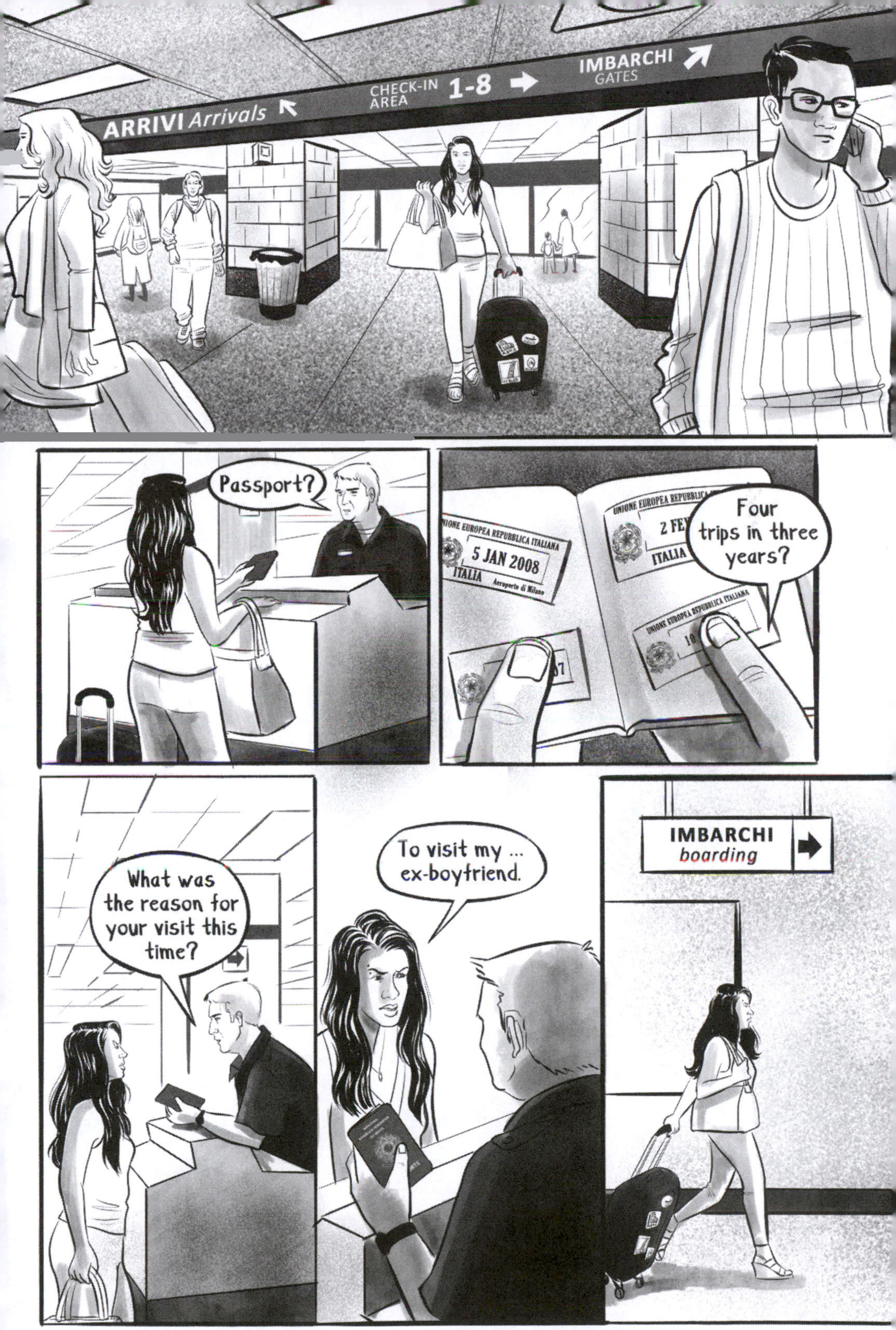

ARRIVI Arrivals
CHECK-IN AREA 1-8
IMBARCHI GATES
Passport?
UNIONE EUROPEA REPUBBLICA ITALIANA 5 JAN 2008 ITALIA Aeroporto di Milano
Four trips in three years?
What was the reason for your visit this time?
To visit my ... ex-boyfriend.
IMBARCHI boarding

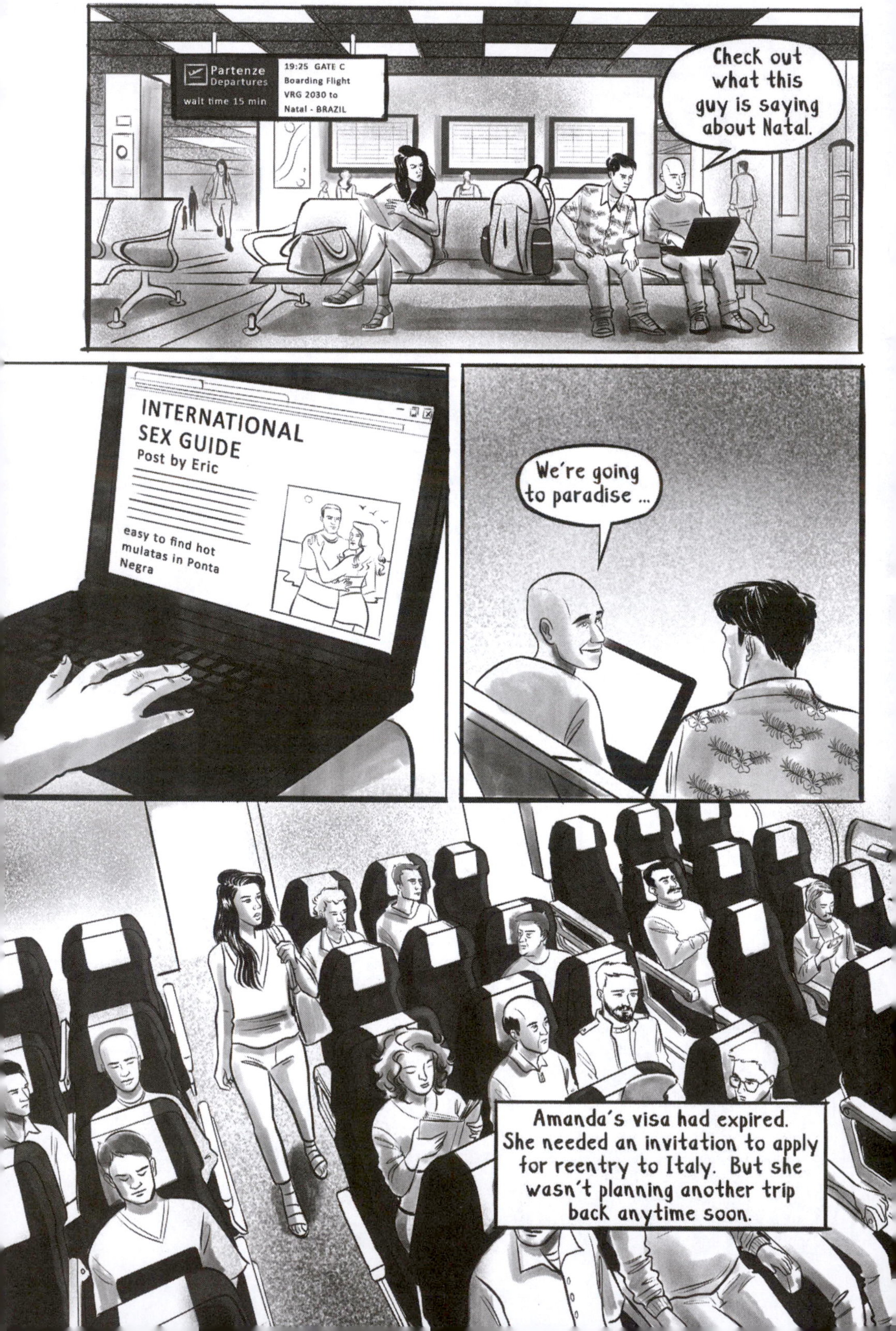
Partenze
Departures
wait time 15 min
19:25 GATE C
Boarding Flight
VRG 2030 to
Natal - BRAZIL
Check out what this guy is saying about Natal.
INTERNATIONAL SEX GUIDE
Post by Eric
easy to find hot mulatas in Ponta Negra
We're going to paradise ...
Amanda's visa had expired. She needed an invitation to apply for reentry to Italy. But she wasn't planning another trip back anytime soon.

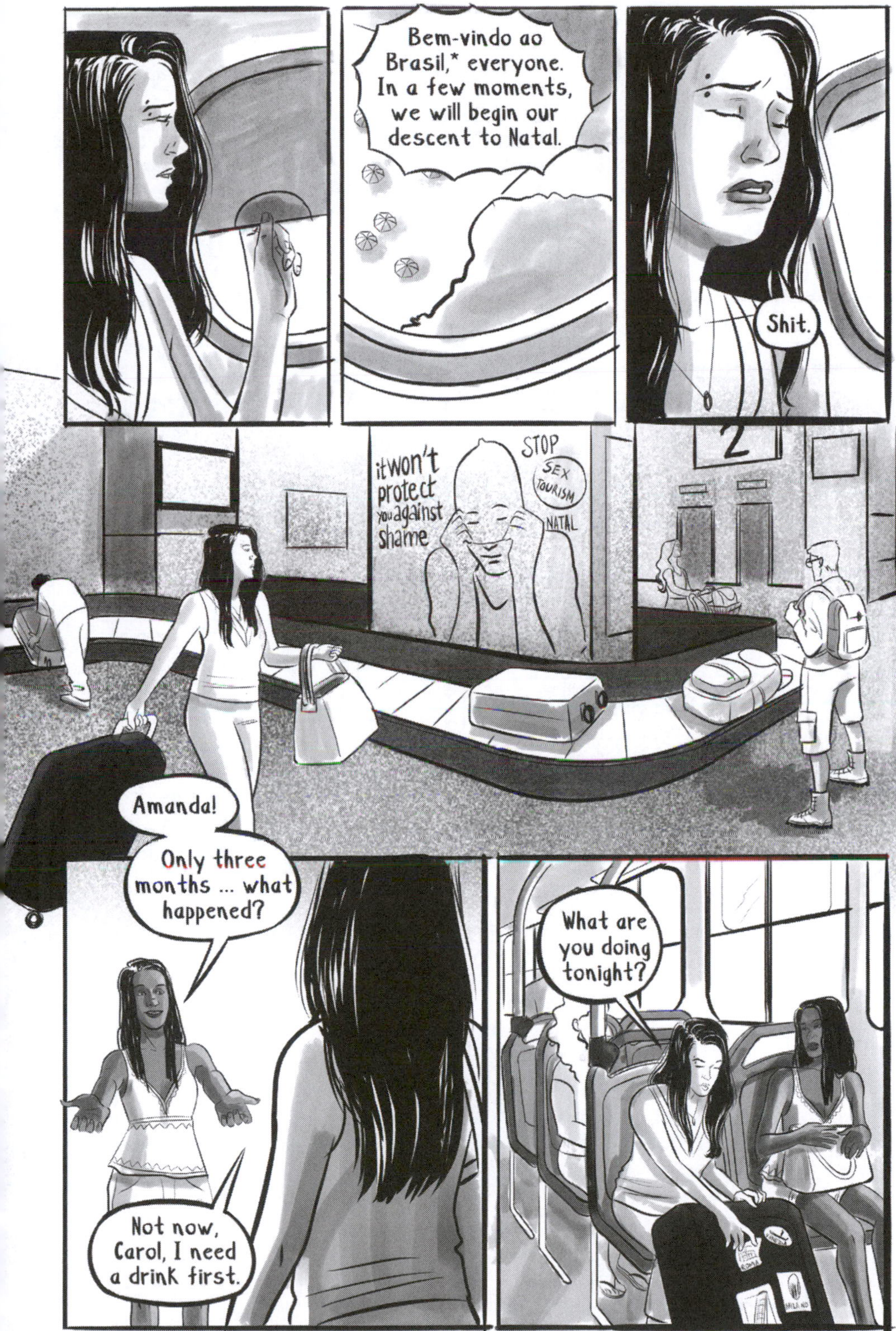
Bem-vindo ao Brasil,* everyone. In a few moments, we will begin our descent to Natal.
Shit.
it won't protect you against shame
STOP SEX TOURISM NATAL
Amanda!
Only three months ... what happened?
Not now, Carol, I need a drink first.
What are you doing tonight?

*bem-vindo ao Brasil = welcome to Brazil

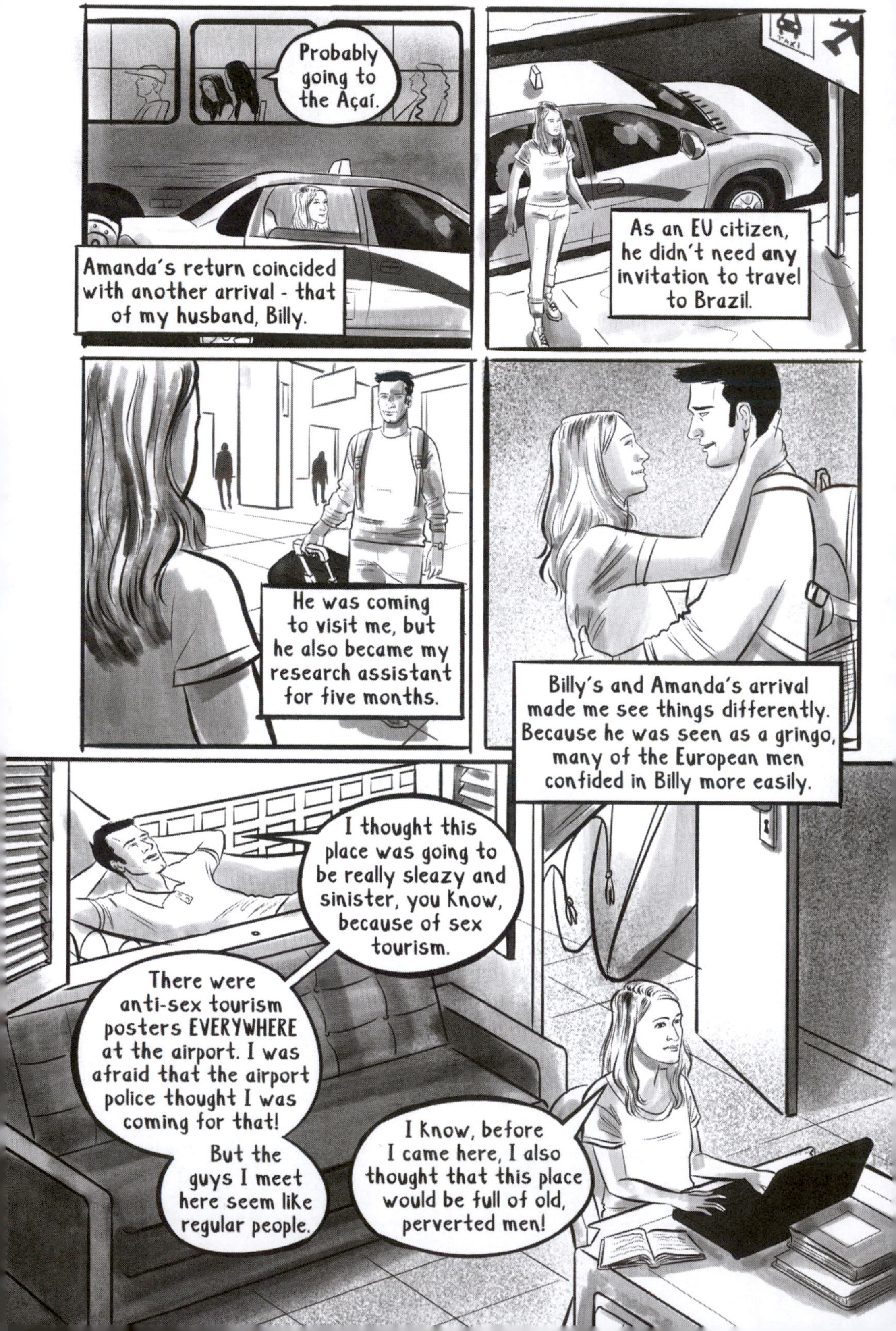
Probably going to the Açaí.
Amanda's return coincided with another arrival - that of my husband, Billy.
As an EU citizen, he didn't need any invitation to travel to Brazil.
He was coming to visit me, but he also became my research assistant for five months.
Billy's and Amanda's arrival made me see things differently. Because he was seen as a gringo, many of the European men confided in Billy more easily.
I thought this place was going to be really sleazy and sinister, you know, because of sex tourism.
There were anti-sex tourism posters EVERYWHERE at the airport. I was afraid that the airport police thought I was coming for that!
But the guys I meet here seem like regular people.
I know, before I came here, I also thought that this place would be full of old, perverted men!

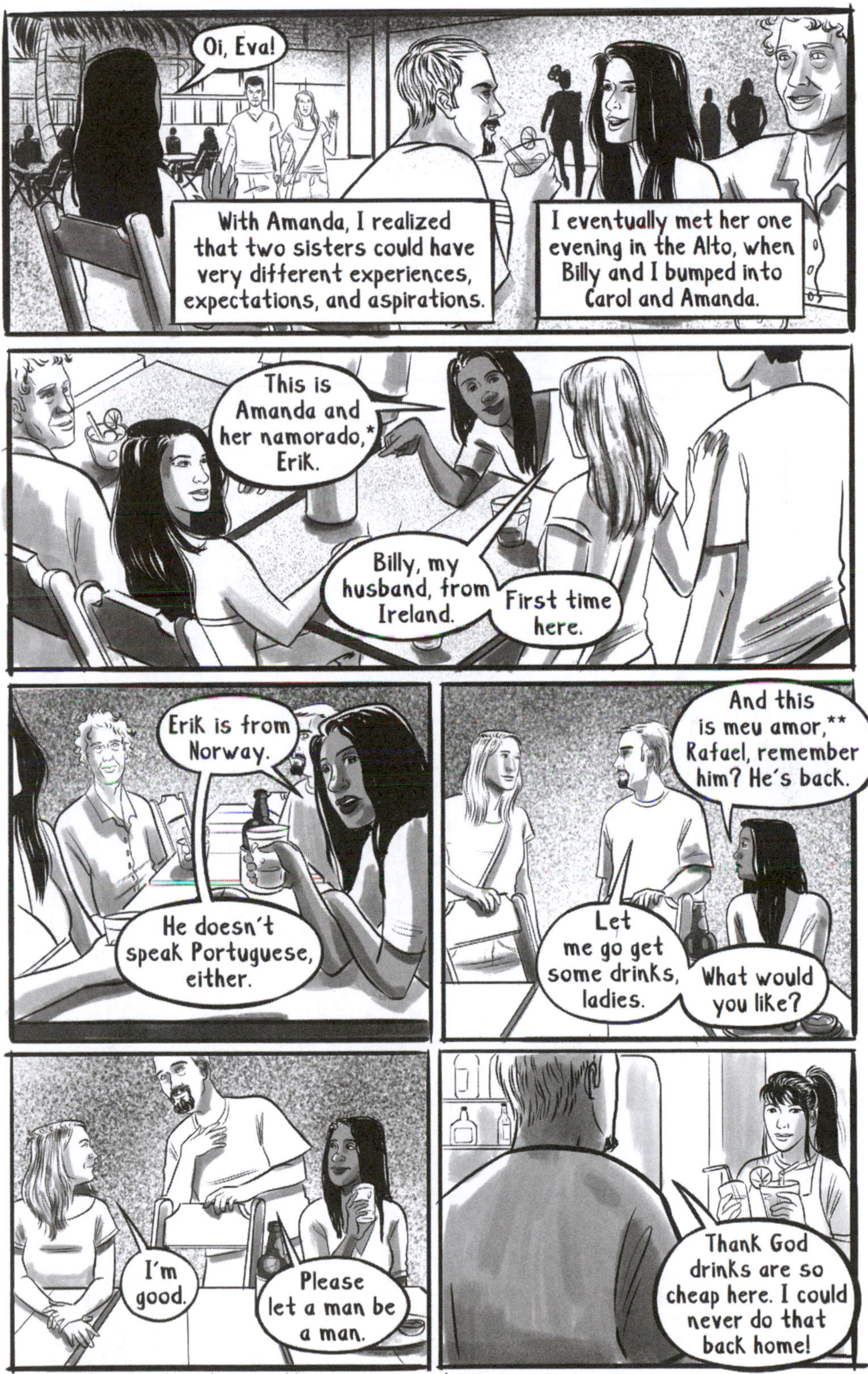
Oi, Eva!
With Amanda, I realized that two sisters could have very different experiences, expectations, and aspirations.
I eventually met her one evening in the Alto, when Billy and I bumped into Carol and Amanda.
This is Amanda and her namorado,* Erik.
Billy, my husband, from Ireland.
First time here.
Erik is from Norway.
He doesn't speak Portuguese, either.
And this is meu amor,** Rafael, remember him? He's back.
Let me go get some drinks, ladies.
What would you like?
I'm good.
Please let a man be a man.
Thank God drinks are so cheap here. I could never do that back home!

*namorado = boyfriend **meu amor = my love

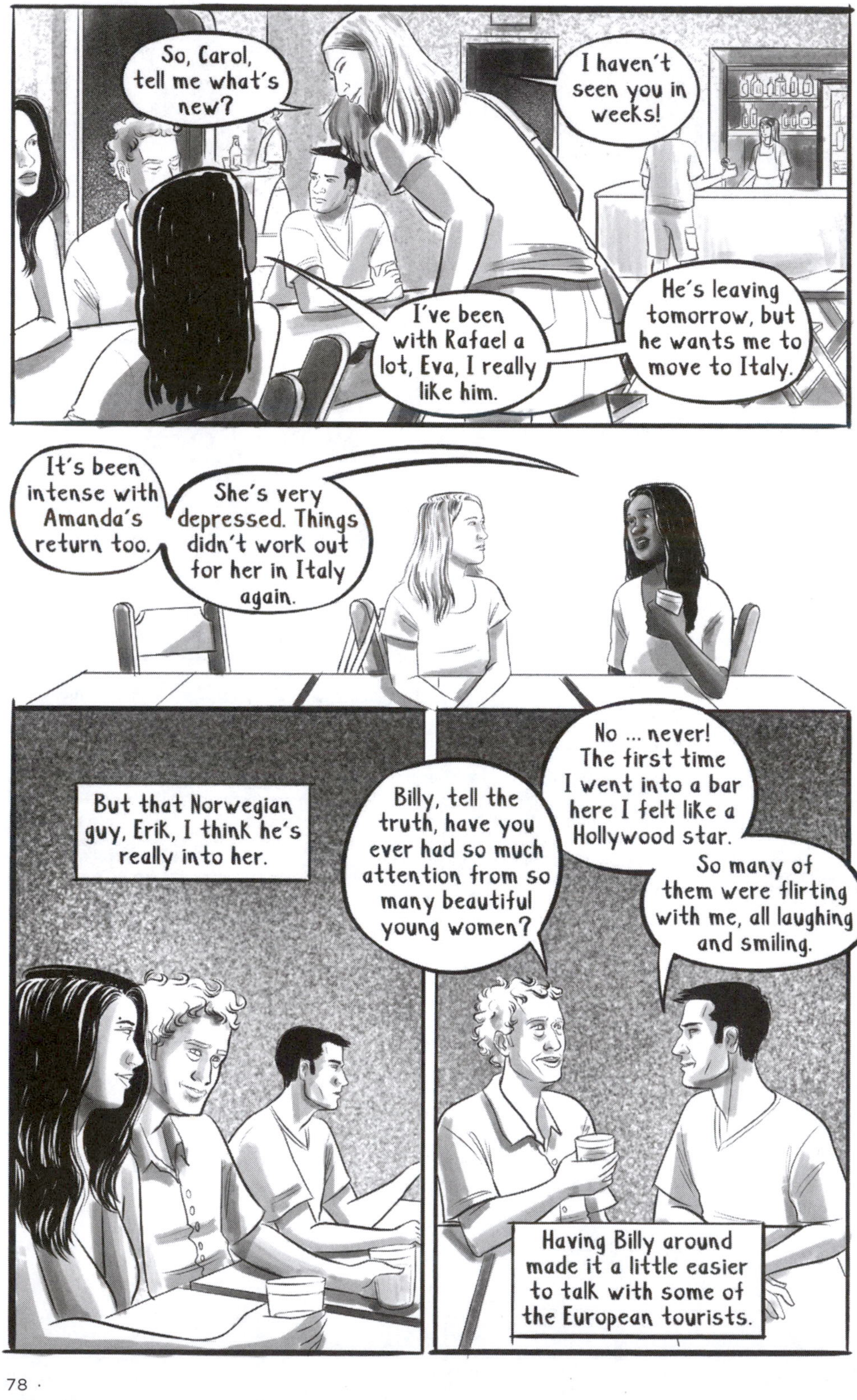

So, Carol, tell me what's new?
I haven't seen you in weeks!
I've been with Rafael a lot, Eva, I really like him.
He's leaving tomorrow, but he wants me to move to Italy.
It's been intense with Amanda's return too.
She's very depressed. Things didn't work out for her in Italy again.
But that Norwegian guy, Erik, I think he's really into her.
Billy, tell the truth, have you ever had so much attention from so many beautiful young women?
No ... never! The first time I went into a bar here I felt like a Hollywood star.
So many of them were flirting with me, all laughing and smiling.
Having Billy around made it a little easier to talk with some of the European tourists.

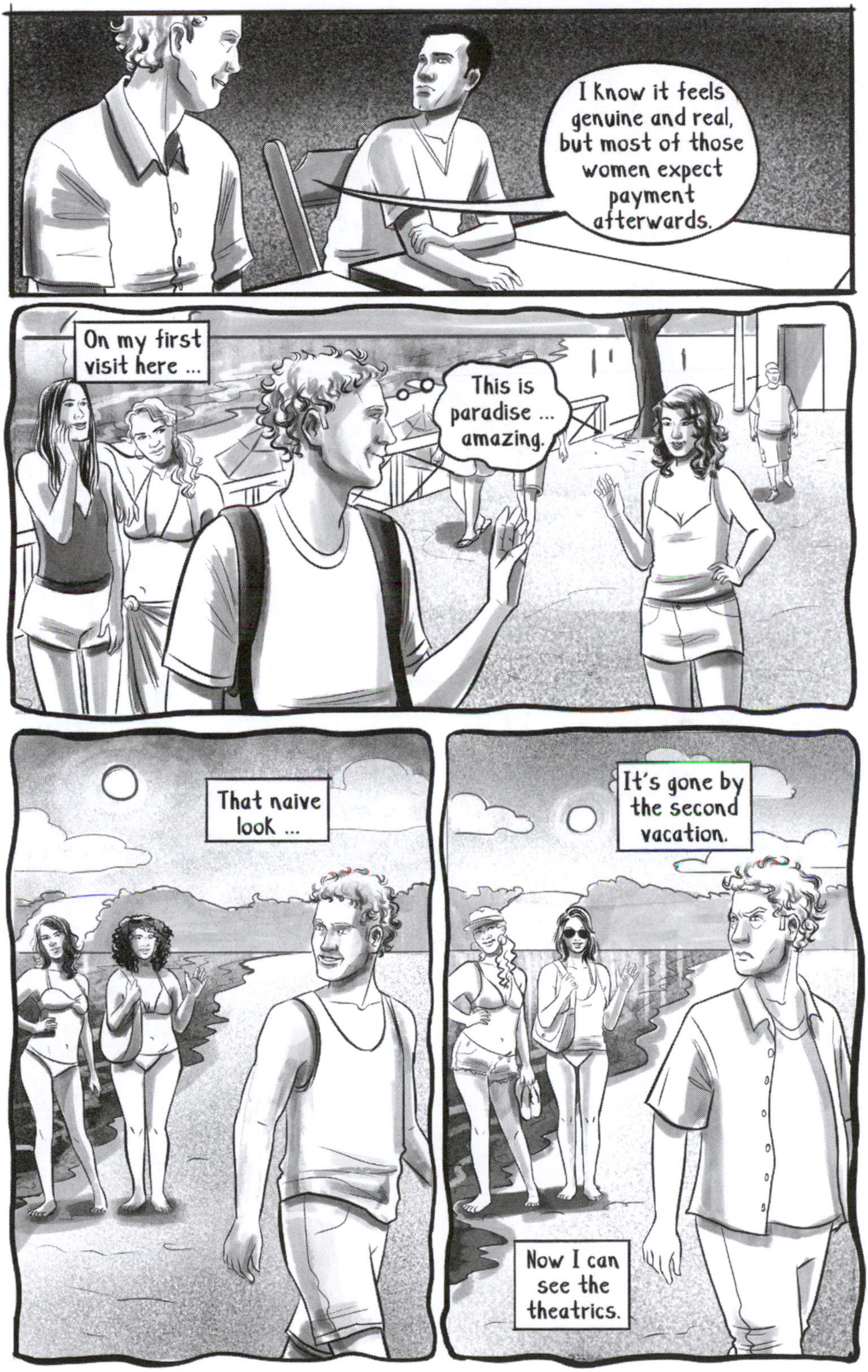
I know it feels genuine and real, but most of those women expect payment afterwards.
On my first visit here ...
This is paradise ... amazing.
That naive look ...
It's gone by the second vacation.
Now I can see the theatrics.

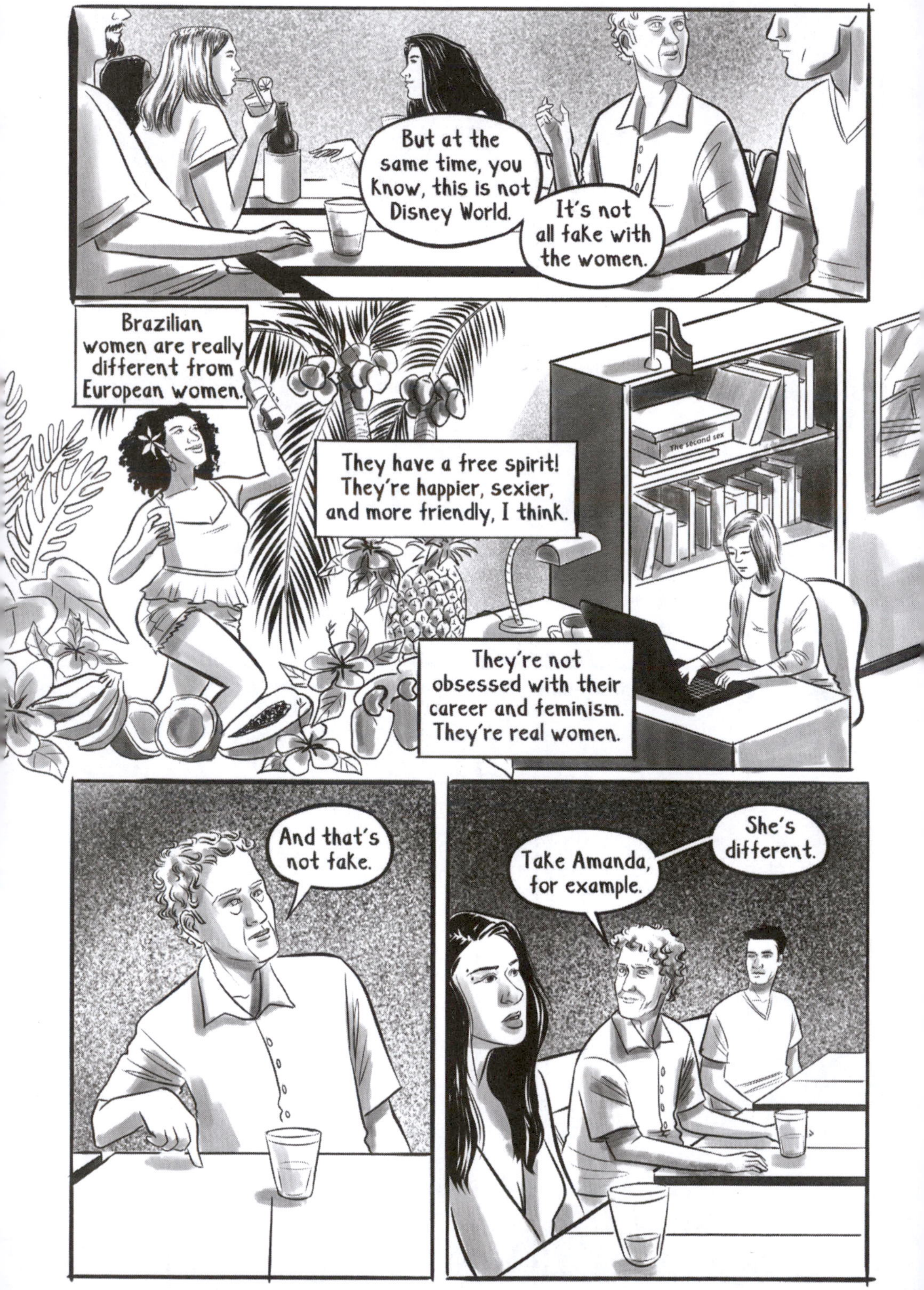
But at the same time, you know, this is not Disney World.
It's not all fake with the women.
Brazilian women are really different from European women.
They have a free spirit! They're happier, sexier, and more friendly, I think.
The second sex
They're not obsessed with their career and feminism. They're real women.
And that's not fake.
Take Amanda, for example.
She's different.

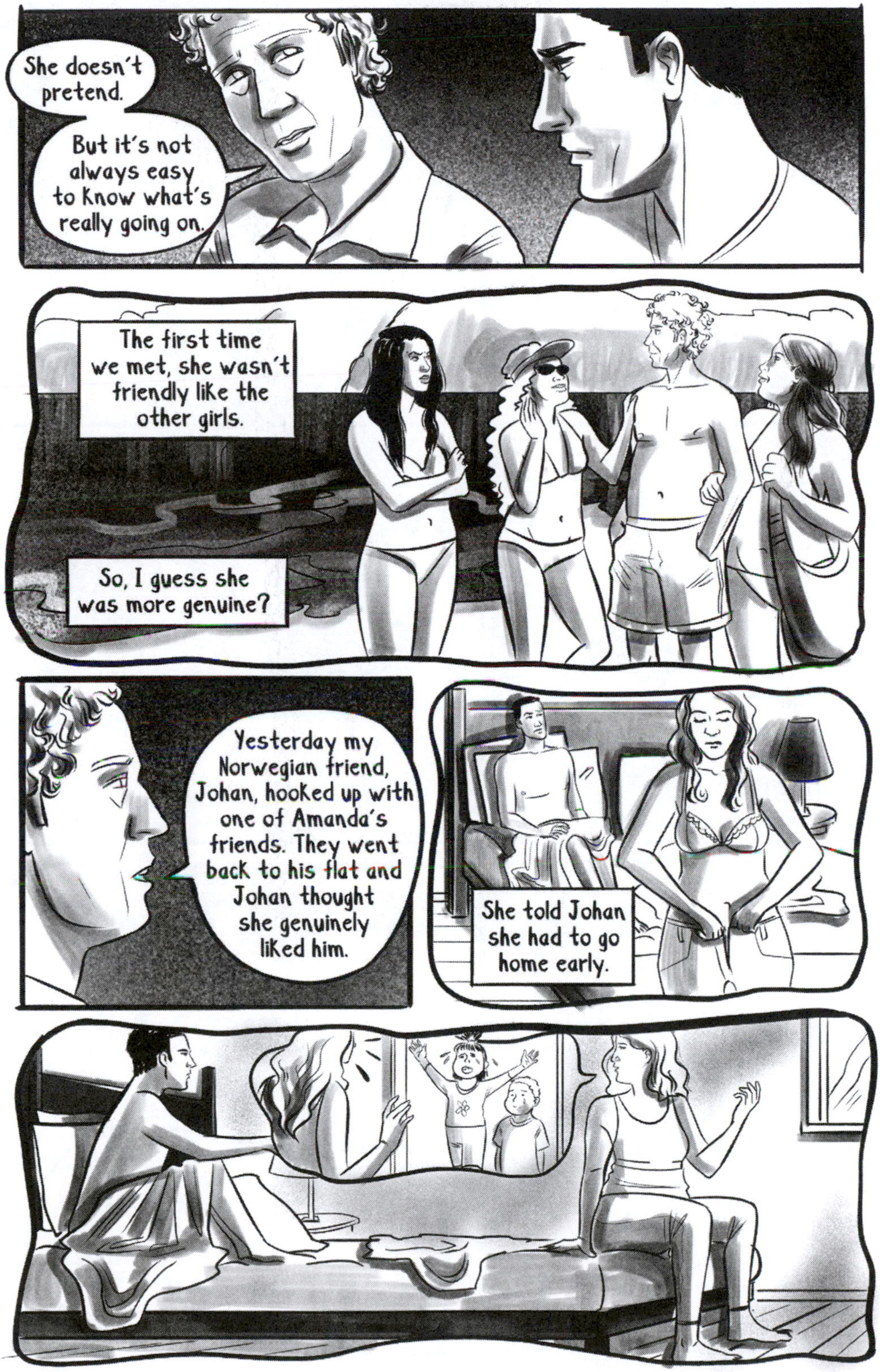
She doesn't pretend.
But it's not always easy to know what's really going on.
The first time we met, she wasn't friendly like the other girls.
So, I guess she was more genuine?
Yesterday my Norwegian friend, Johan, hooked up with one of Amanda's friends. They went back to his flat and Johan thought she genuinely liked him.
She told Johan she had to go home early.

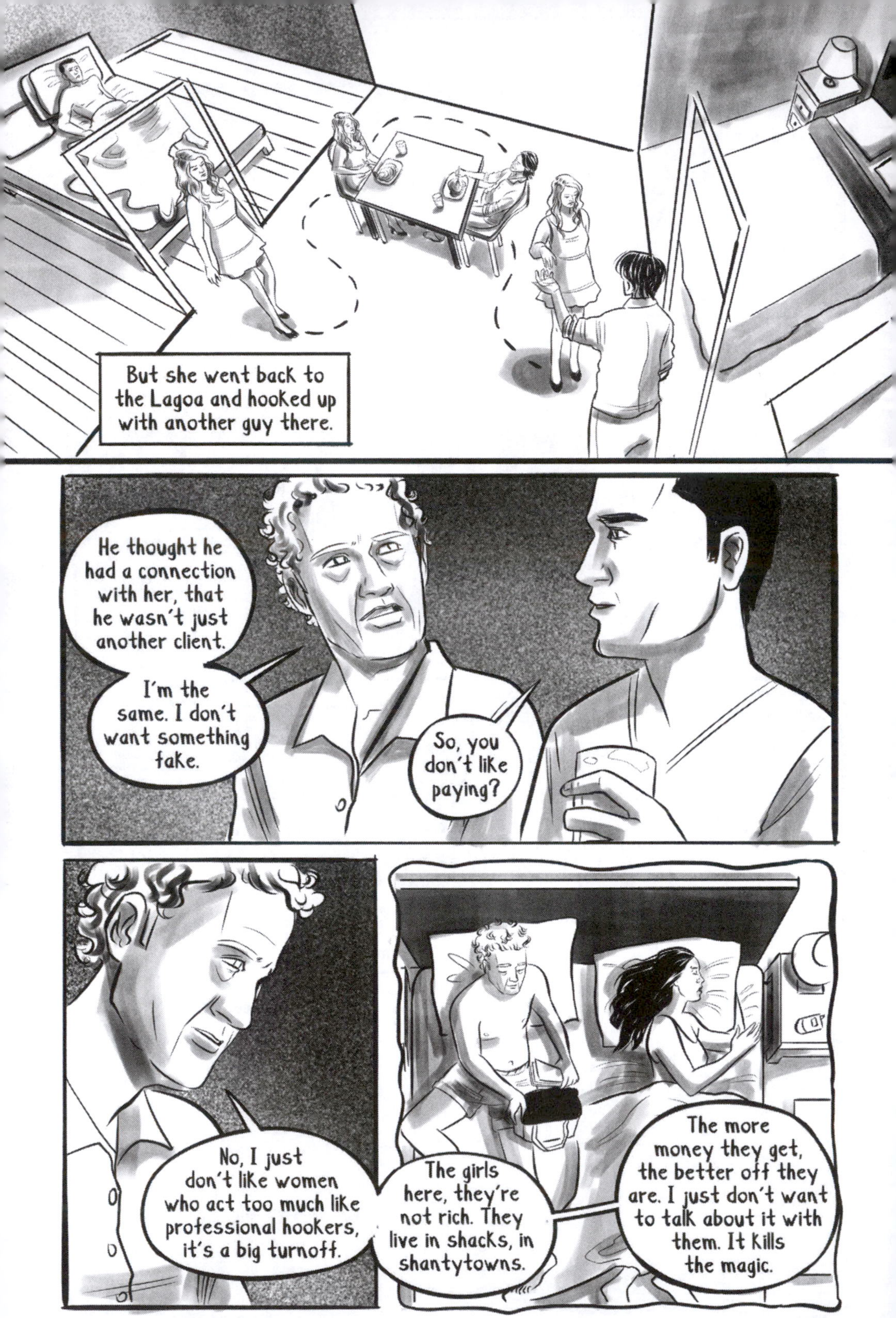

But she went back to the Lagoa and hooked up with another guy there.
He thought he had a connection with her, that he wasn't just another client.
I'm the same. I don't want something fake.
So, you don't like paying?
No, I just don't like women who act too much like professional hookers, it's a big turnoff.
The girls here, they're not rich. They live in shacks, in shantytowns.
The more money they get, the better off they are. I just don't want to talk about it with them. It kills the magic.

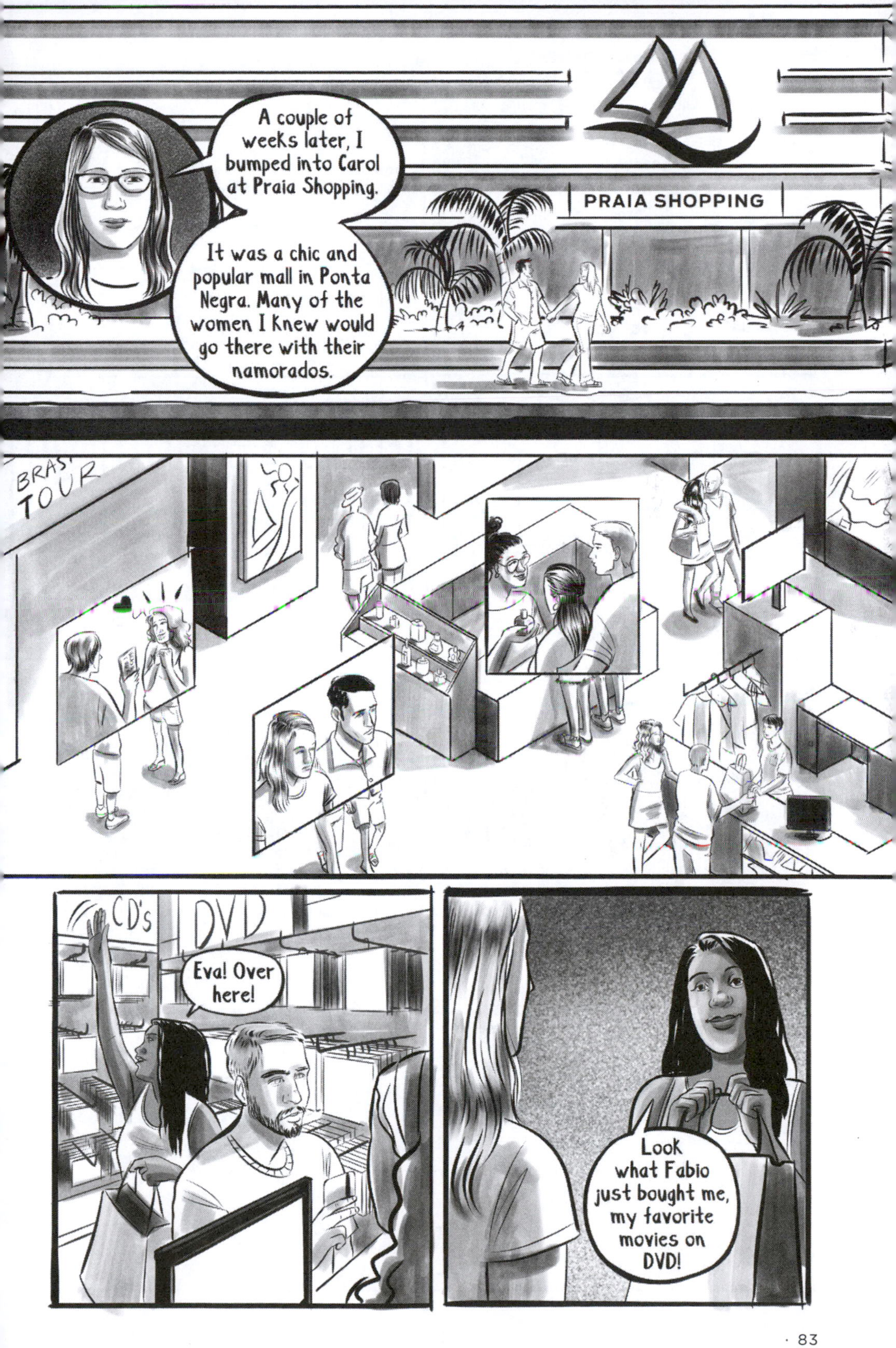
A couple of weeks later, I bumped into Carol at Praia Shopping.
It was a chic and popular mall in Ponta Negra. Many of the women I knew would go there with their namorados.
PRAIA SHOPPING
TOUR
CD's
DVD
Eva! Over here!
Look what Fabio just bought me, my favorite movies on DVD!

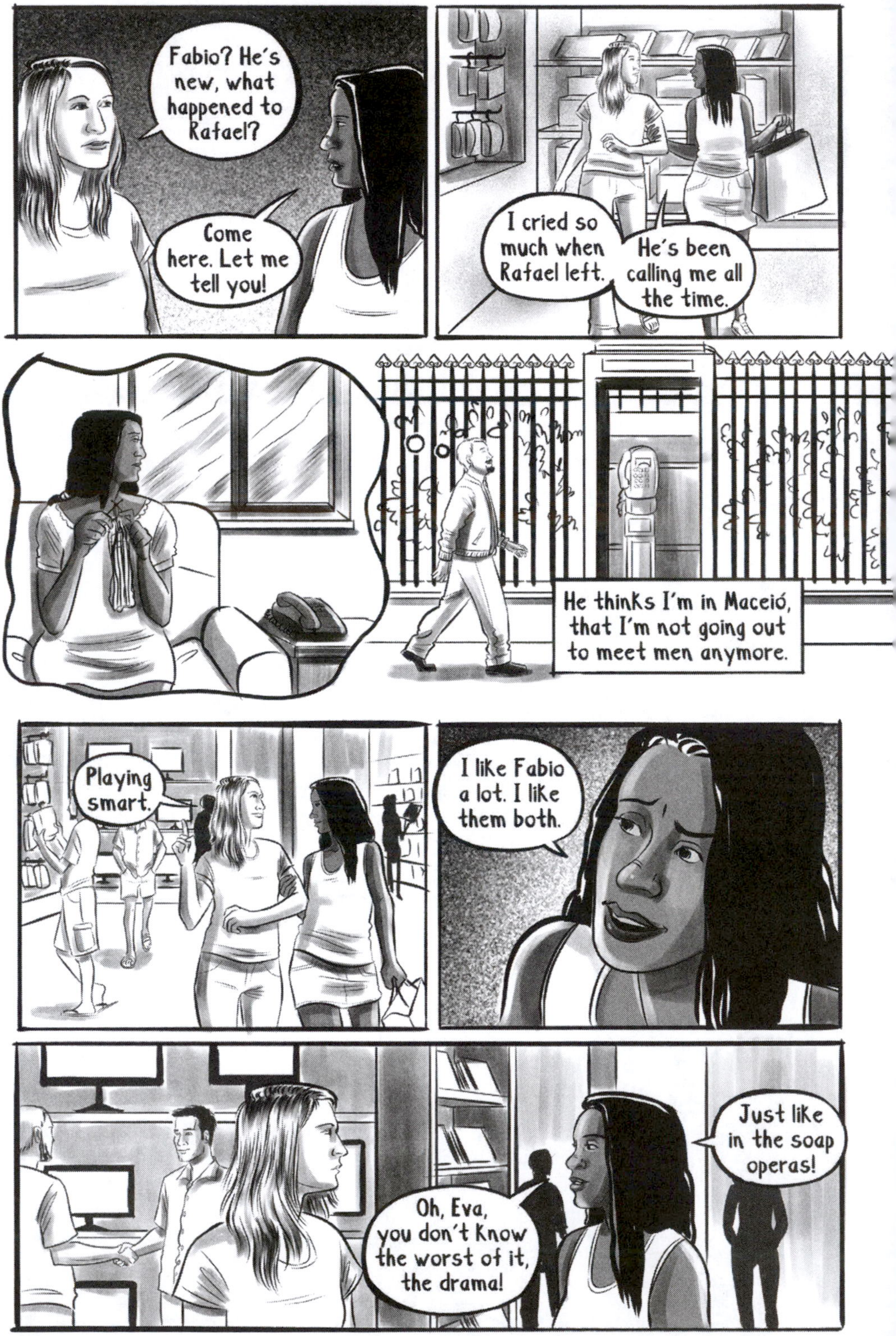
Fabio? He's new, what happened to Rafael?
Come here. Let me tell you!
I cried so much when Rafael left.
He's been calling me all the time.
He thinks I'm in Maceió, that I'm not going out to meet men anymore.
Playing smart.
I like Fabio a lot. I like them both.
Just like in the soap operas!
Oh, Eva, you don't know the worst of it, the drama!

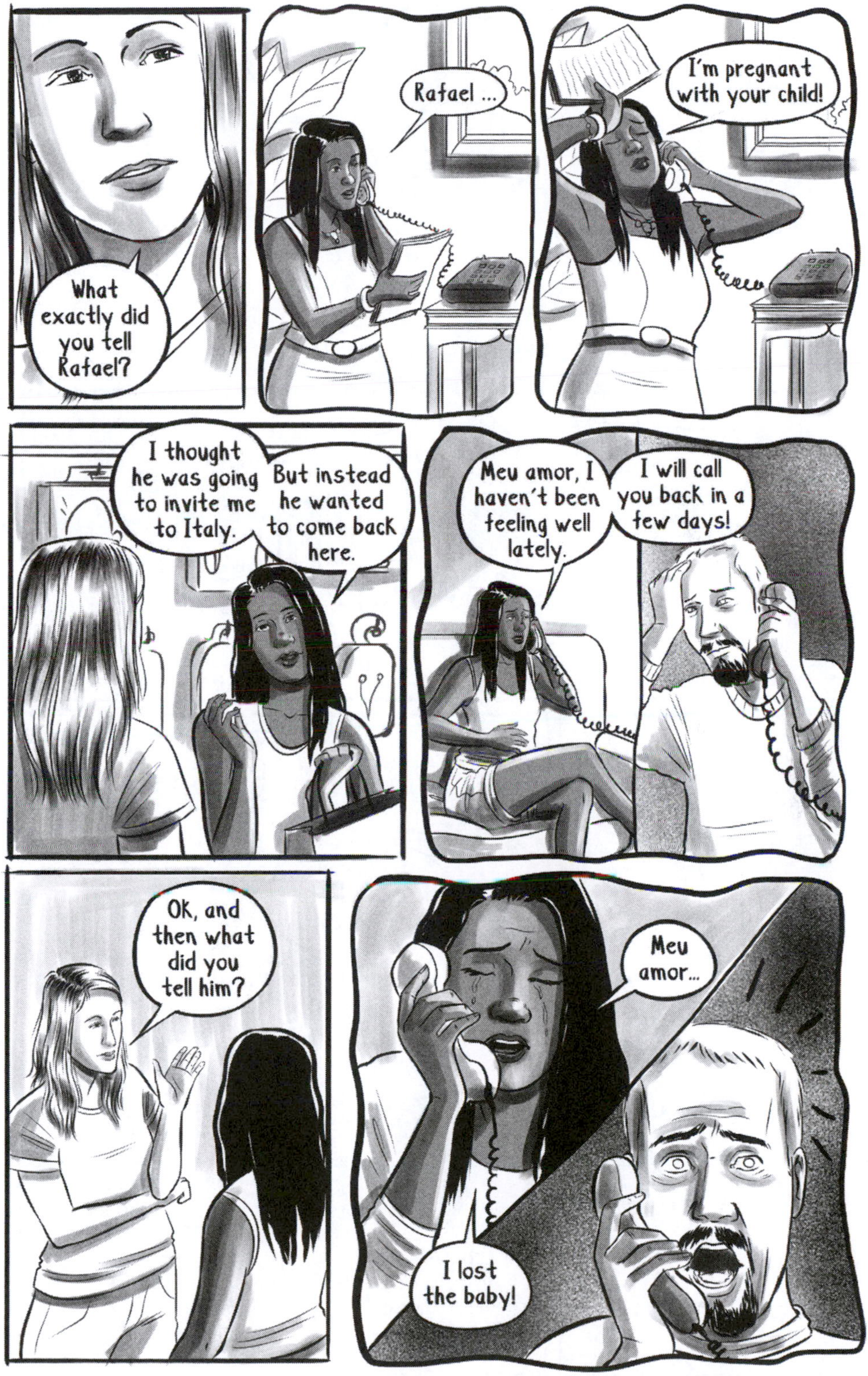
What exactly did you tell Rafael?
Rafael ...
I'm pregnant with your child!
I thought he was going to invite me to Italy.
But instead he wanted to come back here.
Meu amor, I haven't been feeling well lately.
I will call you back in a few days!
OK, and then what did you tell him?
Meu amor...
I lost the baby!

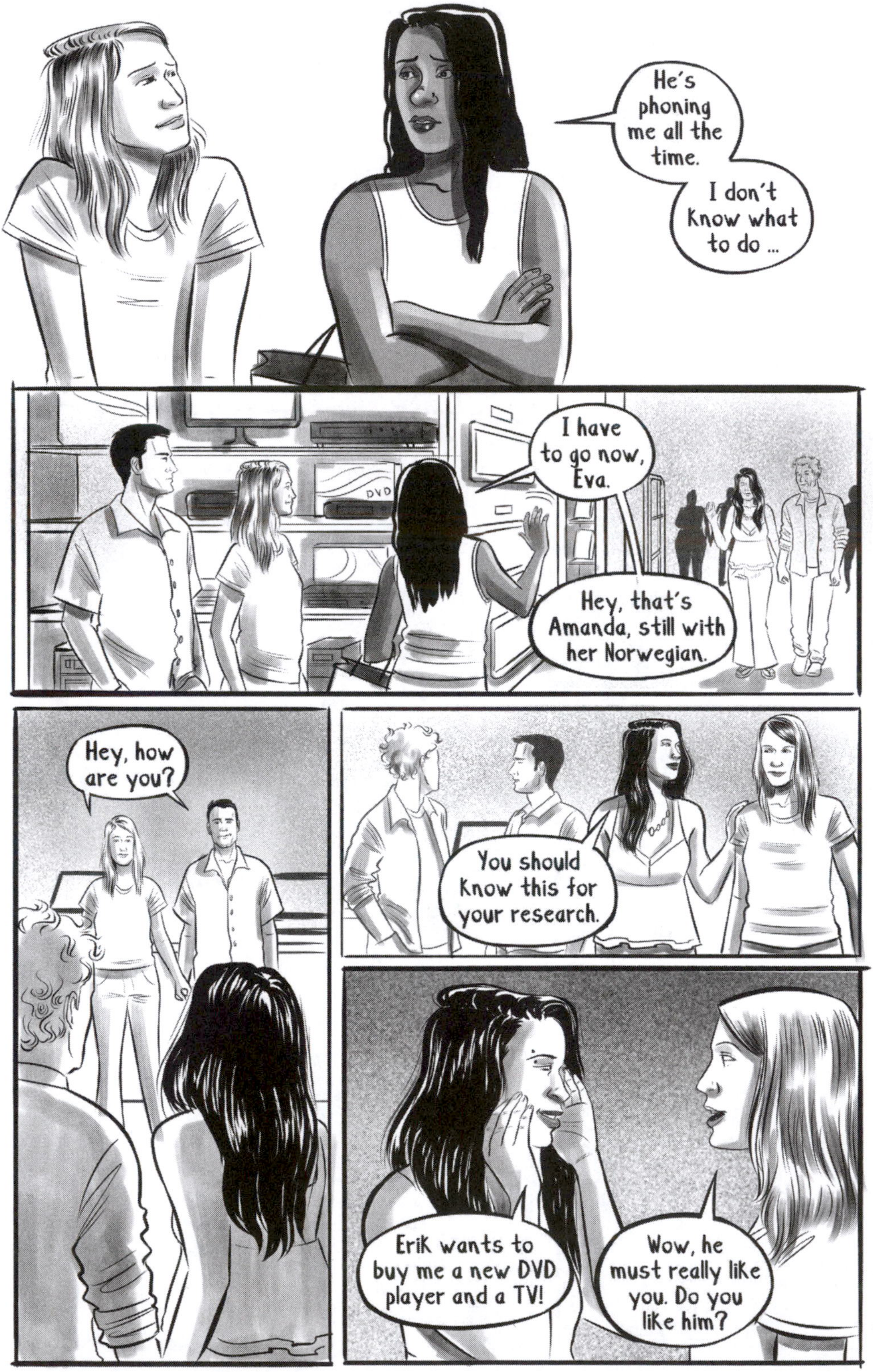
He's phoning me all the time.
I don't know what to do ...
I have to go now, Eva.
Hey, that's Amanda, still with her Norwegian.
Hey, how are you?
You should know this for your research.
Erik wants to buy me a new DVD player and a TV!
Wow, he must really like you. Do you like him?

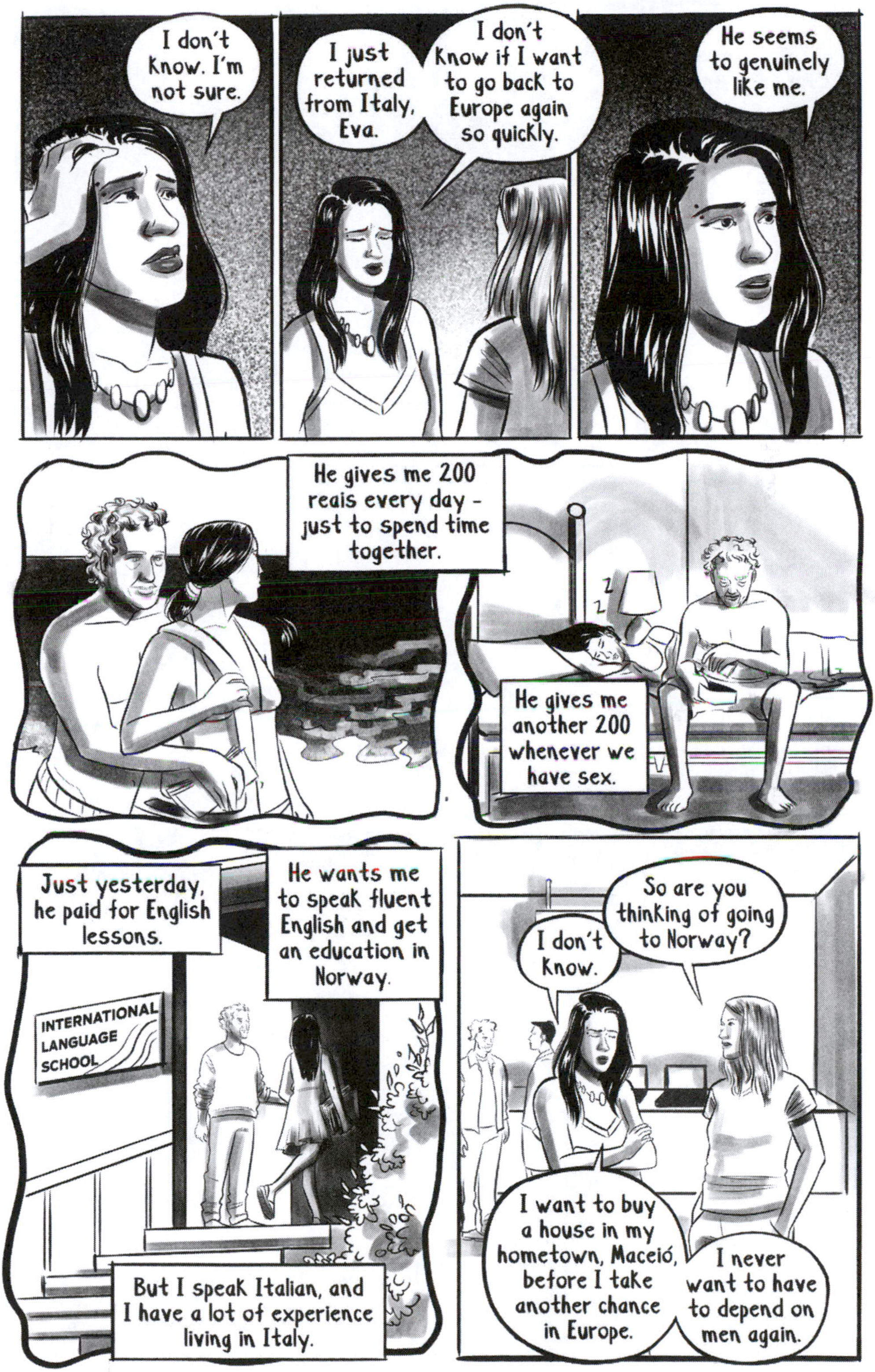
I don't know. I'm not sure.
I just returned from Italy, Eva.
I don't know if I want to go back to Europe again so quickly.
He seems to genuinely like me.
He gives me 200 reais every day - just to spend time together.
He gives me another 200 whenever we have sex.
Just yesterday, he paid for English lessons.
He wants me to speak fluent English and get an education in Norway.
INTERNATIONAL LANGUAGE SCHOOL
But I speak Italian, and I have a lot of experience living in Italy.
So are you thinking of going to Norway?
I don't know.
I want to buy a house in my hometown, Maceió, before I take another chance in Europe.
I never want to have to depend on men again.

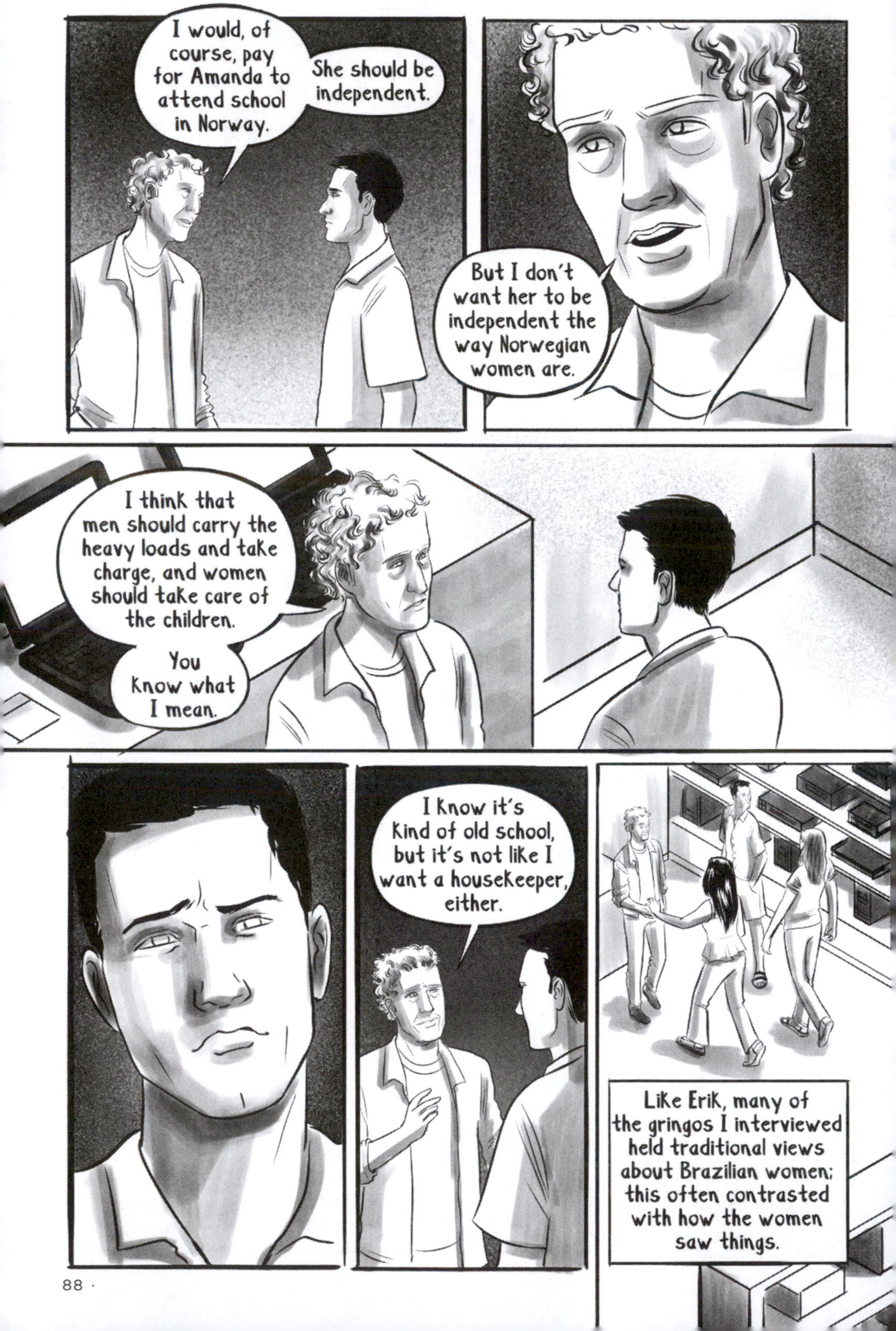

I would, of course, pay for Amanda to attend school in Norway.
She should be independent.
But I don't want her to be independent the way Norwegian women are.
I think that men should carry the heavy loads and take charge, and women should take care of the children.
You know what I mean.
I know it's kind of old school, but it's not like I want a housekeeper, either.
Like Erik, many of the gringos I interviewed held traditional views about Brazilian women; this often contrasted with how the women saw things.

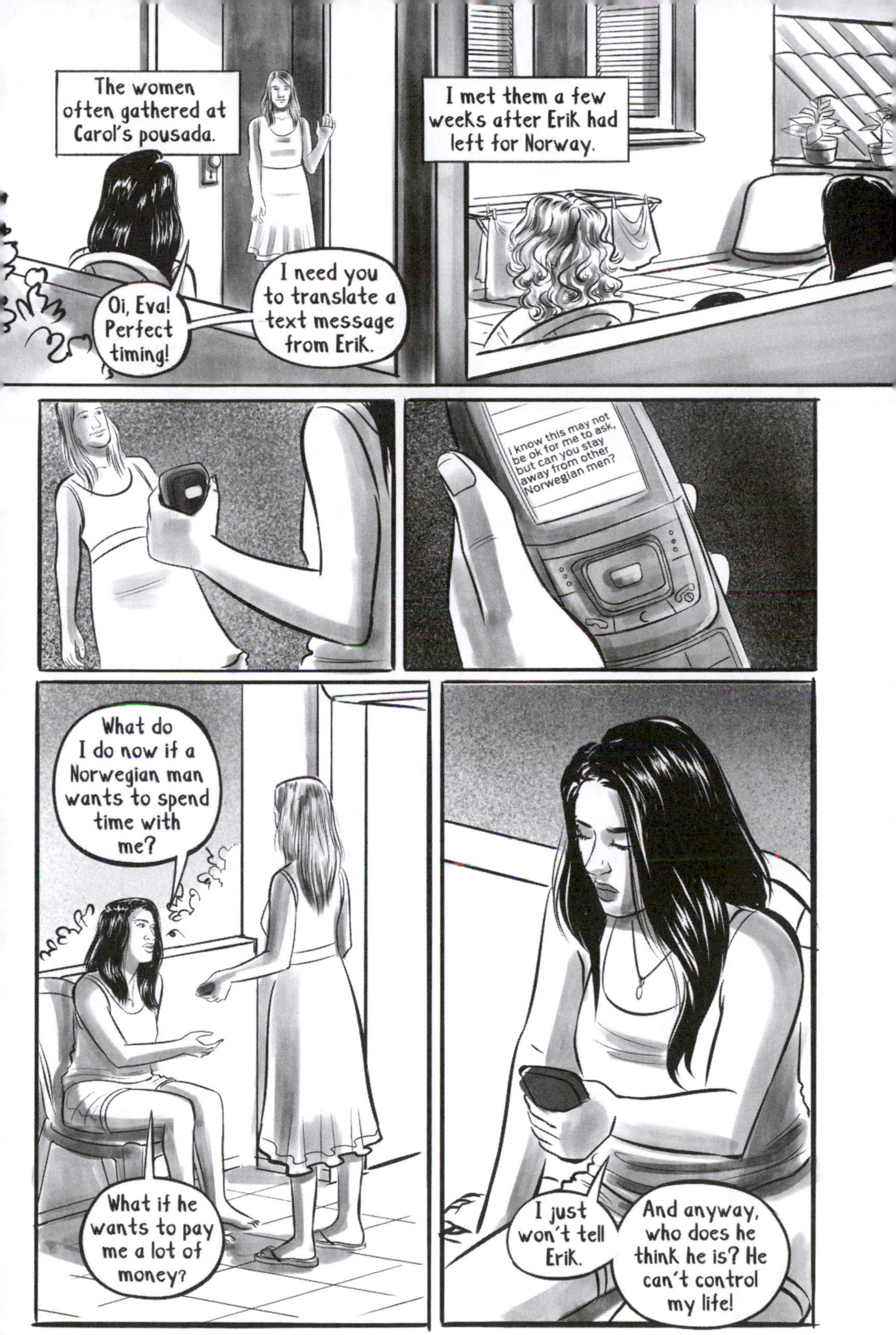
The women often gathered at Carol's pousada.
Oi, Eva! Perfect timing!
I need you to translate a text message from Erik.
I met them a few weeks after Erik had left for Norway.
i know this may not be ok for me to ask, but can you stay away from other Norwegian men?
What do I do now if a Norwegian man wants to spend time with me?
What if he wants to pay me a lot of money?
I just won't tell Erik.
And anyway, who does he think he is? He can't control my life!

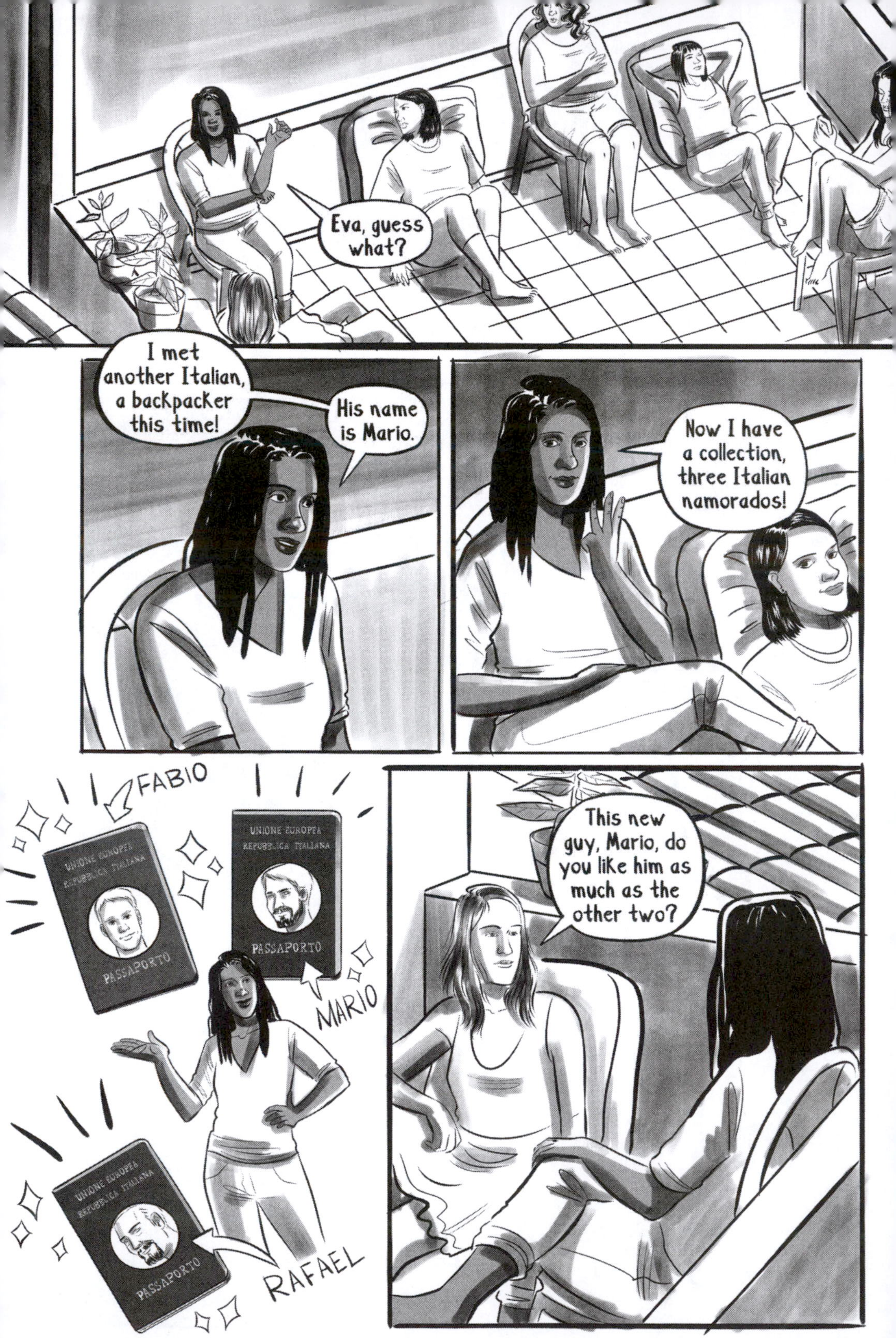
Eva, guess what?
I met another Italian, a backpacker this time!
His name is Mario.
Now I have a collection, three Italian namorados!
FABIO
UNIONE EUROPEA
REPUBBLICA ITALIANA
PASSAPORTO
UNIONE EUROPEA
REPUBBLICA ITALIANA
PASSAPORTO
MARIO
UNIONE EUROPEA
REPUBBLICA ITALIANA
PASSAPORTO
RAFAEL
This new guy, Mario, do you like him as much as the other two?

It was really different with Mario, I went de graça with him every time.

But he never gave me anything in return, not a penny!

He knew I had to spend a lot of time in the bars and clubs - that costs money!

Not even a goodbye gift before he left for Italy.

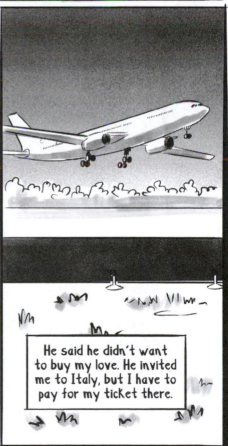

He said he didn't want to buy my love. He invited me to Italy, but I have to pay for my ticket there.

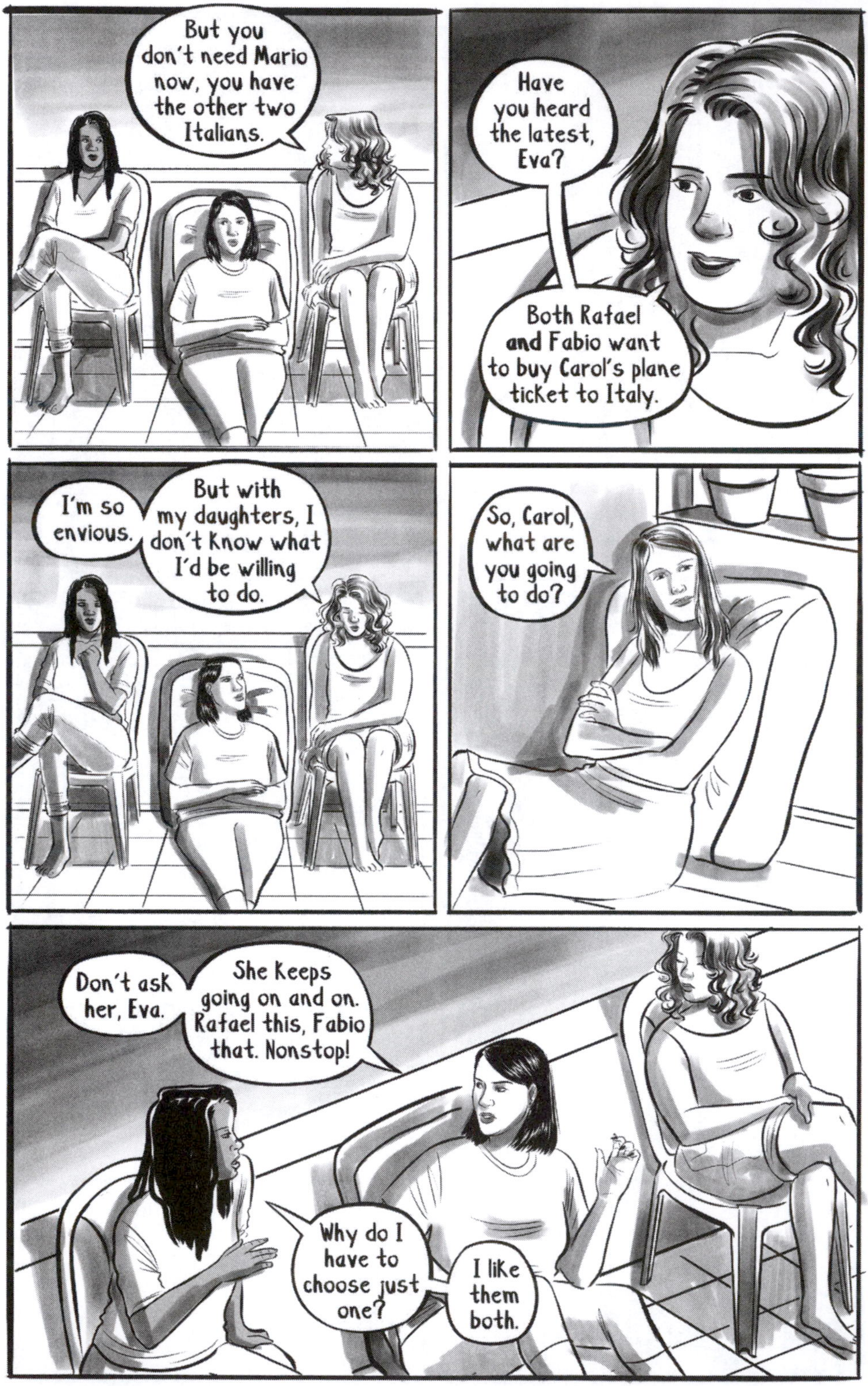
But you don't need Mario now, you have the other two Italians.
Have you heard the latest, Eva?
Both Rafael and Fabio want to buy Carol's plane ticket to Italy.
I'm so envious.
But with my daughters, I don't know what I'd be willing to do.
So, Carol, what are you going to do?
Don't ask her, Eva.
She keeps going on and on. Rafael this, Fabio that. Nonstop!
Why do I have to choose just one?
I like them both.

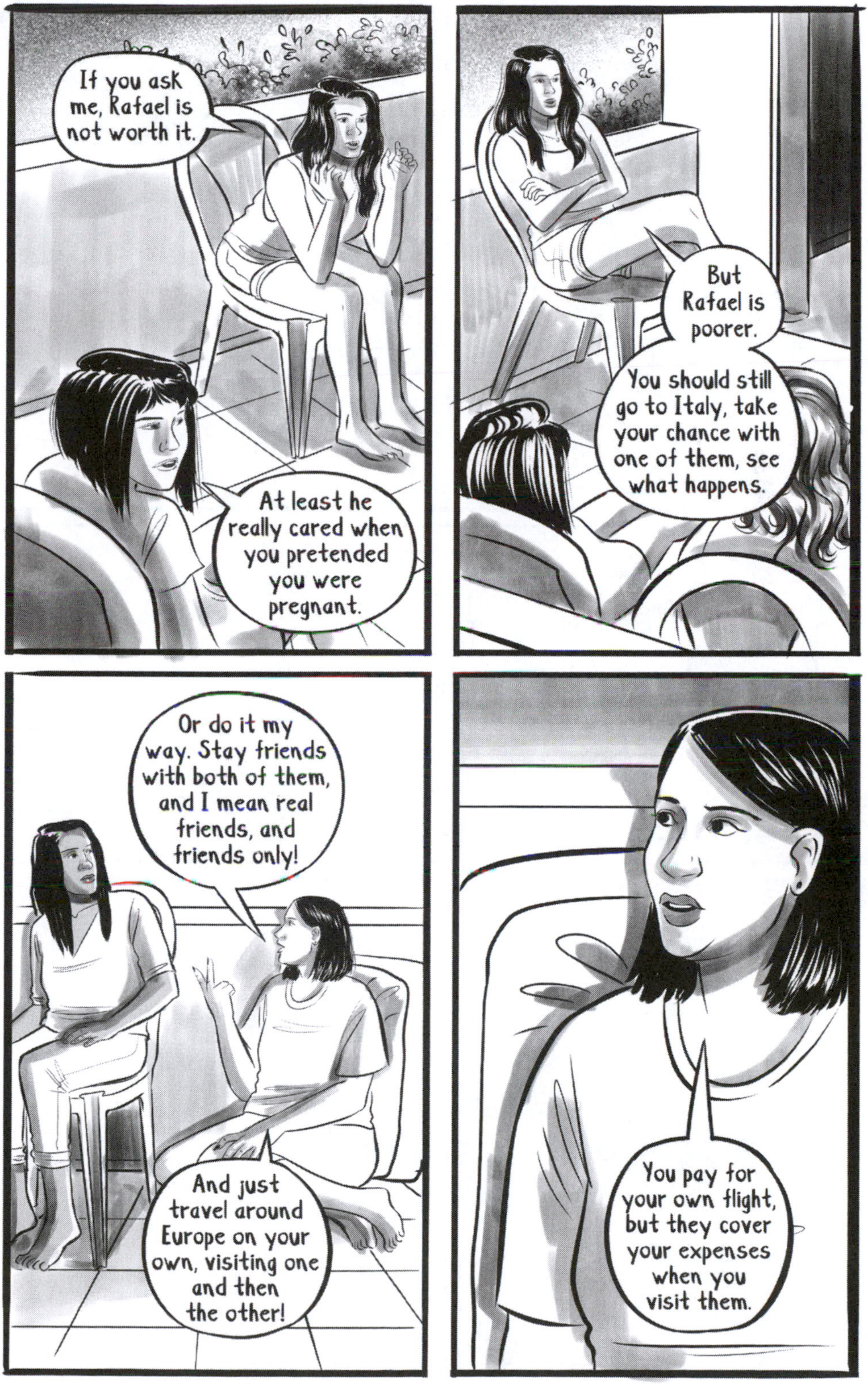
If you ask me, Rafael is not worth it.
At least he really cared when you pretended you were pregnant.
But Rafael is poorer.
You should still go to Italy, take your chance with one of them, see what happens.
Or do it my way. Stay friends with both of them, and I mean real friends, and friends only!
And just travel around Europe on your own, visiting one and then the other!
You pay for your own flight, but they cover your expenses when you visit them.

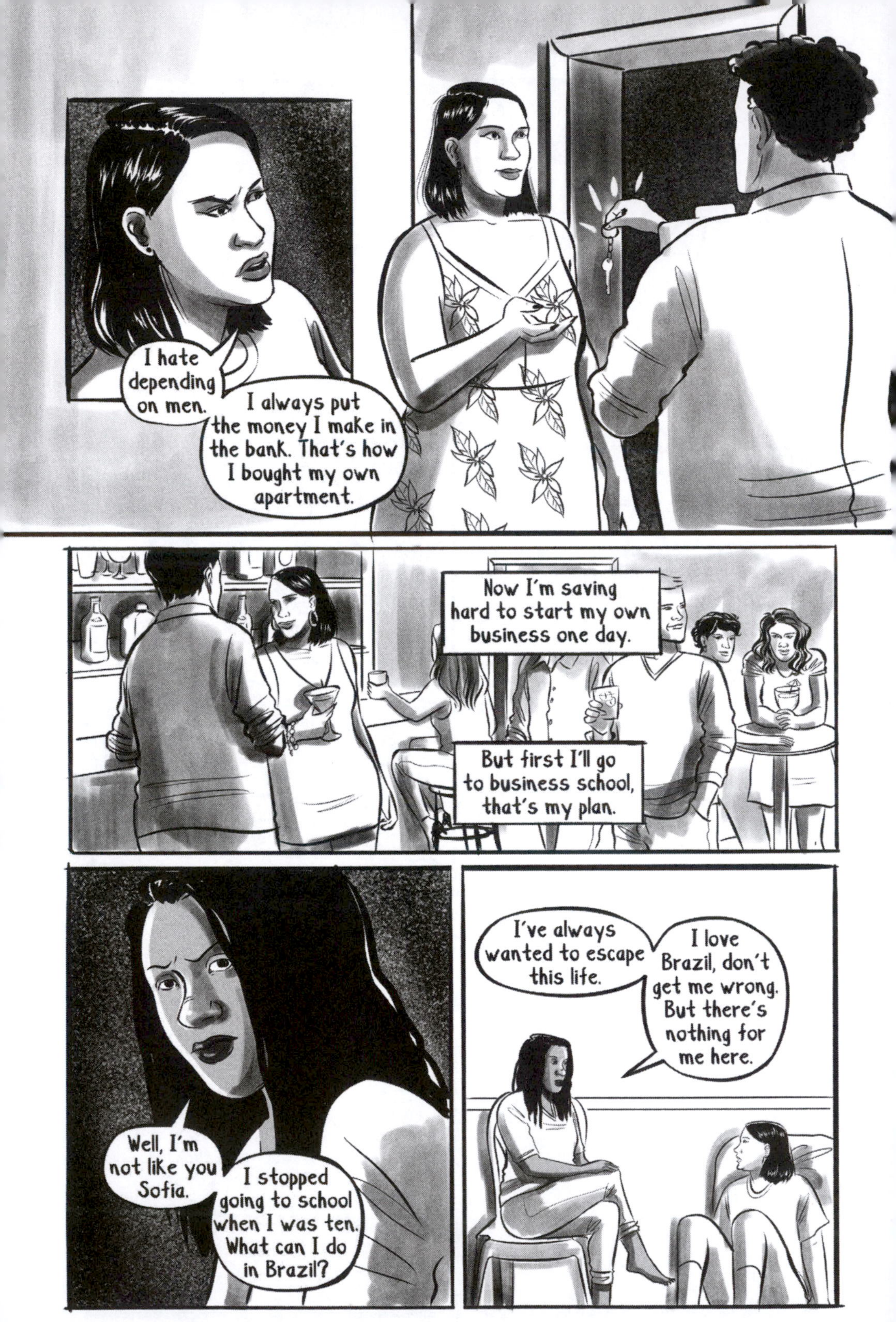
I hate depending on men.
I always put the money I make in the bank. That's how I bought my own apartment.
Now I'm saving hard to start my own business one day.
But first I'll go to business school, that's my plan.
Well, I'm not like you Sofia.
I stopped going to school when I was ten. What can I do in Brazil?
I've always wanted to escape this life.
I love Brazil, don't get me wrong. But there's nothing for me here.

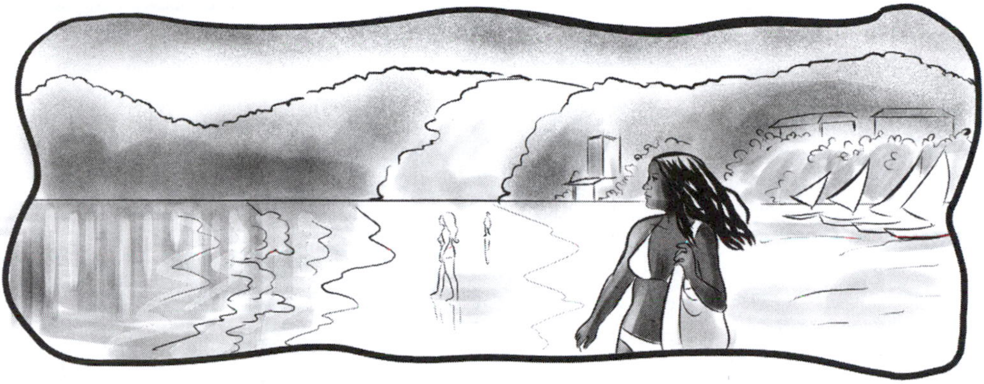

WHEN I CAME TO PONTA NEGRA BEACH LAST JULY,
I MET SO MANY GRINGOS, MADE SO MUCH MONEY.

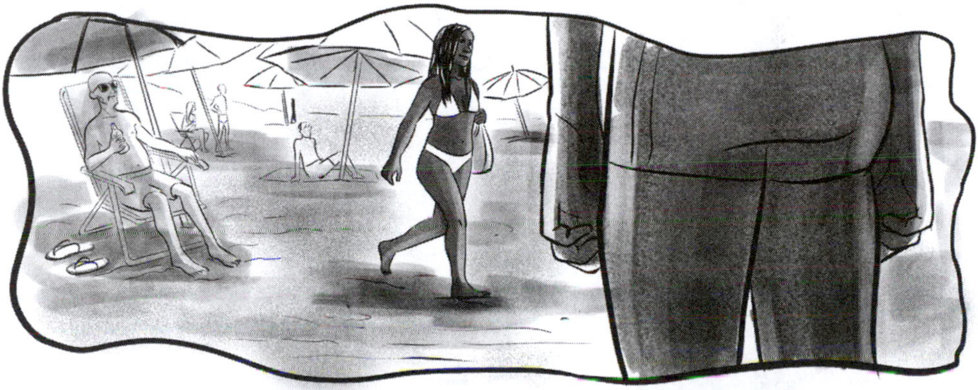

IT WAS MUCH, MUCH BETTER THAN CLEANING THE HOUSES OF
THOSE RICH BRAZILIANS WHO TREAT US LIKE THEIR SLAVES!

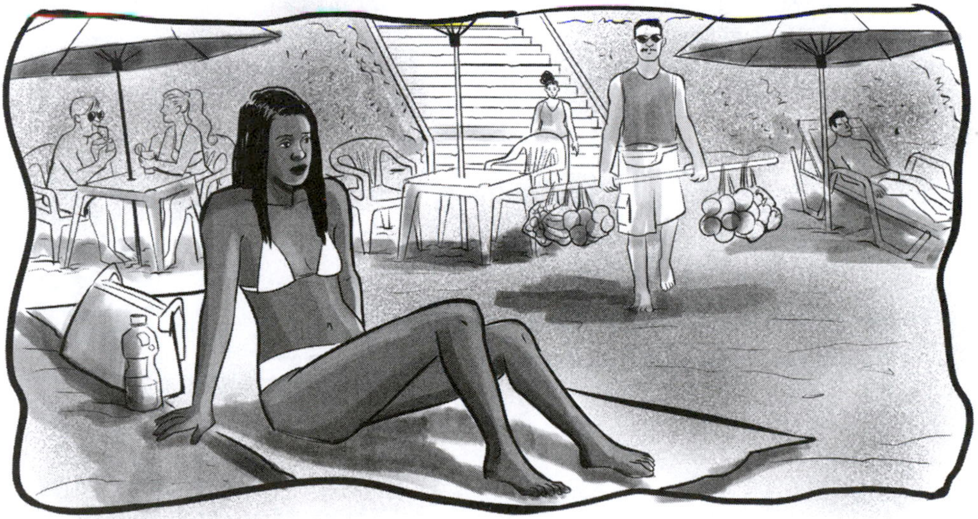

BUT THEN I DIDN'T WANT THIS LIFE ANYMORE, EITHER.

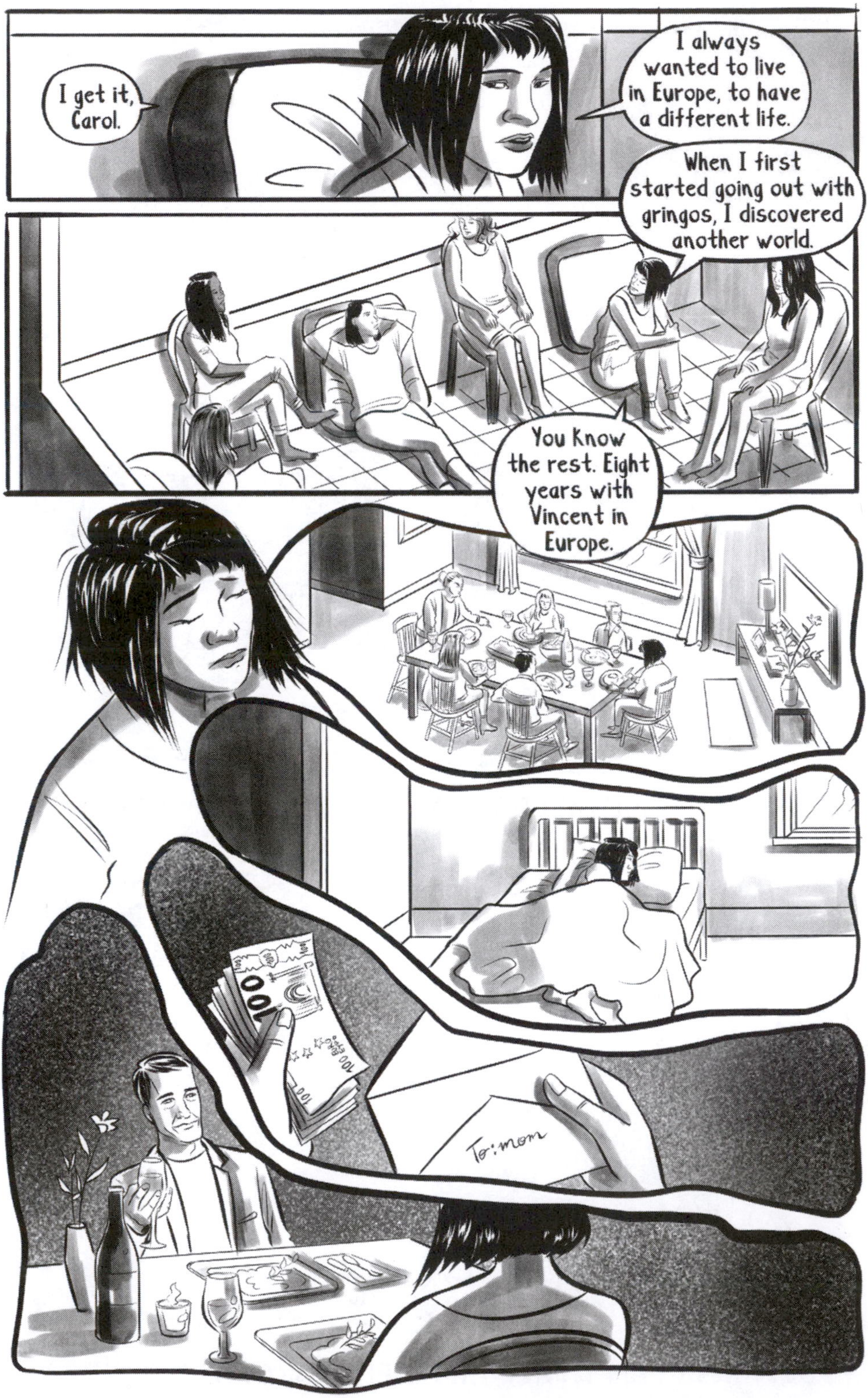
I get it, Carol.
I always wanted to live in Europe, to have a different life.
When I first started going out with gringos, I discovered another world.
You know the rest. Eight years with Vincent in Europe.
To: mom

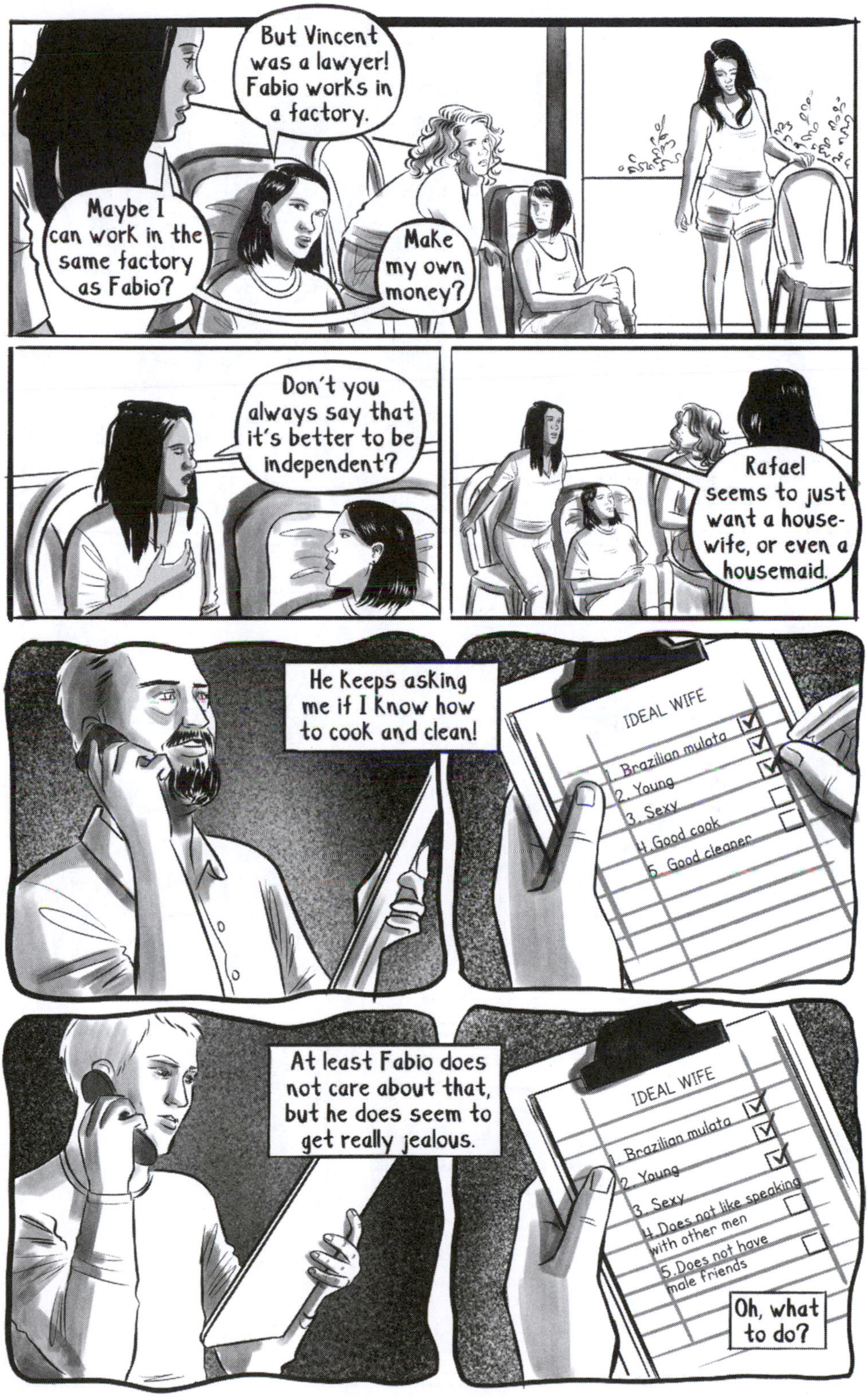

But Vincent was a lawyer! Fabio works in a factory.
Maybe I can work in the same factory as Fabio?
Make my own money?
Don't you always say that it's better to be independent?
Rafael seems to just want a house-wife, or even a housemaid.
He keeps asking me if I know how to cook and clean!
IDEAL WIFE
1. Brazilian mulata
2. Young
3. Sexy
4. Good cook
5. Good cleaner
At least Fabio does not care about that, but he does seem to get really jealous.
IDEAL WIFE
1. Brazilian mulata
2. Young
3. Sexy
4. Does not like speaking with other men
5. Does not have male friends
Oh, what to do?

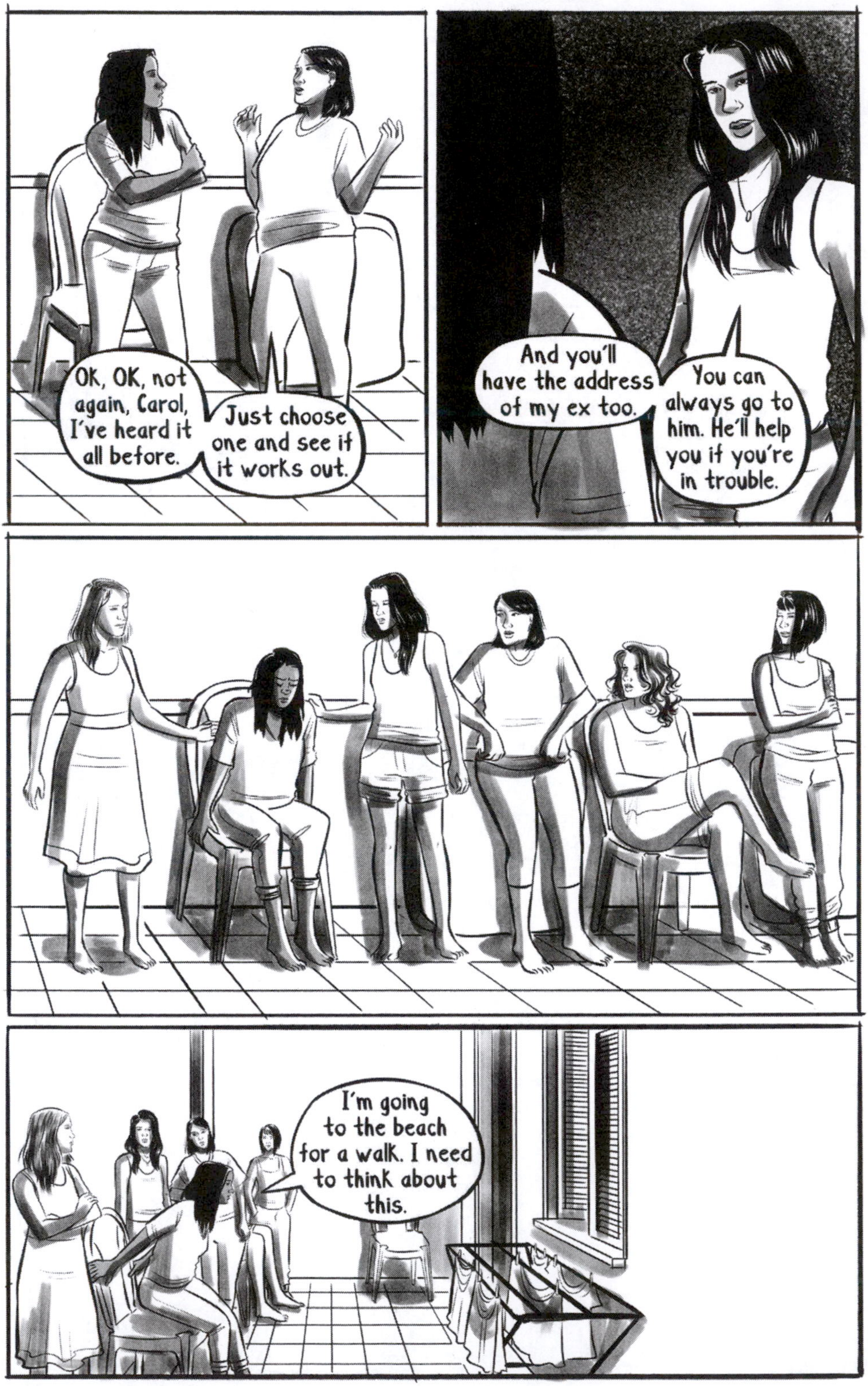
OK, OK, not again, Carol, I've heard it all before.
Just choose one and see if it works out.
And you'll have the address of my ex too.
You can always go to him. He'll help you if you're in trouble.
I'm going to the beach for a walk. I need to think about this.

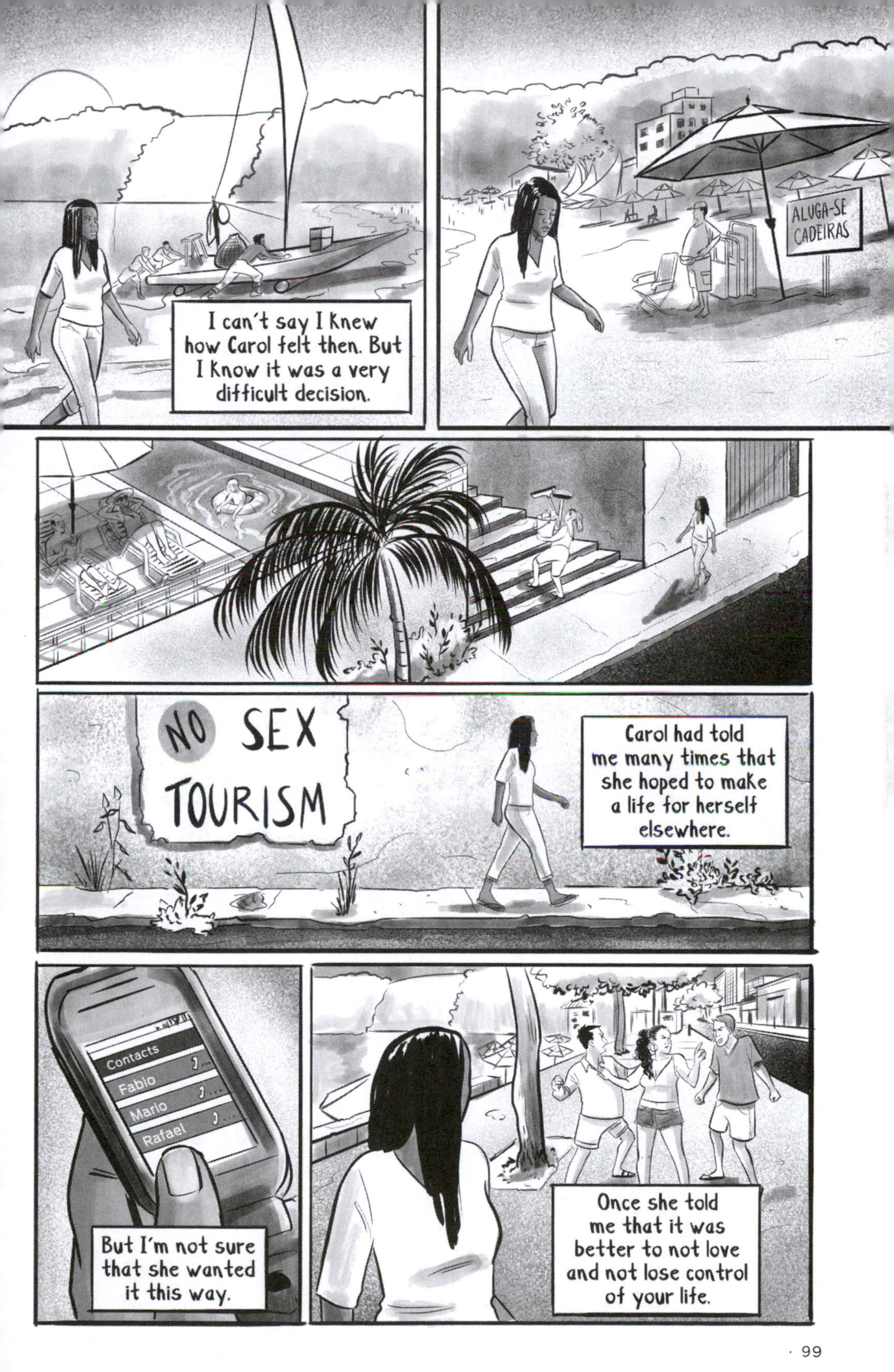
I can't say I knew how Carol felt then. But I know it was a very difficult decision.
ALUGA-SE CADEIRAS
NO SEX TOURISM
Carol had told me many times that she hoped to make a life for herself elsewhere.
Contacts
Fabio
Mario
Rafael
But I'm not sure that she wanted it this way.
Once she told me that it was better to not love and not lose control of your life.

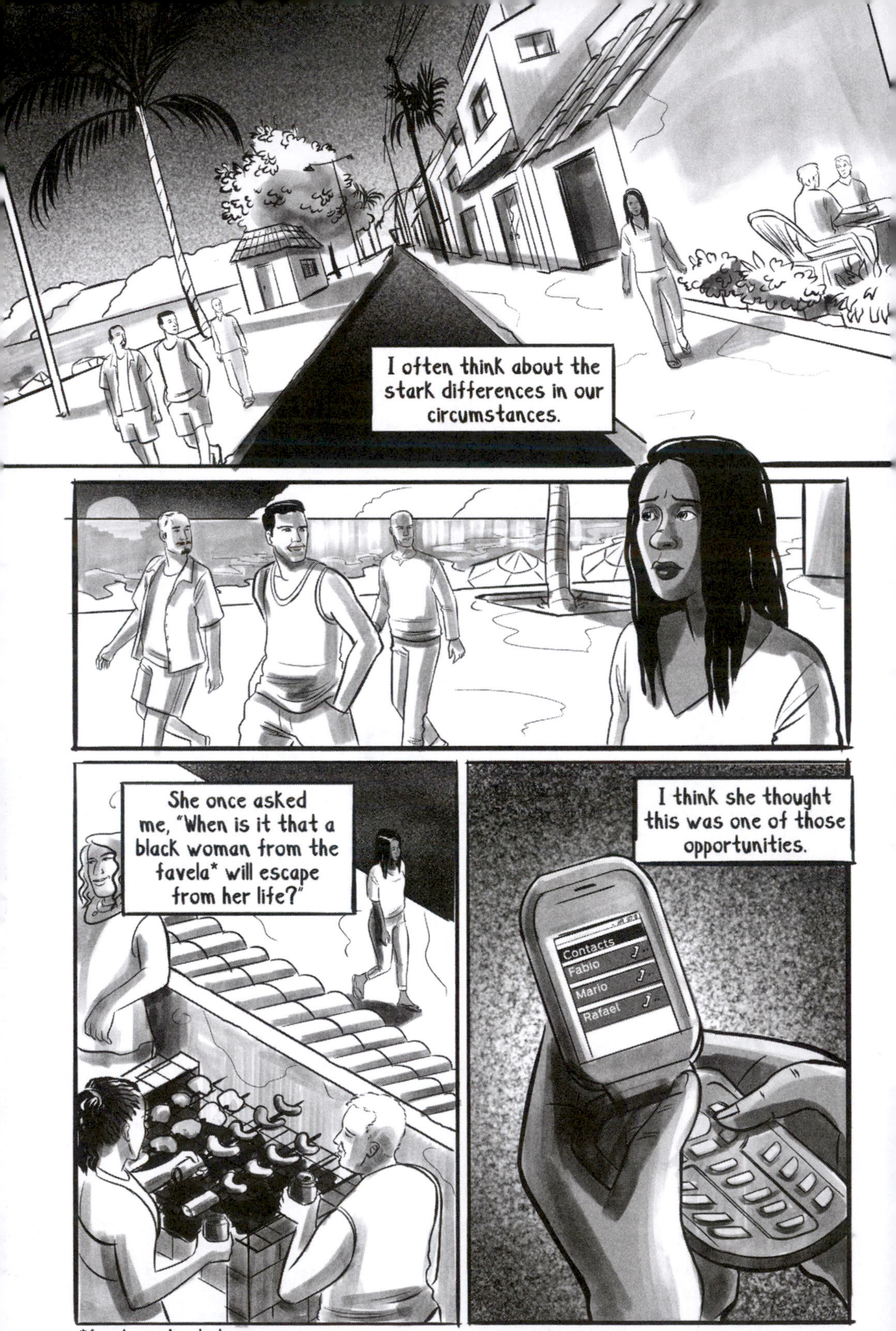
I often think about the stark differences in our circumstances.
She once asked me, "When is it that a black woman from the favela* will escape from her life?"
I think she thought this was one of those opportunities.
Contacts
Fabio
Mario
Rafael

*favela = shantytown

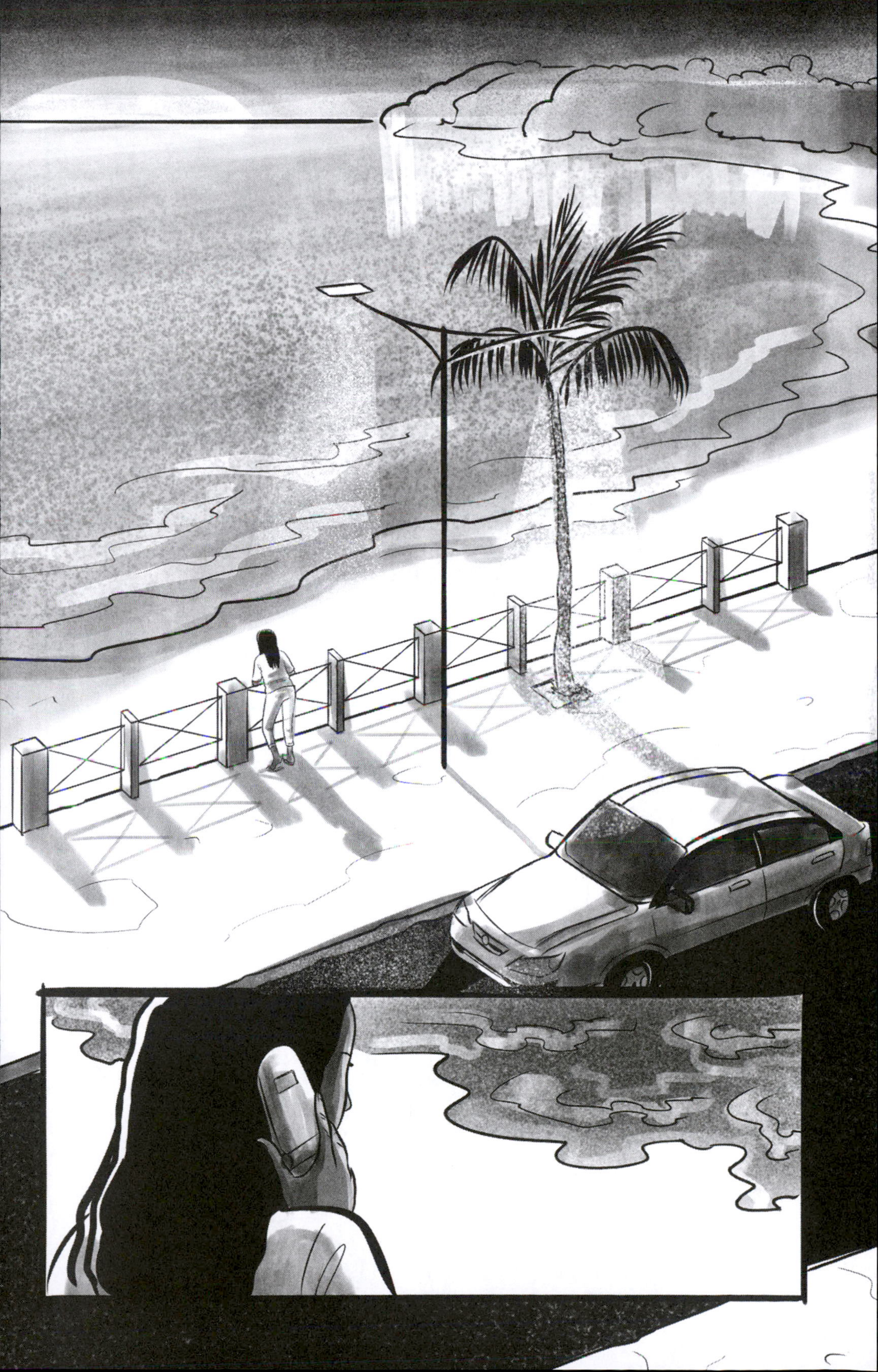

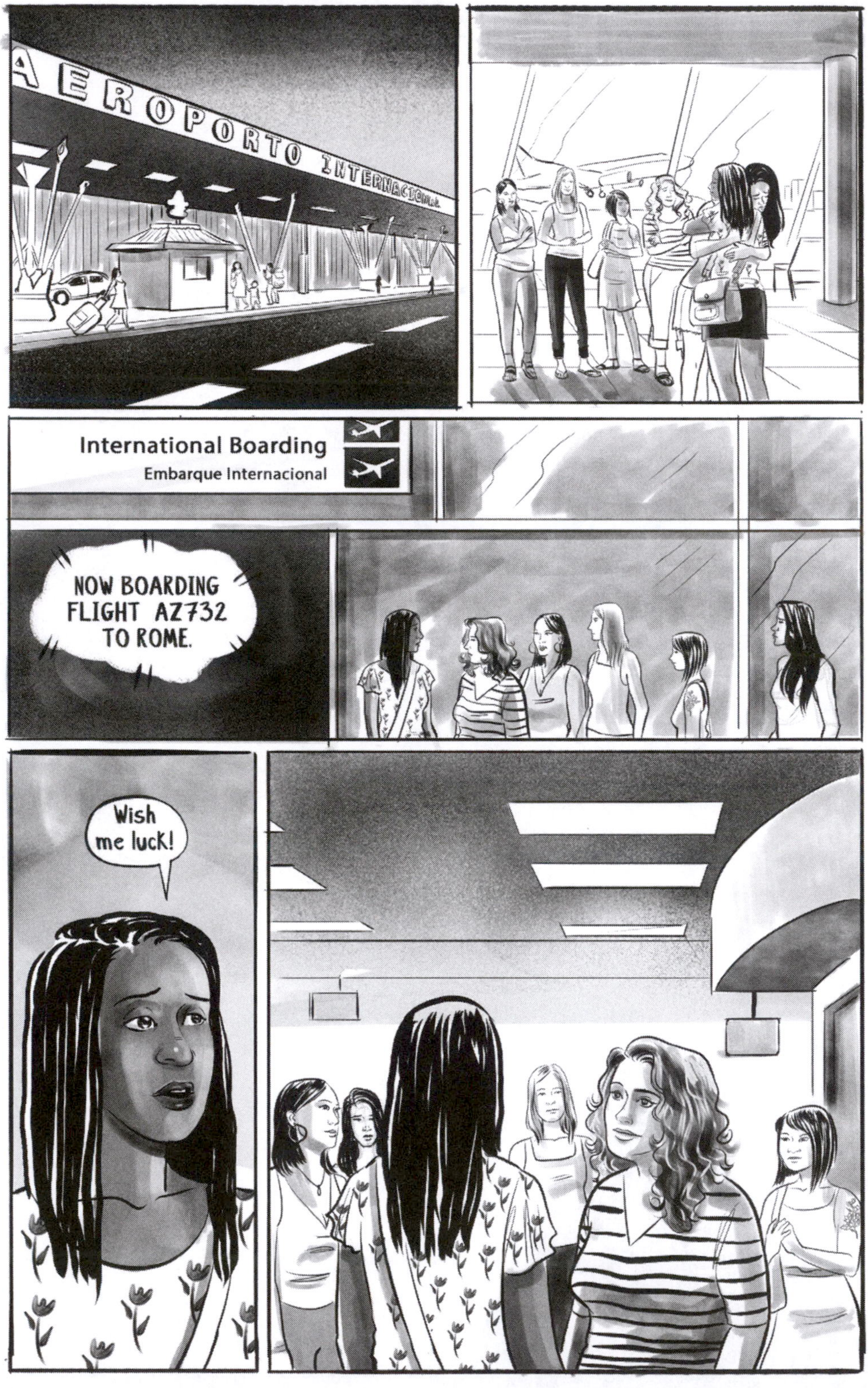
AEROPORTO INTERNACIONAL
International Boarding
Embarque Internacional
NOW BOARDING FLIGHT AZ732 TO ROME.
Wish me luck!

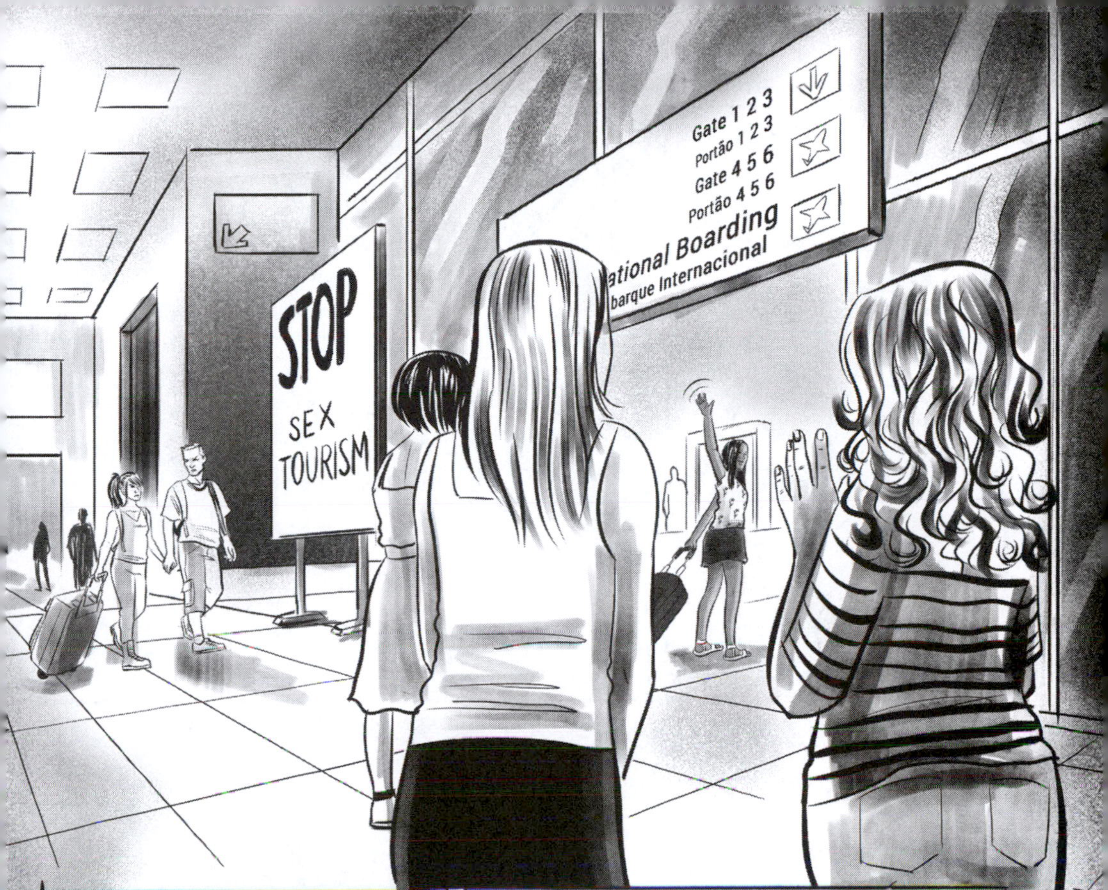
STOP
SEX
TOURISM
Gate 1 2 3
Portão 1 2 3
Gate 4 5 6
Portão 4 5 6
ational Boarding
barque Internacional

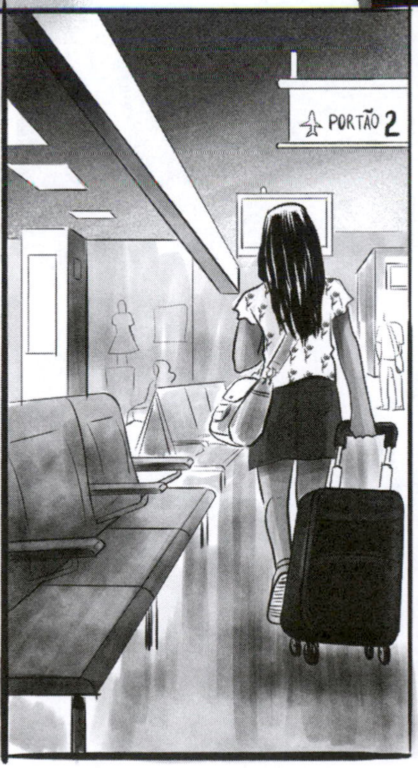
PORTÃO 2

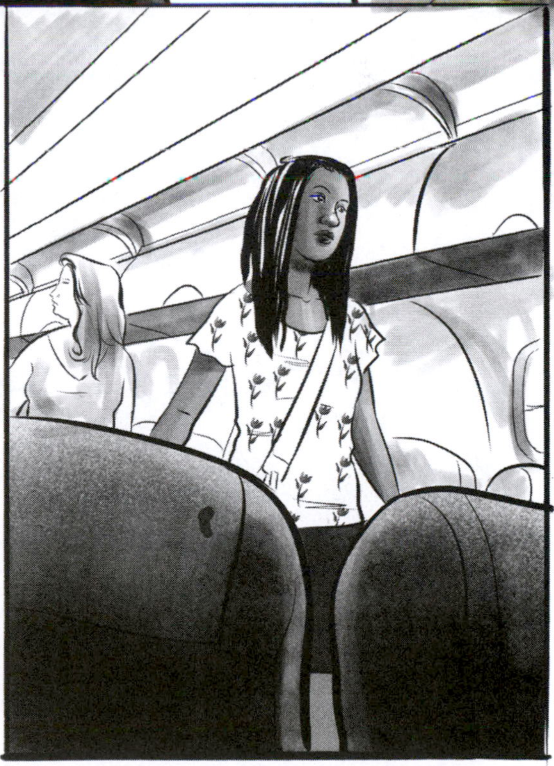

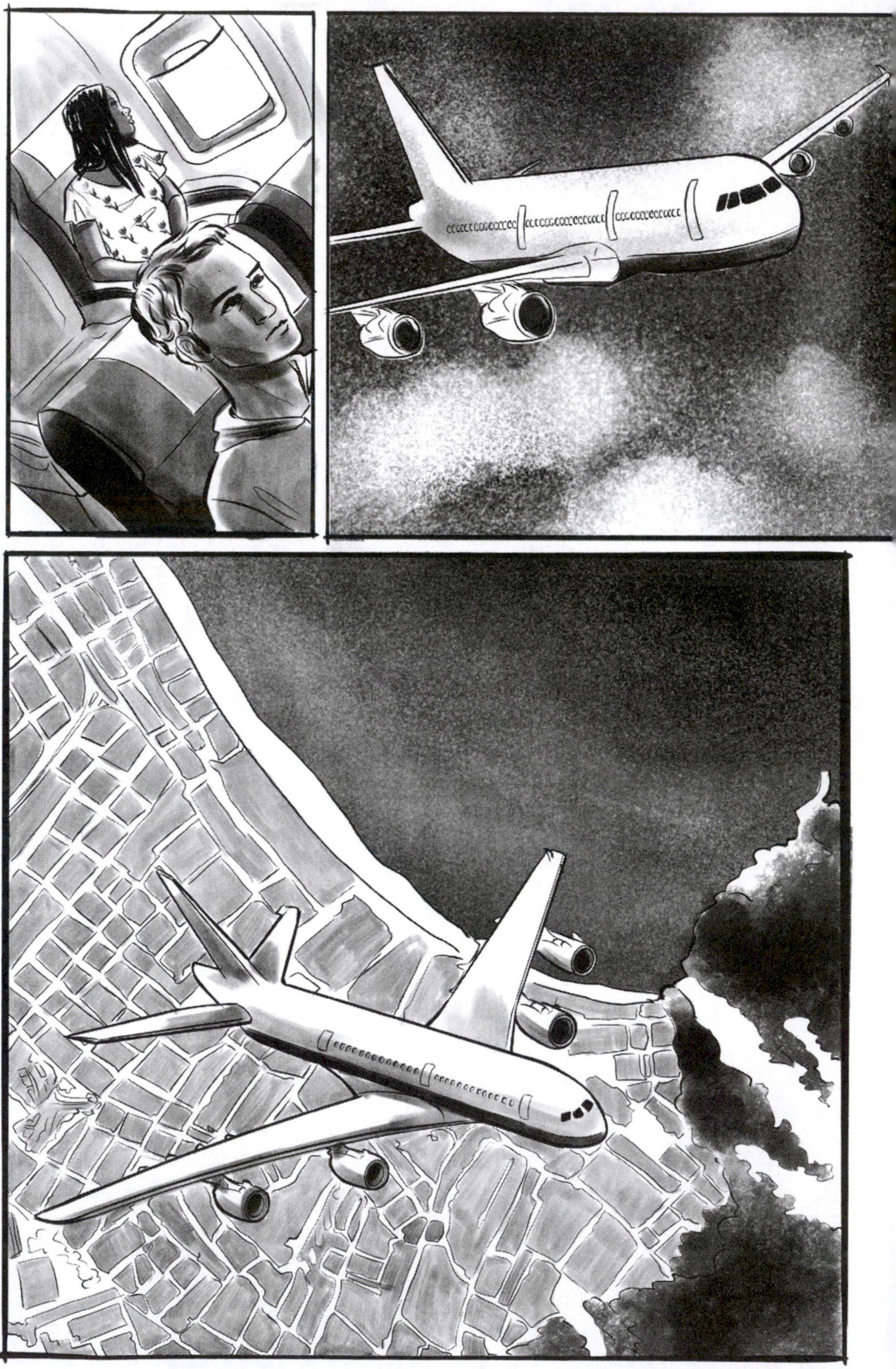

EPILOGUE

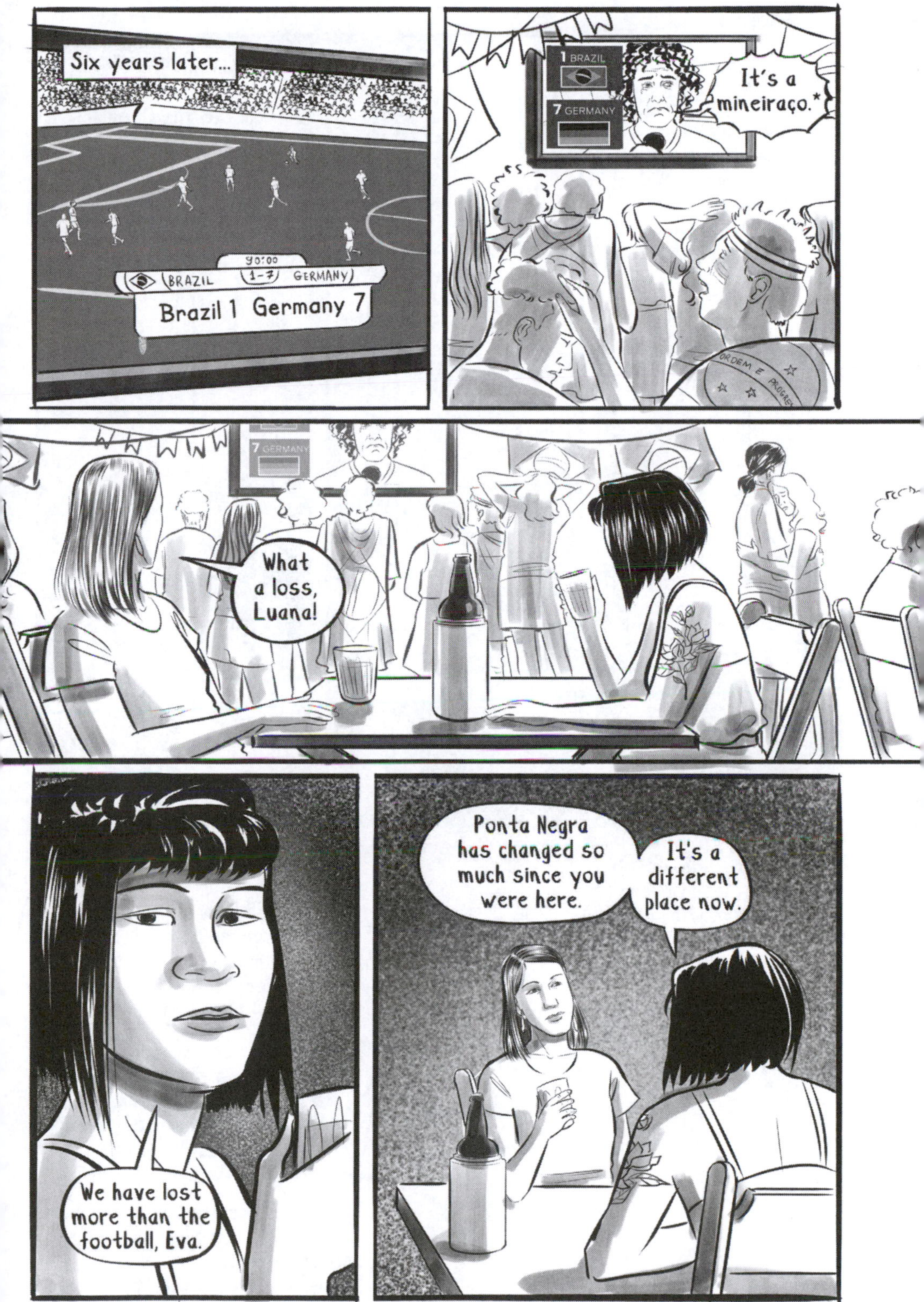
Six years later...
90:00
BRAZIL
1-7
GERMANY
Brazil 1 Germany 7
1 BRAZIL
7 GERMANY
It's a mineiraço.*
ORDEM E PROGRE
7 GERMANY
What a loss, Luana!
We have lost more than the football, Eva.
Ponta Negra has changed so much since you were here.
It's a different place now.

*mineiraço = national shame, how Brazil's loss against Germany came to be known

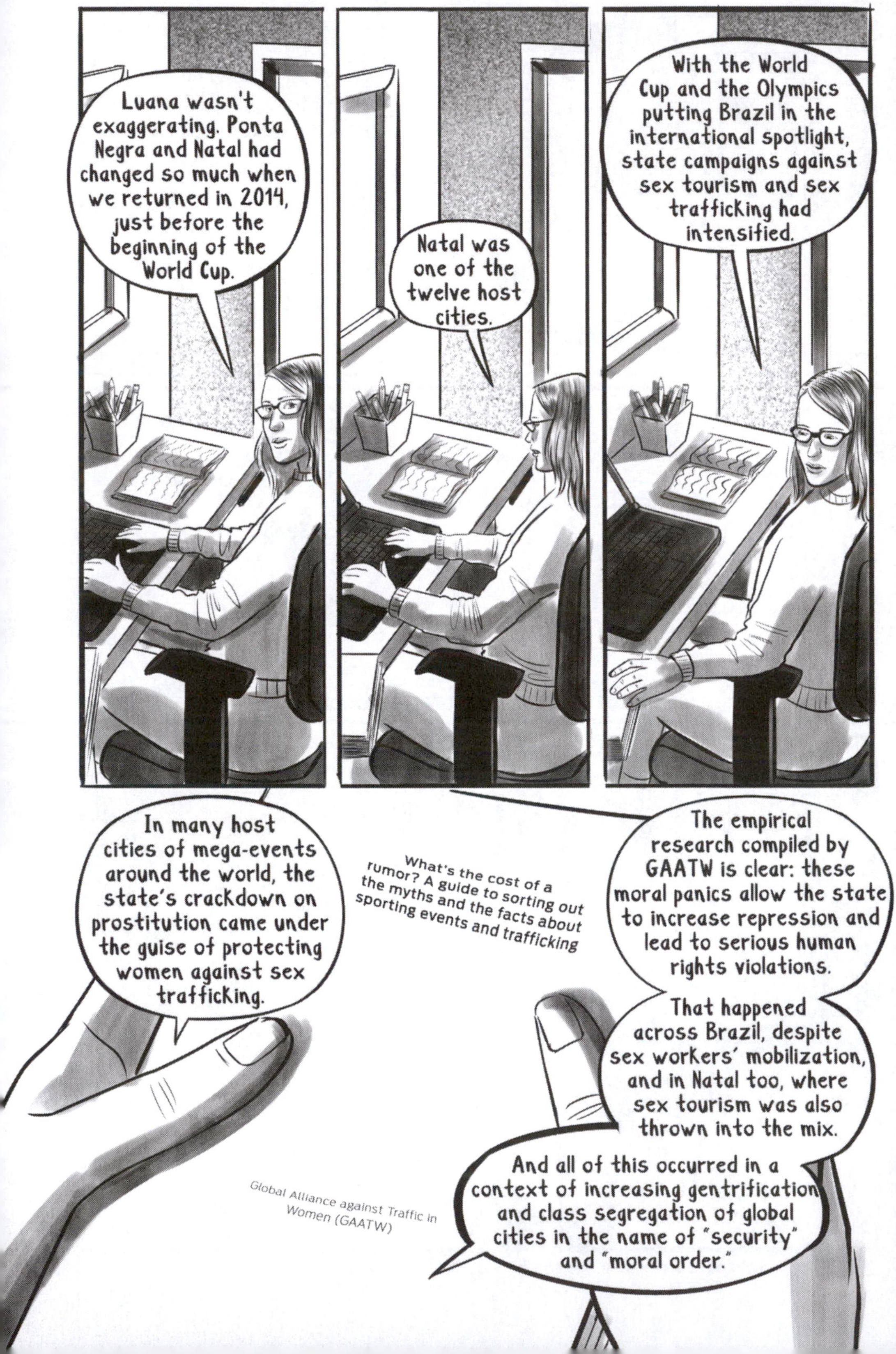
Luana wasn't exaggerating. Ponta Negra and Natal had changed so much when we returned in 2014, just before the beginning of the World Cup.
Natal was one of the twelve host cities.
With the World Cup and the Olympics putting Brazil in the international spotlight, state campaigns against sex tourism and sex trafficking had intensified.
In many host cities of mega-events around the world, the state's crackdown on prostitution came under the guise of protecting women against sex trafficking.
What's the cost of a rumor? A guide to sorting out the myths and the facts about sporting events and trafficking
The empirical research compiled by GAATW is clear: these moral panics allow the state to increase repression and lead to serious human rights violations.
Global Alliance against Traffic in Women (GAATW)
That happened across Brazil, despite sex workers' mobilization, and in Natal too, where sex tourism was also thrown into the mix.
And all of this occurred in a context of increasing gentrification and class segregation of global cities in the name of "security" and "moral order."

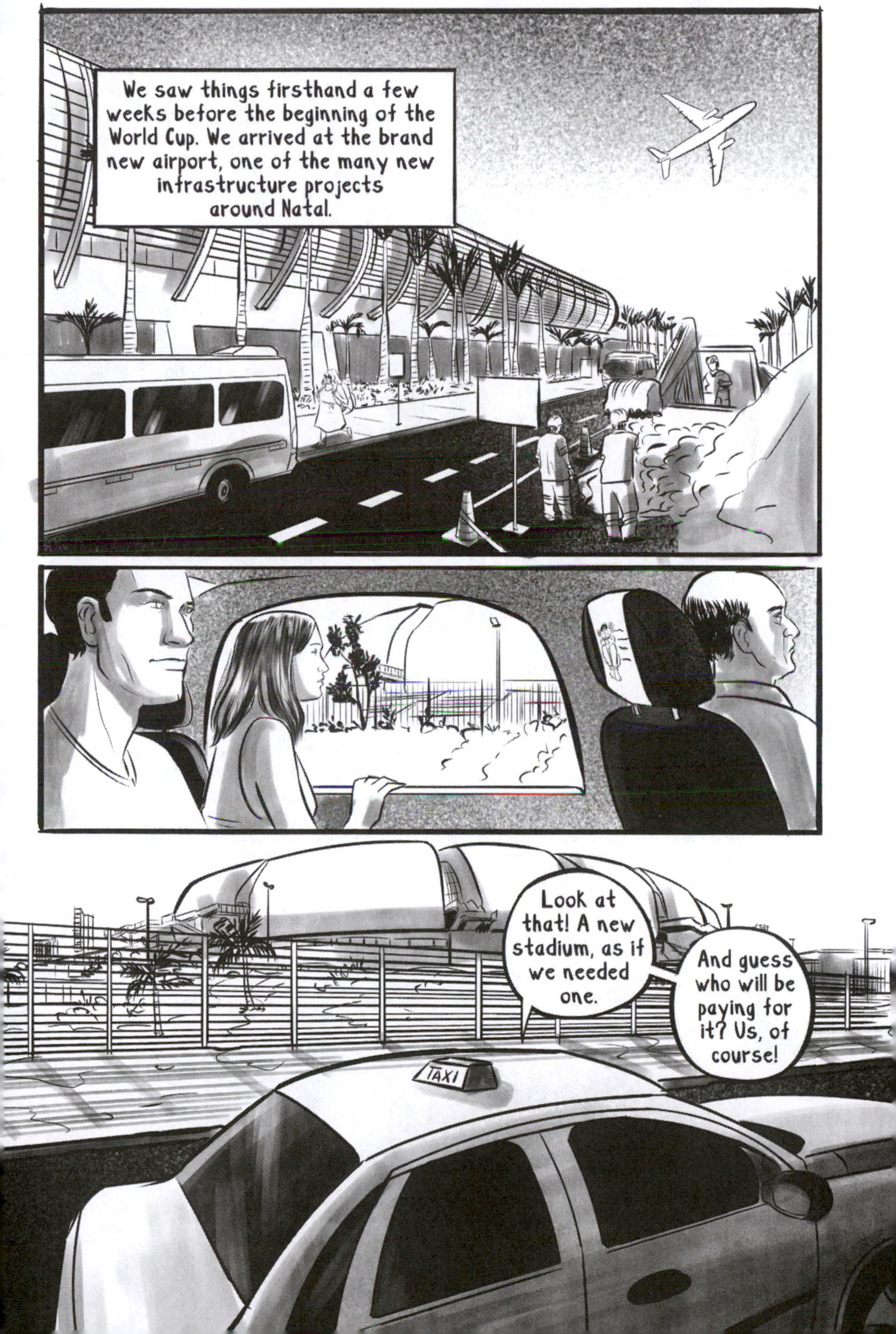
We saw things firsthand a few weeks before the beginning of the World Cup. We arrived at the brand new airport, one of the many new infrastructure projects around Natal.
Look at that! A new stadium, as if we needed one.
And guess who will be paying for it? Us, of course!
TAXI

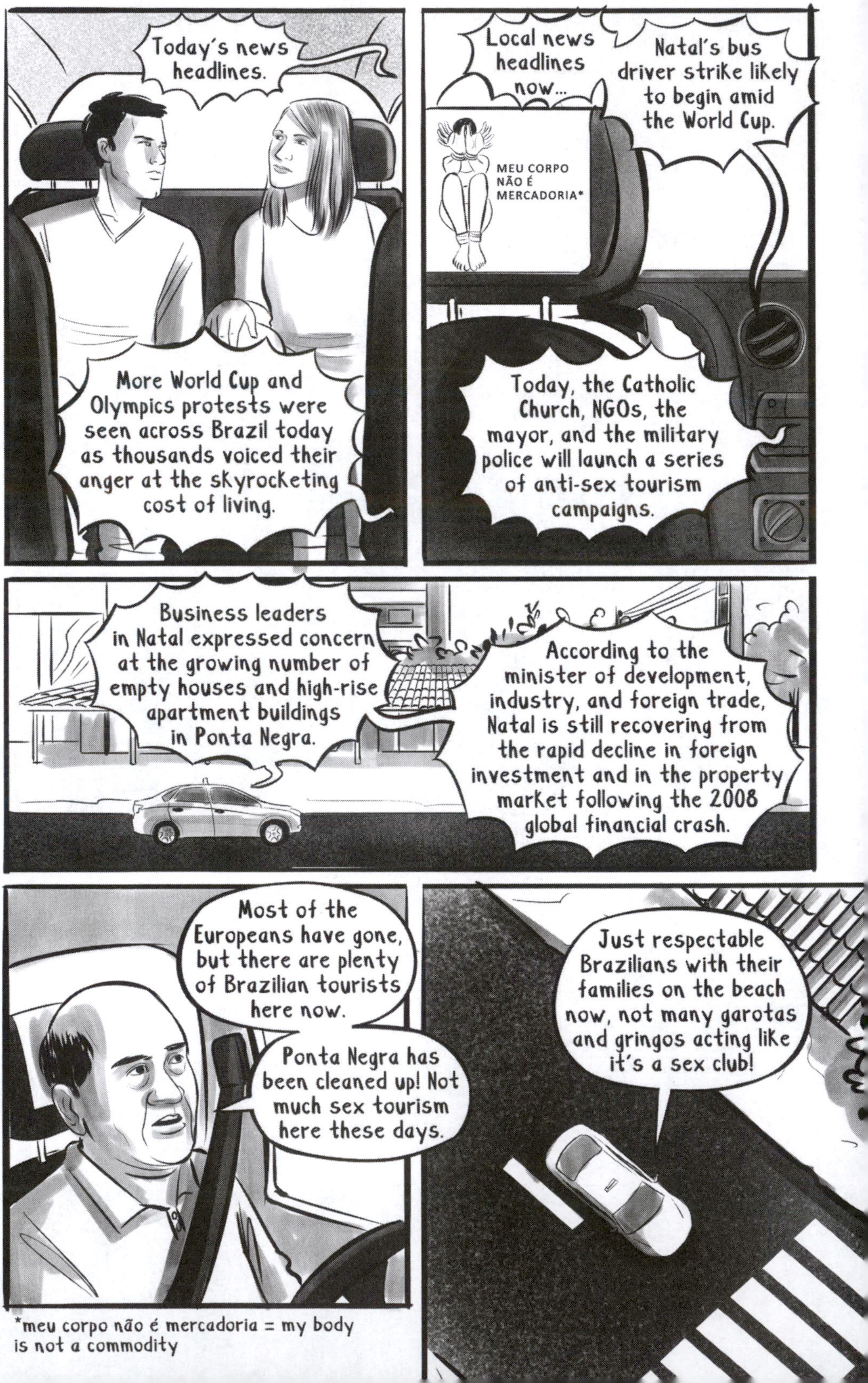
Today's news headlines.
More World Cup and Olympics protests were seen across Brazil today as thousands voiced their anger at the skyrocketing cost of living.
Local news headlines now...
Natal's bus driver strike likely to begin amid the World Cup.
MEU CORPO NÃO É MERCADORIA*
Today, the Catholic Church, NGOs, the mayor, and the military police will launch a series of anti-sex tourism campaigns.
Business leaders in Natal expressed concern at the growing number of empty houses and high-rise apartment buildings in Ponta Negra.
According to the minister of development, industry, and foreign trade, Natal is still recovering from the rapid decline in foreign investment and in the property market following the 2008 global financial crash.
Most of the Europeans have gone, but there are plenty of Brazilian tourists here now.
Ponta Negra has been cleaned up! Not much sex tourism here these days.
Just respectable Brazilians with their families on the beach now, not many garotas and gringos acting like it's a sex club!

*meu corpo não é mercadoria = my body is not a commodity

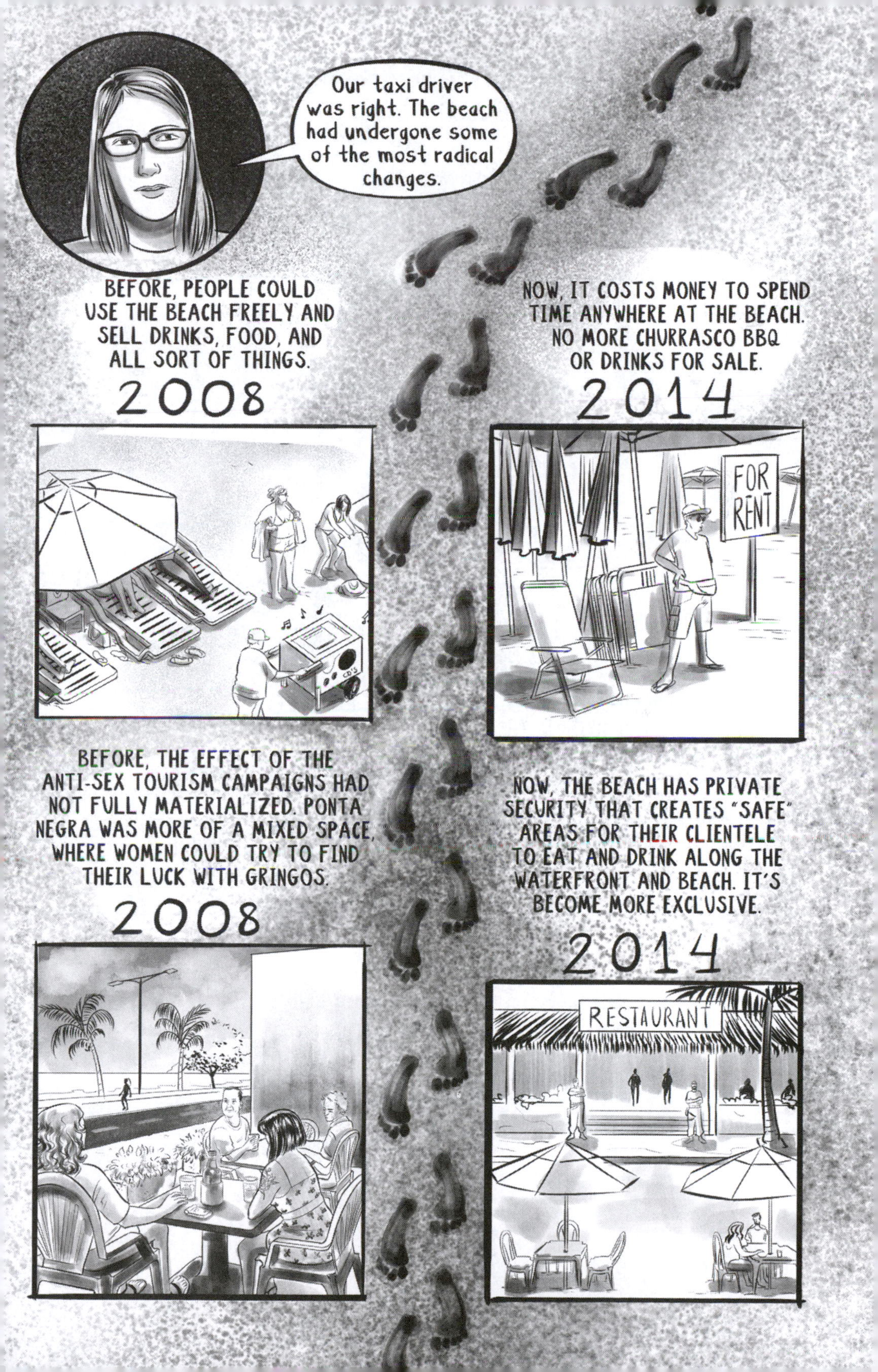
Our taxi driver was right. The beach had undergone some of the most radical changes.
BEFORE, PEOPLE COULD USE THE BEACH FREELY AND SELL DRINKS, FOOD, AND ALL SORT OF THINGS.
2008
CD'S
NOW, IT COSTS MONEY TO SPEND TIME ANYWHERE AT THE BEACH. NO MORE CHURRASCO BBQ OR DRINKS FOR SALE.
2014
FOR RENT
BEFORE, THE EFFECT OF THE ANTI-SEX TOURISM CAMPAIGNS HAD NOT FULLY MATERIALIZED. PONTA NEGRA WAS MORE OF A MIXED SPACE, WHERE WOMEN COULD TRY TO FIND THEIR LUCK WITH GRINGOS.
2008
NOW, THE BEACH HAS PRIVATE SECURITY THAT CREATES "SAFE" AREAS FOR THEIR CLIENTELE TO EAT AND DRINK ALONG THE WATERFRONT AND BEACH. IT'S BECOME MORE EXCLUSIVE.
2014
RESTAURANT

THE CRACKDOWN AND CAMPAIGNS AGAINST SEX TOURISM DID LEAD TO MORE SURVEILLANCE ON THE BEACH, AND MORE POLICE ON THE STREETS, FOR A TIME.

2008

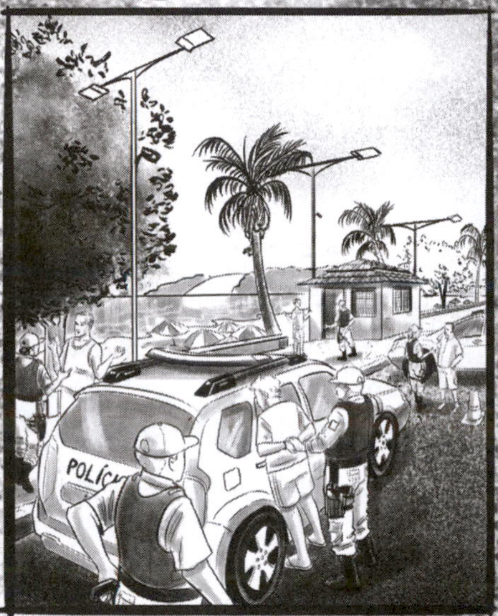

BUT THE WORLD CUP SAW A RETURN TO AND HUGE INCREASE IN THE VISIBLE POLICE AND MILITARY PRESENCE IN NATAL AND PONTA NEGRA.

2014

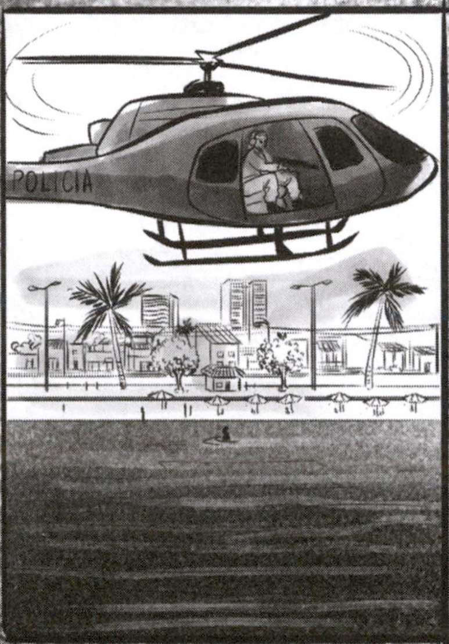
POLICIA

THE 2008 FINANCIAL CRASH CAUSED A MASSIVE DROP IN THE NUMBER OF EUROPEAN TOURISTS COMING TO NATAL. PONTA NEGRA WAS HIT HARD.

2008

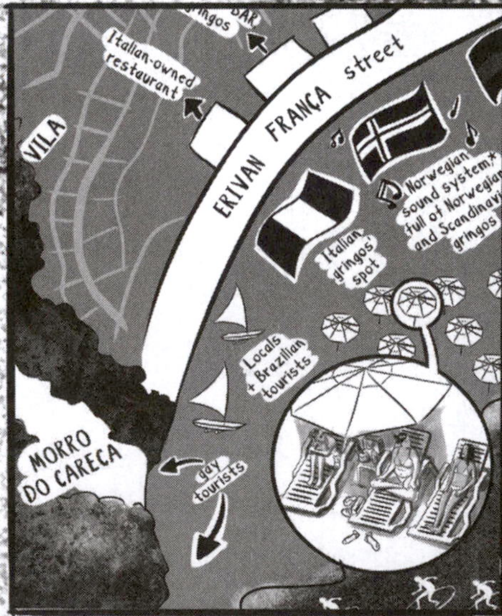
BAR
Italian-owned restaurant
ERIVAN FRANÇA street
VILA
Norwegian sound system*
Italian gringos' spot
Locals + Brazilian tourists
MORRO DO CARECA
gay tourists

MEETING FOREIGN TOURISTS TO DATE OR MARRY, AND SAIR DESSA VIDA, WAS INCREASINGLY LESS LIKELY NOW FOR THE WOMEN I MET IN PONTA NEGRA. IT WAS A VERY DIFFERENT "SCENE" THAN BEFORE.

2014

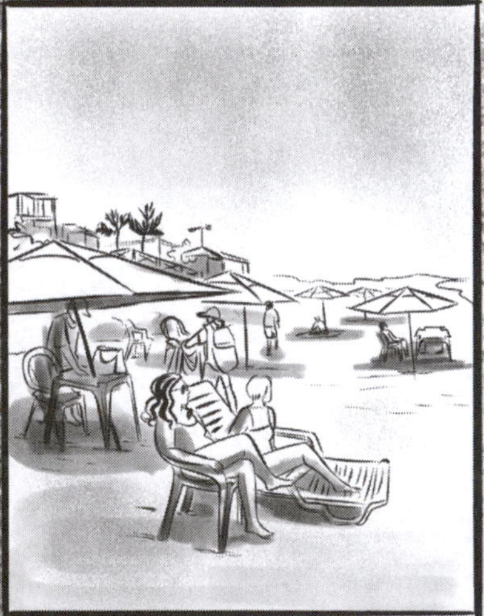

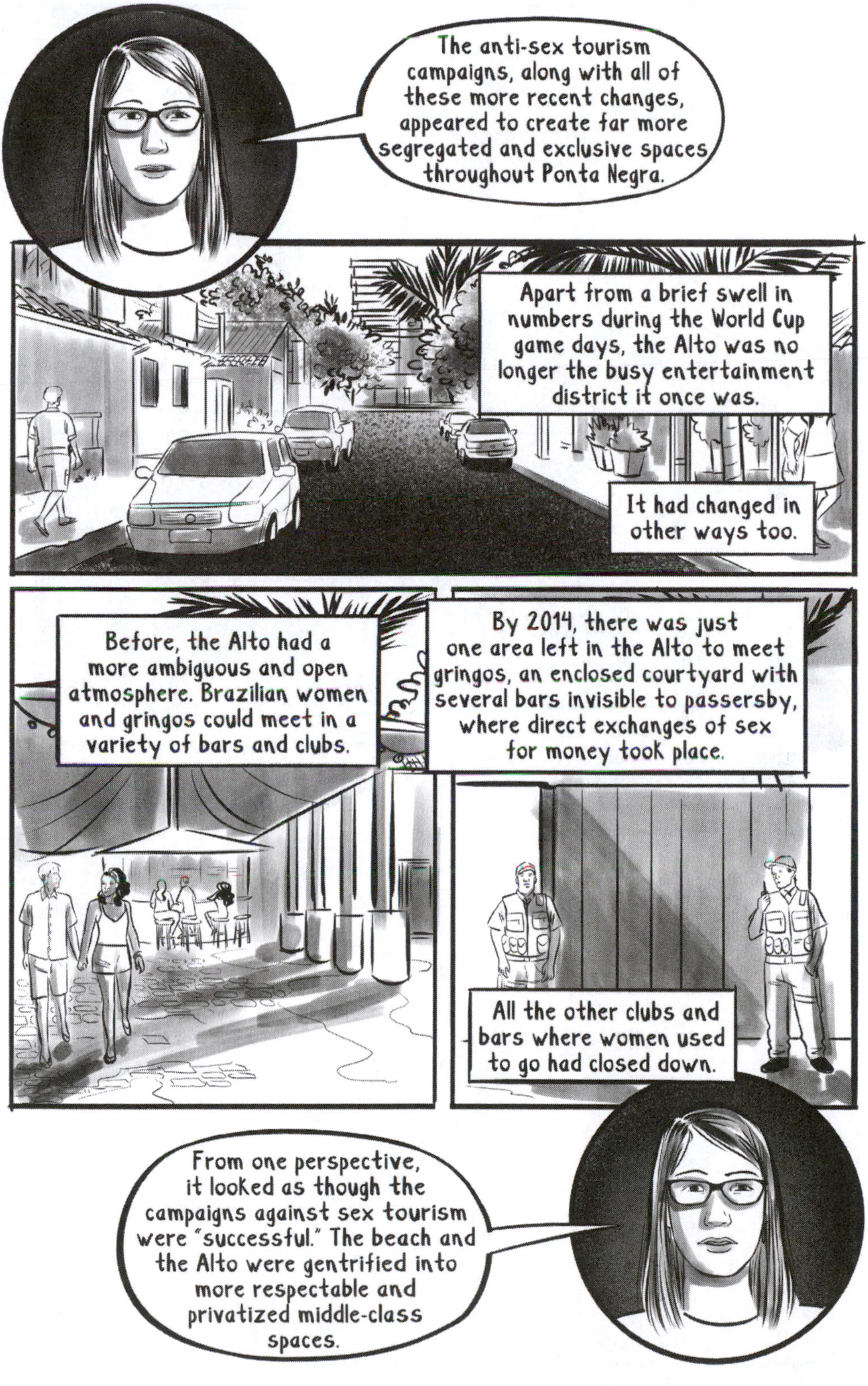
The anti-sex tourism campaigns, along with all of these more recent changes, appeared to create far more segregated and exclusive spaces throughout Ponta Negra.
Apart from a brief swell in numbers during the World Cup game days, the Alto was no longer the busy entertainment district it once was.
It had changed in other ways too.
Before, the Alto had a more ambiguous and open atmosphere. Brazilian women and gringos could meet in a variety of bars and clubs.
By 2014, there was just one area left in the Alto to meet gringos, an enclosed courtyard with several bars invisible to passersby, where direct exchanges of sex for money took place.
All the other clubs and bars where women used to go had closed down.
From one perspective, it looked as though the campaigns against sex tourism were "successful." The beach and the Alto were gentrified into more respectable and privatized middle-class spaces.

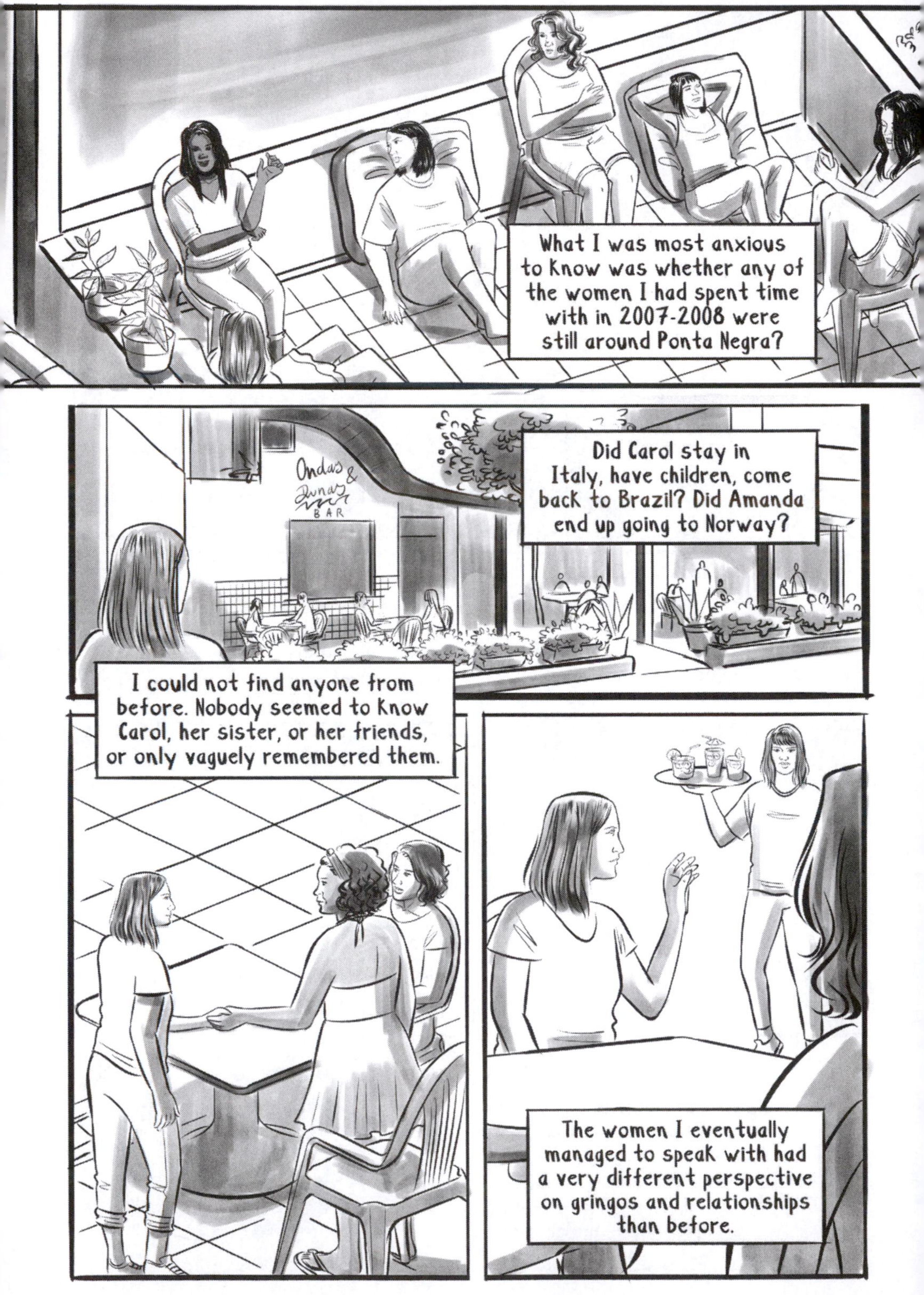

What I was most anxious to Know was whether any of the women I had spent time with in 2007-2008 were still around Ponta Negra?
Ondas & Dunas BAR
Did Carol stay in Italy, have children, come back to Brazil? Did Amanda end up going to Norway?
I could not find anyone from before. Nobody seemed to Know Carol, her sister, or her friends, or only vaguely remembered them.
The women I eventually managed to speak with had a very different perspective on gringos and relationships than before.

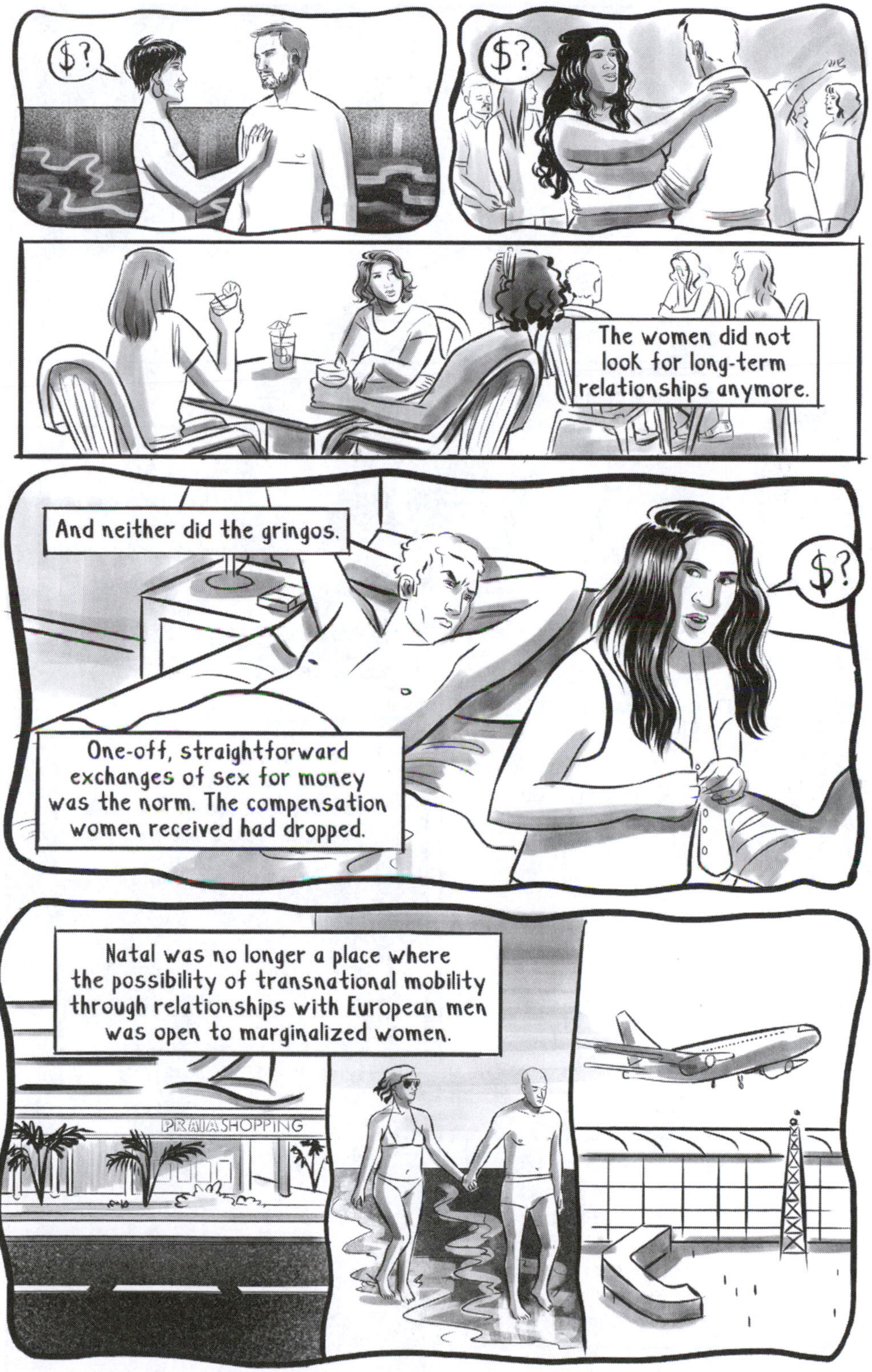
$?
$?
The women did not look for long-term relationships anymore.
And neither did the gringos.
$?
One-off, straightforward exchanges of sex for money was the norm. The compensation women received had dropped.
Natal was no longer a place where the possibility of transnational mobility through relationships with European men was open to marginalized women.
PRAIA SHOPPING

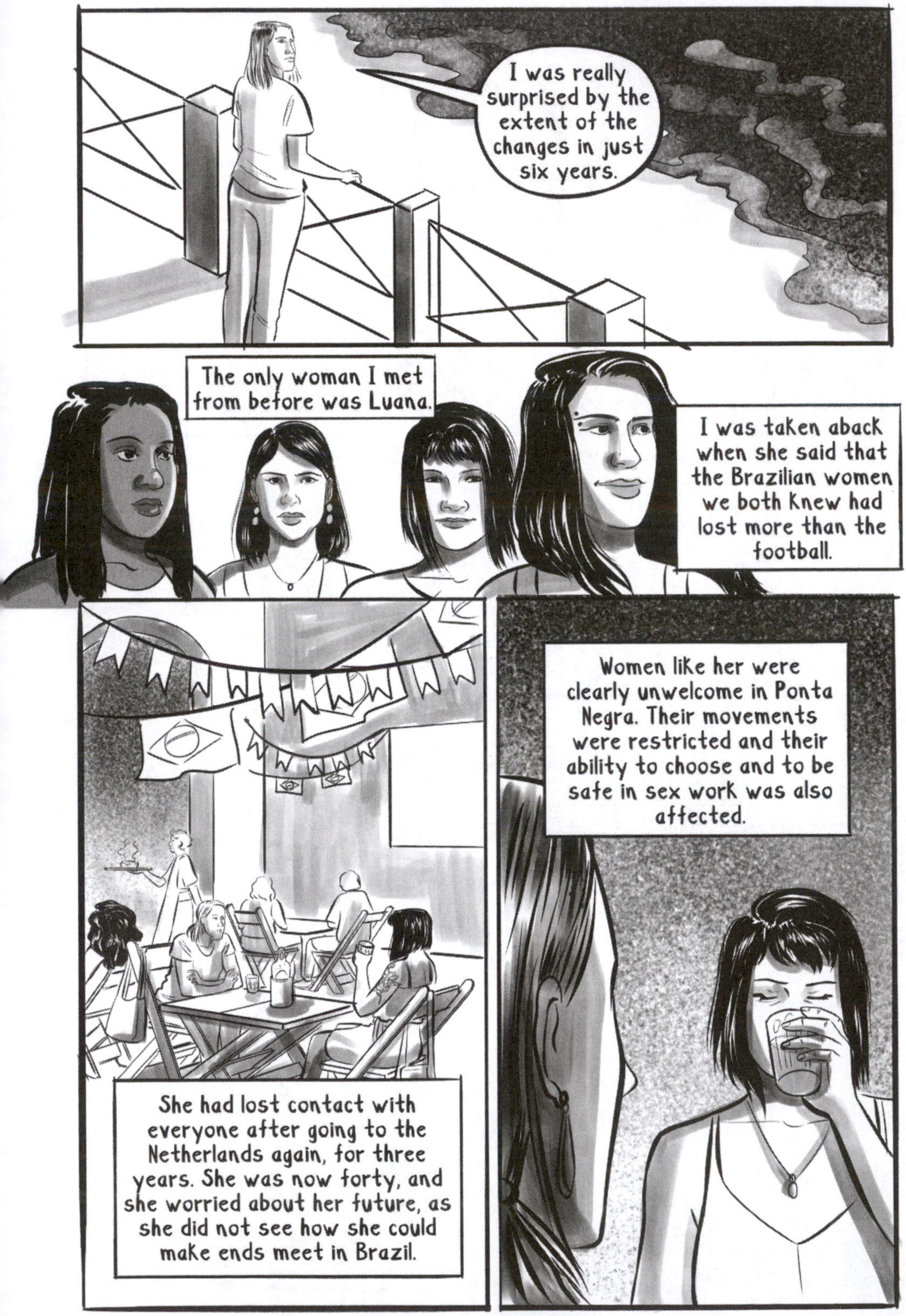
I was really surprised by the extent of the changes in just six years.
The only woman I met from before was Luana.
I was taken aback when she said that the Brazilian women we both knew had lost more than the football.
She had lost contact with everyone after going to the Netherlands again, for three years. She was now forty, and she worried about her future, as she did not see how she could make ends meet in Brazil.
Women like her were clearly unwelcome in Ponta Negra. Their movements were restricted and their ability to choose and to be safe in sex work was also affected.

AN INTENSIFIED POLICE PRESENCE EXACERBATED THINGS FURTHER IN PONTA NEGRA.

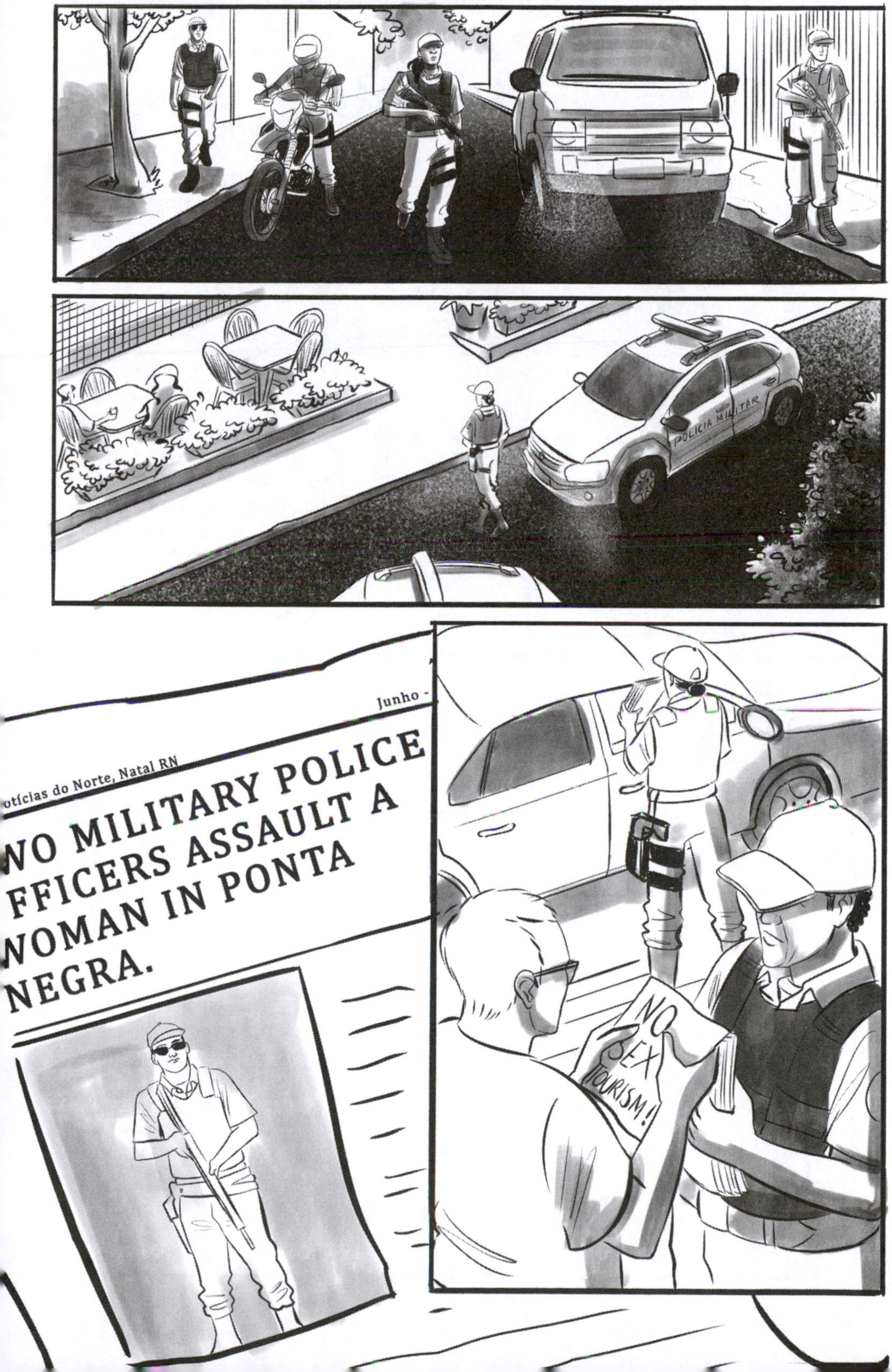
POLICIA MILITAR
Junho -
otícias do Norte, Natal RN
NO MILITARY POLICE
FFICERS ASSAULT A
WOMAN IN PONTA
NEGRA.
NO SEX TOURISM!

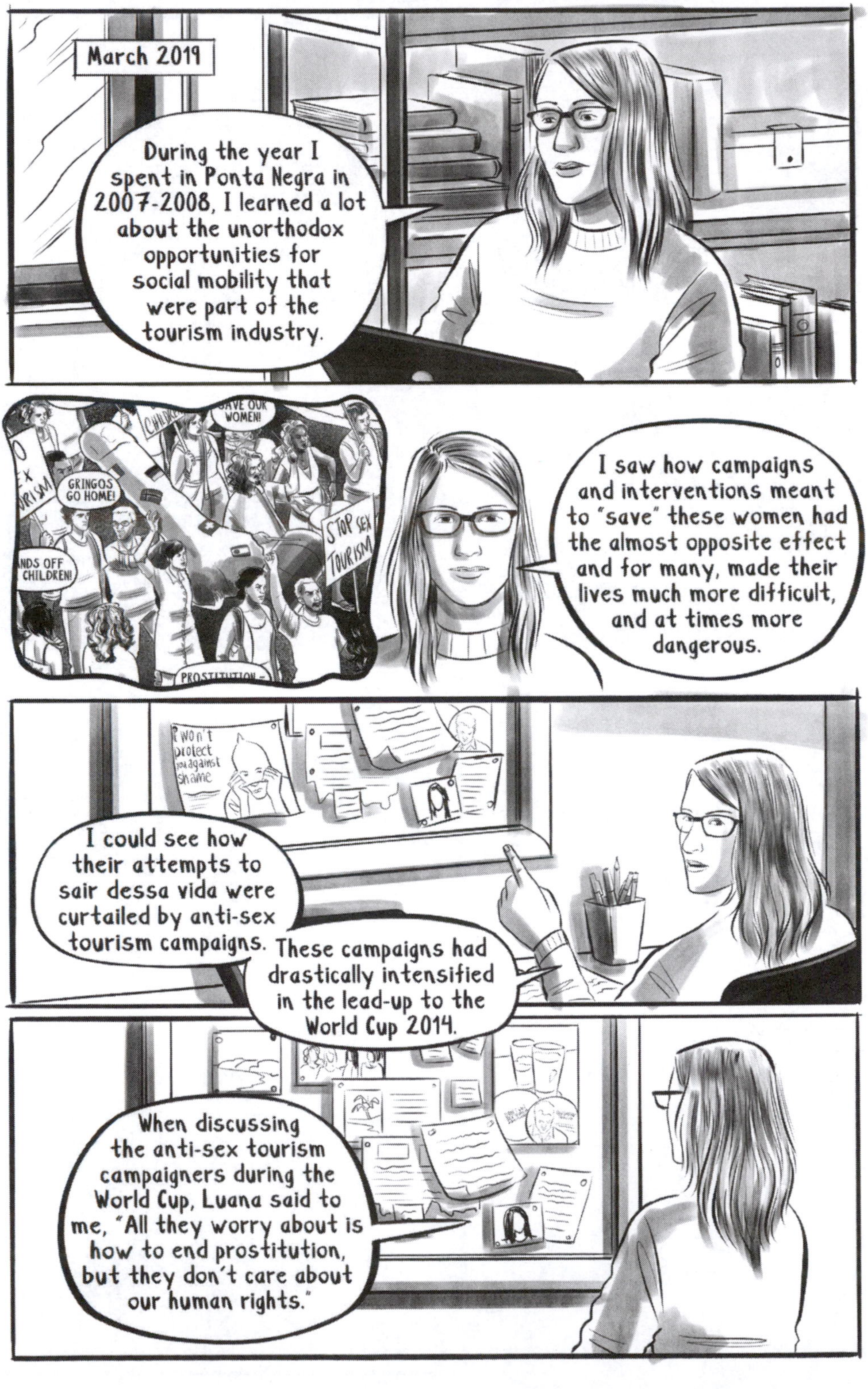

March 2019
During the year I spent in Ponta Negra in 2007-2008, I learned a lot about the unorthodox opportunities for social mobility that were part of the tourism industry.
SAVE OUR WOMEN!
GRINGOS GO HOME!
STOP SEX TOURISM
I saw how campaigns and interventions meant to "save" these women had the almost opposite effect and for many, made their lives much more difficult, and at times more dangerous.
I won't protect you against shame
I could see how their attempts to sair dessa vida were curtailed by anti-sex tourism campaigns.
These campaigns had drastically intensified in the lead-up to the World Cup 2014.
When discussing the anti-sex tourism campaigners during the World Cup, Luana said to me, "All they worry about is how to end prostitution, but they don't care about our human rights."

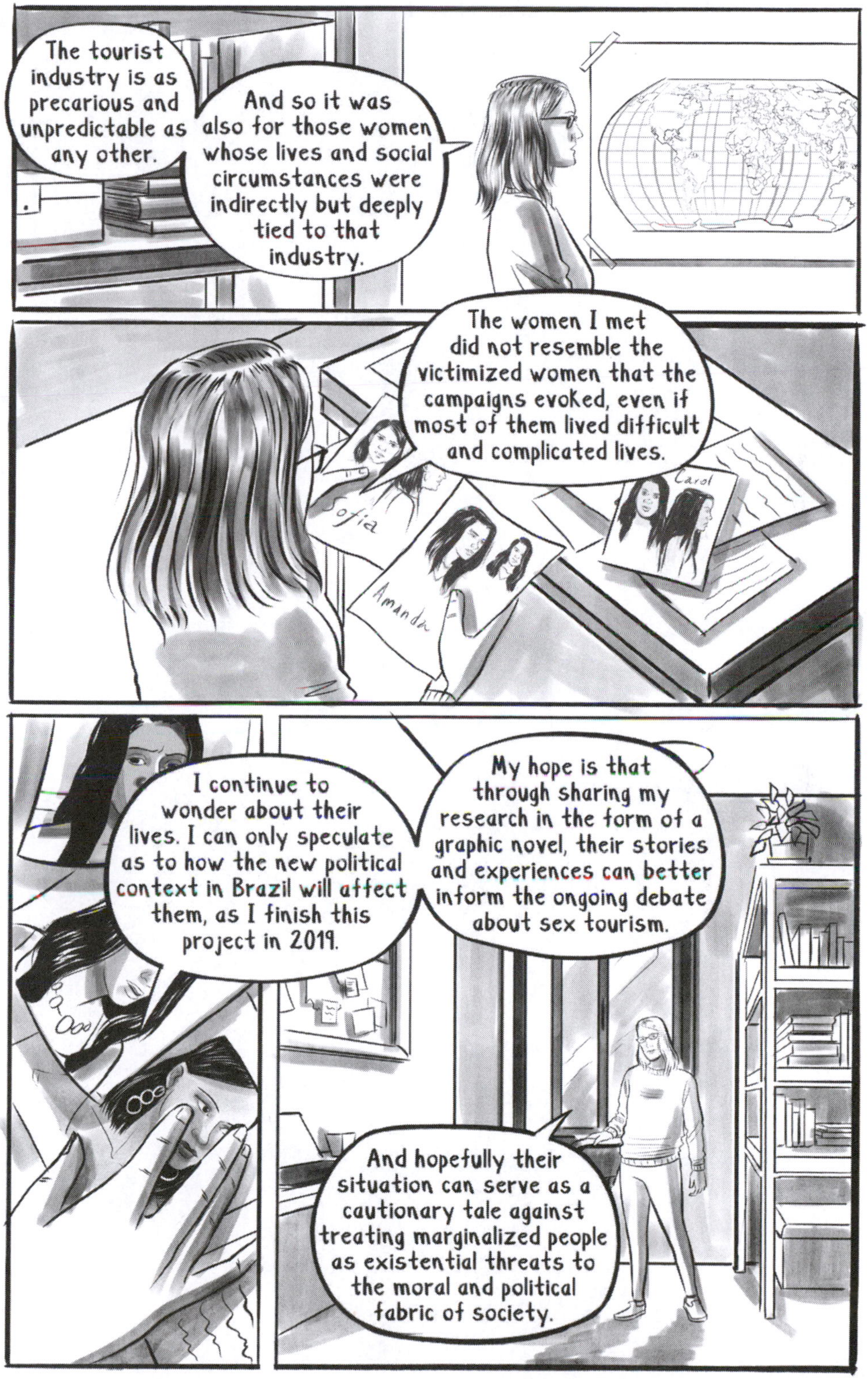

The tourist industry is as precarious and unpredictable as any other.
And so it was also for those women whose lives and social circumstances were indirectly but deeply tied to that industry.
The women I met did not resemble the victimized women that the campaigns evoked, even if most of them lived difficult and complicated lives.
Carol
Sofia
Amanda
I continue to wonder about their lives. I can only speculate as to how the new political context in Brazil will affect them, as I finish this project in 2019.
My hope is that through sharing my research in the form of a graphic novel, their stories and experiences can better inform the ongoing debate about sex tourism.
And hopefully their situation can serve as a cautionary tale against treating marginalized people as existential threats to the moral and political fabric of society.

READING GUIDE AND DISCUSSION QUESTIONS

The Story

1. Let's begin by trying to understand what's happening in the story: What are some of the reasons Carol is leaving Brazil to live in Italy?
2. What does she think about her life in Brazil? About her job as a domestic worker? About the *gringos* (or foreign men) she has met?
3. What about her friends: What do they think of Carol's eventual departure? How do they imagine and/or remember Europe? How are their views similar to and/or different than Carol's?
4. For Carol and her friends, what are some of the opportunities in and enticements of meeting foreign men? What are some of the challenges?
5. What does the graphic story suggest about the centrality of mobility (social, economic, spatial, etc.) and the aspirations to transform one's life?
6. What are the main changes in Ponta Negra between 2008 and 2014? What are the implications of these changes for women who seek to engage in sexual/intimate relationships with foreign men, including local *garotas de programa* (middle-class sex workers)?

Everyday Experiences of Sex Tourism

1. Carol's experiences do not occur in isolation. There are larger, structural forces that mediate her experiences. What are these forces, and how do they play out in her life? What about the lives of her friends?

2. How would you describe Ponta Negra as a place? What do you think it feels like to live in Ponta Negra for Carol and her friends?
3. What happens once these women arrive in Ponta Negra – what kinds of experiences do they have? Compare Carol's experiences with those of her friends.
4. What are the different forms of labor made apparent in the story?
5. What are the things women do to establish long-term ties with foreign men?
6. How do their practices challenge the public/private, work/leisure, love/money, fake/authentic dichotomies?
7. What forms of exclusion, inequality, stigmatization, discrimination, and marginalization do Carol and her friends experience in Ponta Negra?
8. Why do Brazilian women like Carol say they want to *sair dessa vida* (get out of this life)? What do they mean by this? What do they see as oppressing them?

Anti–Sex Tourism Mobilization and Intervention

1. What are the different anti–sex tourism strategies made apparent in the graphic story?
2. How and why is the mobilization and intervention against sex tourism in Natal harmful to some local Brazilian women, such as Carol and her friends? In other words, what's wrong with the opposition to sex tourism in Natal?
3. What lies behind this mobilization – that is, what are some of the underlying motivations and reasons for opposing sex tourism, as expressed by some campaigners, residents, and bar and restaurant owners?
4. What are the links between sexism, racism, classism, and the anti–sex tourism mobilization?
5. How do media, state, and NGO campaigns depict women in sex tourism?
6. How might the experiences of Carol and her friends in sex tourism depart from these depictions?

Gringo Love?

1. How do women discuss what they do with foreign tourists? What role does romance, love, affection, and intimacy play in these encounters? What about money?

2. What about the gringos – the foreign tourists – what are they looking for with Brazilian women in Ponta Negra? What are their motivations?

3. What are some of the tensions around money and payment for both Brazilian women and foreign men?

4. How do the Brazilian women and foreign men in the story imagine one another? How are their mutual desires racialized and gendered? What are some of the tensions and contradictions in these mutual imaginings?

5. What is the role of "gringo love" (love with foreign men) in women's attempts to *sair dessa vida*?

6. What are these women's aspirations for a better future? How do they envision achieving these aspirations?

Ethnography in Graphic Form

1. Eva, the anthropologist, is the narrator in *Gringo Love*. Why do you think this is the case? How does it affect the story?

2. What is made more noticeable, visible, with this medium that may be more difficult to accomplish with other modes of ethnography? What are some of the limitations of using graphic novels to represent ethnography?

3. What do you think about the partial fictionalization of ethnography? Aren't anthropologists supposed to collect data and represent their findings as accurately as possible?

4. What do you think are some of the ethical issues involved in producing an ethnography as a graphic novel?

Beyond *Gringo Love*

1. What were some of the common assumptions and stereotypes about sex tourism you had that were challenged by this graphic story? Assumptions about Brazil? About women involved in sex tourism? About the foreign tourists?

2. What are some of the issues you think may apply elsewhere? Are there parallels with practices of gentrification, public invisibility, and anti-prostitution in other places and communities?

3. How does the graphic story speak to your own experiences of travel and mobility?

APPENDIX 2

THE MAKING OF *GRINGO LOVE*

The Creation Process

The process of making *Gringo Love* has been a complex, collaborative endeavor with William Flynn (hereafter, Billy) – who first had the idea of using this medium to adapt my research and helped with the "translation" of written research work into a visual narrative – and Débora Santos, the Brazilian graphic artist who illustrated the book. Billy's primary role was to find ways of adapting my research into graphic form, including working with me to develop a narrative, to create dialogues, and to find visually compelling ways of representing my ideas. This involved both developing the narrative arc for the overall story as well as elaborating, page by page, the sequencing of events. We then provided Débora with a very thorough and detailed panel-by-panel written script, which she illustrated in draft form while adding her own creative gaze to it. A Brazilian woman from the northeast, Débora transformed our script into rich, detailed, familiar beach and street scenes. She also made suggestions to alter the composition of a page or single panel and to vary the scenes and rhythm, typically also adding visual elements we had not thought about that further enrich the story and readers' visual experience. Billy and I would then look at her layouts and provide feedback and suggestions for adjustments, in a back-and-forth manner that included many iterations of the story, until we eventually moved into the final artwork. We learned, in the making of *Gringo Love*, about what works well and not so well in the graphic form, and we now have a sense of the complexities of meaning-making in comics and graphic novels. For readers curious to know more about these aspects and our collaboration, I discuss them in more detail in a two-part blog post on the Teaching Culture blog: http://www .utpteachingculture.com/anthropology-otherwise-thoughts-on-a-graphic -novel-experiment/.

Our approach was largely based on adapting my ethnographic research into graphic form, an adaptation that occurred after the research was complete. Our primary sources for creating the story were my fieldnotes and interview excerpts – in other words, *texts*. Initially, I constructed a narrative arc based on actual events and people I knew, with dialogue based on things they had said to me, taken verbatim. Yet the dialogues were clumsy and heavy, the storyline hard to build. In making *Gringo Love*, I had to shift my too-discursively-inclined self, as an anthropologist who had been, perhaps, too willing to be disciplined to think in a primarily textual mode. Meaning-making in comics happens through the juxtaposition of image + text, a fine balancing act, so that neither image nor text reduces or overpowers the other (McCloud 1993). While making *Gringo Love*, I was constantly humbled and made aware of the intricacies of trying to find this fine balance. It requires a constant awareness of the interactions between image and text, and what happens when they come together to co-constitute meanings (Sousanis 2015). I eventually had to let go of my use of verbatim quotes and exactitude, even if I remained committed to render, as much as possible, the integrity of the ethnographic fieldwork and "ethnography as deep-knowledge about particular social location" (Cerwonka and Malkki 2007, 27). The medium, as many have said before me, makes possible meaningful rendering of complex subjective experiences at the intersection of larger sociopolitical realities (Hathaway 2011). Indeed, I became interested in the potential of graphic novels and comics to tell anthropology otherwise in part from my own nascent interest in reading graphic novels at the intersection of biography and history or engaging with complex social issues – for instance, *Fun Home*, by Alison Bechdel (2006), *Persepolis*, by Marjane Satrapi (2007), or *Maus*, by Art Spiegelman (1991). These graphic novels made a lasting impression on me as a reader because of their capacity to generate affective knowledge – ways of knowing that rely on our own experiences, that allow us to "feel with" others. I, too, wanted to leave readers with an impression of what Ponta Negra felt like, especially for women negotiating the economy of sex tourism. I also thought that a graphic novel could be the ideal medium to undo existing myths around sex tourism, especially about sexualized victims, given the global circulation of graphic images about sex tourism that are also deeply affective. I felt I ought to engage the same visual mode, even if what I wish to generate in my readers is distinct from the affective politics that are common in visual representations of sex tourism.

As I worked on the project, my understanding of what constitutes the integrity of the field shifted and I eventually moved more toward fictionalization, partly for narrative purposes and partly because the medium lends itself very well to a blurred line between fiction and reality (see, for instance, Hamdy and Nye 2017; Galman 2019). Like other works of ethnographic fiction, the ethno-graphic novel allows the author to take some "liberties with reality" (Hecht 2006, 8), while still evoking the rigor of ethnographic observations and engagements. In my case, the graphic story, while partly fictionalized, draws on my extensive ethnographic experiences, encounters, and engagements during fieldwork and remains an attempt to retell what I have learned, mediated by my positionalities, standpoints, and orientations. In order to build a coherent and more engaging story, I ended up modifying the timeline of events and creating interactions and dialogues between characters that did not actually happen in the way I narrate them. I have also merged features and experiences of different people into single characters, in part for narrative purposes but also to protect the identities of the people with whom I conducted research, as graphic descriptions may elicit memories and feelings of recognition for those familiar with Ponta Negra in 2007–8 and 2014. Many aspects about the characters are also fictive, like their age, hometowns, time spent in Europe/Brazil, relationship to one another, and nationalities (in the case of foreign men). Except for a few landmark places – like the various neighborhoods of Ponta Negra, the shopping mall, or the beach – I have also changed the names of restaurants, bars, and nightclubs. *Gringo Love* still tells the tale of my research, drawing extensively on my encounters, but its relationship to truth and fiction is a blurry one.

The graphic novel also situates Eva, the anthropologist, as part of the story and as narrator to engage readers on ethnography as a research process that is situated, embodied, and grounded in particular vantage points (Behar and Gordon 1995; Cerwonka and Malkki 2007; Haraway 1988). As narrator, Eva presents women's experiences against the backdrop of various misguided interventions by authorities, local organizations, and anti–sex tourism campaigners that attempt to either rescue them or erase them from public visibility. My optics are thus apparent in the choices that I make about how to tell this story and what to tell. A vision, as Donna Haraway suggests, implies the power to see. As she tells us, "there is no unmediated photograph or passive camera obscura in scientific accounts of bodies and machines; there are only highly specific visual possibilities, each with a wonderfully detailed, active, partial way of organizing worlds" (1988, 583). The particular and specific optics I embody are not seamless, either. If personhood is the condition for understanding in ethnography (Cerwonka and Malkki 2007), then an engagement with the notion of complex personhood (Gordon 1997) further complicates *both* my positioning and my attempts to narrate the life of others. As sociologist Avery Gordon suggests, complex personhood involves the recognition that people's lives are at once straightforward and full of meaningful complexities, that "all people (albeit in specific forms whose specificity is sometimes everything) remember and forget, are beset by contradiction, and recognize and misrecognize themselves and others" (1997, 4). This also means, for Gordon, that subjective experiences don't always map clearly onto existing social structures. How do I tell a coherent story of "sex tourism" as lived and experienced, while remaining aware of the twists and turns that exceed neat social categories? For anthropologists, complex personhood is made apparent in the messiness of everyday lives as we take part in them through ethnography. Anthropologist Danilyn Rutherford (2012) hints at those tensions in her proposal to embrace what she terms "kinky empiricism," an appeal to realize that one of the strengths of anthropology concerns its ability to render the empirical in unique ways because of its methods and ethics that create obligations and the truth claims that come with such a sense of obligation (2012, 465). This form of engagement, she suggests, also involves skepticism and doubt, as kinky empiricism "eats away at certainty as well as good conscience" (2012, 468). As she puts it, "every observation is haunted by a multiplicity of places and times" (471) – a haunting that I experienced vividly in the making of *Gringo Love*, perhaps given how the drawings conjure up the real even while transforming it, making social life tractable despite its contradictions, ambiguities, uncertainties, and disjunctures.

The Research Process

The graphic novel – while partly fictionalized – draws extensively on two periods of ethnographic research I conducted. In this section, I further detail the methodology behind the knowledge that made its way into the graphic story. Let me begin with the extensive fieldwork I conducted in 2007–8 for my dissertation, upon which the graphic novel largely draws.

FIELDWORK IN PONTA NEGRA (2007–8)

Between July 2007 and June 2008, I conducted ethnographic research in the tourist district of Ponta Negra, where I lived and engaged in participant observation in spaces frequented by Brazilian women and foreign men, mainly Europeans, such as bars, nightclubs, restaurants, shopping malls, Internet cafes, and beaches. There, I interacted over many months with several Brazilian women and also conducted open-ended interviews with 27 women[1] to complement my observations and our ongoing conversations. Some of the women I was close to never agreed to a formal, tape-recorded interview but still volunteered to share aspects of their life through informal conversations over an extended period of time. Other women continuously shared about their experiences. It is these long-term, informal exchanges that form the basis of my main ethnographic insights and the content that found its way into the graphic novel. I also talked to dozens of foreign men and conducted 15 formal, open-ended interviews with them (11 tourists and 4 expats). Additionally, I interviewed people whose lives had been impacted by the sex-tourist economy, such as local residents, informal workers in the tourism industry, business owners, NGO workers, the head of ASPRO-RN (the local association of sex workers), and various activists, and I engaged in informal conversations with many more.

---

1 These interviews were all tape-recorded, except for one with a tourist who requested that I take written notes. The Brazilian women I interviewed were between 18 and 38 years of age, and most of them were in their early to late twenties, with an average age of 27. None of the women I interviewed had gone to university but three had professional degrees (for instance, in nursing and hairdressing). Fifteen women had high school diplomas (all of them from public institutions); of the remaining 12 women, half had completed their primary-school education, and the remaining six women had frequented schools only briefly. Most of these women came from impoverished households. Nineteen of the 27 women I interviewed had children (between one and four, with an average of two children per woman, most of them toddlers or of elementary-school age). Of the 19 women who had children, seven had a child with a foreigner.

In Ponta Negra, I spent most of my time conducting participant observation – that is, taking part in the everyday life of the sex-tourist economy
and hanging out in the spaces where foreign tourists and Brazilian women
sought to meet one another.[2] This included the beach, where I spent time
almost every day, either alone or with a group of Brazilian women I had met
previously. The beach had distinct social spaces. For instance, close to the
Morro do Careca, local fishermen would come back with their *jangadas*
(wooden fishing boats) after fishing at sea, kids from the impoverished Vila
would play in the waves or in the sand, and Brazilian tourists would commonly frequent this quieter side of the beach. On the opposite end, where
the Via Costeira begins, upper middle-class and upper-class hotels directly
facing the beach attracted more affluent Brazilian and European tourists,
including couples, families, and groups of female/male friends. The busiest
segment of the beach was located next to Erivan França Street, a one-way
street with buildings only on the far side, facing the beach. Along this segment some areas stood out, because they attracted almost exclusively foreign
men and Brazilian women seeking to meet one another. There was a Norwe-
gian-friendly spot where the local, handmade sound systems played
Norwegian music, and there were other spots known for attracting either
Spanish or Italian male tourists. This is where I concentrated my partici-
pant-observation activities, and these spaces are featured in the graphic story
and easy to find on the maps.

On Erivan França Street there was an important point of encounter, especially in the early evening, between Brazilian women and foreign men, and I
fictionalized this spot in the graphic story as the Ondas & Dunas Bar. I frequented the venue almost every day, sometimes just for a few minutes (when
there were very few people or to catch up with someone met previously) and
other times, I would spend a couple of hours there. The first few times I went
there, I sat alone, a little awkwardly, feeling like a misfit in this space. Yet I
rarely remained alone, as there was always someone inviting me to join his or
her table (both foreign men and Brazilian women). After a few weeks, the
Brazilian women who regularly frequented Ponta Negra's beach and bars to
meet foreign men recognized me and invited me to join their tables.

---

2 I focused on heteronormative sexual encounters between local women and tourist men, given
   their predominance, hypervisibility, and the moral panic surrounding them; readers interested
   in non-normative relationships and queering sex tourism in Brazil may consider the work of
   Williams (2013) and Mitchell (2016).

Brazilian women seeking to meet foreign men also spent the early evening preparing for the night out, and I took part in this activity from time to time with a few Brazilian women, especially with those who lived nearby my rented apartment.[3] As we saw in the graphic story, women would discuss the upcoming night and the foreign men they dated or had paid sex with, and they would offer tips and advice to each other. These intimate conversations provided further insights into the ambiguity and complexity of their practices and allowed me to witness additional dimensions of their lives, including the emotional and embodied labor they perform daily, as shown in this book.

The nightlife in Ponta Negra commonly began after 10:00 p.m. and ended in the early hours of the morning. I found this rhythm tiring, and many women commented on their difficulty to maintain this routine on a regular basis. I conducted participant observation in most of the nightclubs and bars (about a dozen) but eventually I opted to concentrate on those catering to and/or attracting Brazilian women and foreign men. These included two small bars with tropical themes (such bars kept opening and closing down, so in the graphic story, I chose to merge the two main bars in which I spent time into the Paraíso). Around midnight, those still interested in staying out would move to one of the few nightclubs in the area – for narrative purposes, in the graphic story I focus on the most popular, which I fictionalized as the Lagoa, but others were also the focus of my observations.

The Alto, as the main entertainment district in Ponta Negra, was also a diversified social space consisting of various bars, restaurants, and nightclubs that catered to both locals and tourists, including bars frequented mainly by students, young professionals, and middle-class Brazilians. The Lagoa, which was locally associated with sex tourism, was a space neither exclusively to pick up someone nor to directly negotiate an exchange of sex for money; rather, Brazilian women and foreign men would also flirt, chat, dance, make out, and so on. Other bars were also sites of various exchanges, even if they presented themselves as more "respectable." I spent three to four nights a week in the bars or clubs, speaking with different groups of people throughout the night, or sitting at the bar and observing what was happening.

---

3 I lived on the edge of the Alto near the Vila. For narrative purposes and to highlight our different socioeconomic means, in the graphic story I located my apartment in the middle-class, residential Conjunto, in contrast to Carol in the more impoverished Vila, where many of the women I knew lived.

SITUATING MYSELF IN THE FIELD (2007-8)

My presence in these various spaces generated some puzzlement: my claim of being an anthropologist conducting research was met with suspicious smiles, flirting, and laughter, and I was at times asked if I was working (as a *garota de programa*)[4] or interested in sex with women. Some also suspected that my research was an excuse to justify my presence in these highly sexualized spaces. These experiences reveal that despite the obvious and dominant heterosexual nature of most tourist venues in Ponta Negra, more complicated sexual desires and encounters also permeated these spaces. At the same time, as a woman, albeit a *foreign* woman, I was sometimes considered competition for the attention of foreign men. Furthermore, women in the bars and clubs did not identify as a collective group (even those who considered themselves *garotas de programa*) and kept a distance from the local association of sex workers. To approach women, I could not rely on the outreach work of local associations or NGOs, as these did not conduct outreach activities in Ponta Negra. Instead, I had to constantly develop new ties, but at times this was hindered by how women tended to identify with a group of women. Once I became close to some women, I was seen as part of their group and it became difficult to get to know other women beyond the usual familiarities. This presented me with the possibility of getting closer to some women while restricting my potential reach to a larger group of them. I think that for the women with whom I got close, I was an odd but nonthreatening companion, since I could provide them with unobtrusive company for the night while they worked and played with the men, especially since women commonly did not like to go out alone.

When my husband, Billy, joined me in the field for the last five months of my fieldwork (late January to June), I recruited him as a research assistant. Billy conducted participant observation in the bars, nightclubs, restaurants, and at the beach on about a dozen occasions. He wrote fieldnotes and told me about his observations and the conversations he had with English-speaking tourists. His experience was distinct from mine, as he could blend in easily in

---

4 *Garota de programa* colloquially refers to a middle-class sex worker or escort. According to Piscitelli, "the word *programas* [plural of *programa*] designates explicit agreements to exchange sexual services for money, including prices, practices and lengths of encounters" (2007b, 491). It is sometimes used interchangeably with *prostituição* (prostitution) but it also may connote middle-class prostitution, including prostitution in nightclubs (Gaspar 1985) or even high-class prostitution, such as escort services (Rohter 2006).

the bars and nightclubs as a European man in his early thirties, matching the demographics of the average foreign tourist. Indeed, when frequenting the bars together, we could pass as a Brazilian/European couple in the eyes of some of the tourists (but not in those of the Brazilians). His encounters with foreign men were thus mediated by his position in the field: based on his perceived identity as a European male tourist, foreign men spoke with him in different ways than they would with me. For instance, a Spanish tourist once told him: "It must be hard to be here with your wife!" as he assumed a shared experience in the bars and nightclubs of Ponta Negra by virtue of being a European man. Importantly, however, these foreign men did more than crudely comment on women's bodies or proudly discuss their sexual prowess, as one might assume. Instead they revealed to Billy their complex emotional attachments to Brazilian women, shared stories of deception or deep affection, or confided about their desire for long-term relationships and their sense of loss of power and desirability back home. As shown in the graphic story, the conversations he had with them thus complemented and corroborated mine in many ways and helped to provide further depth to my ethnographic findings as well as confirm my own understanding of their practices.

COLLABORATIONS

During the field research period, I developed collaborative ties with Lita (Marta Bertrand Galarza), a social sciences student from Spain doing a pilot study on sex tourism in Natal. She spent six weeks in Ponta Negra in the months of August and September and rented an apartment in my building. We agreed to collaborate, though we were working on separate projects, and during these few weeks we went to the bars, nightclubs, restaurants, and beaches together. We conducted five interviews together, discussed our impressions and observations, and shared our fieldnotes. It was also helpful to conduct my observations with another foreign student and woman. This collaboration was particularly fruitful to confirm patterns I had observed in Ponta Negra and it informs my research in various ways, although it did not make its way into the graphic story for narrative purposes.

I also developed a collaborative relationship with the *Coletivo Leila Diniz*, a feminist collective critical of the ways in which the campaigns against sex tourism of various state and non-state actors tended to displace important issues – structural inequalities, lack of job opportunities, and the imbalanced benefits of tourism development. The collective provided me with institutional, intellectual, and emotional support while I was in Natal. Members gave me tours of the neighborhood, helped me find a place to stay, introduced me to key figures in Natal who opposed sex tourism, and provided me with many insights about their experiences as middle-class residents in Ponta Negra. They invited me to take part in some of their reading groups, and I had the opportunity to present my findings to them and to have fruitful intellectual exchanges. I also accompanied the feminist collective to Salvador da Bahia to the *Forum Social Nordestino*, a regional version of the World Social Forum, and took part in sessions addressing sex tourism and/or sex trafficking. I participated in other events in Natal, including public forums and protests, alongside the collective. I deeply admire the critical work done by this group of progressive feminists; while the collective then only indirectly engaged with the issue of sex tourism, the group provided a vital alternative to the widespread moral panic around sex tourism through its critique of the harms of anti–sex tourism mobilizations for local *garotas de programa* (Azevedo 2005).

Finally, as part of my attempt to document the opposition to sex tourism, I interviewed various state and non-state anti–sex tourism campaigners. I had not anticipated finding opposition to sex tourism from local business owners, given the economic benefits sex tourism commonly generates for them. Yet some of them did oppose it, and they tended to cater to a middle-class Brazilian clientele. Besides interviewing owners of bars, restaurants, and hotels campaigning against sex tourism, I also consulted their websites, visited their establishments, and collected their campaign materials. Another strategy was to consult the archive of newspaper articles on sex tourism collected by the local NGO Resposta in their main office in Natal, and I conducted further research through the web search engine of the *Diário de Natal* and *Tribuna do Norte* in order to understand the context that had given rise to the opposition to sex tourism, to get a sense of the public debates on sex tourism, and to document the various responses, interventions, and campaigns that ensued. Through these diverse research strategies, I was able to explore the campaigns from several angles and to situate them within their local political contexts. This analysis also helped to position the campaigns that emerged with the advent of the 2014 World Cup.

THE 2014 WORLD CUP

In 2014, I returned to Natal to conduct ethnographic research for two months: prior to, during, and after the World Cup. As one of the 12 host cities, Natal was the site of many city marketing and campaigning activities, with a renewed focus on mobilization against sex tourism and sex trafficking. My aim was to conduct an ethnographic analysis of these campaigns – that is, to map their empirical effects, paying particular attention to the role of public emotions in mobilizing against sex tourism and trafficking.

A first and key step in this project was to track and analyze the different campaigns, including their web presence, use of social media, alliances, and public interventions. I participated in meetings, public debates, and protests from various organizations. I also conducted interviews with 25 campaigners, including students, feminist activists, religious figures, unionists, NGO workers, politicians, state employees, and bureaucrats. It was difficult to keep track of all the campaigns, as multiple campaigns coexisted and had different groups involved – some against the trafficking of women, others against the sexual exploitation of children, others against sex tourism. Many of them implicitly supported anti-prostitution measures, and several of my interviewees were in favor of further criminalization and police repression in order to end sex tourism.

On this return visit, I tried to locate many of the women I had interviewed previously – for the most part, unsuccessfully. I did meet with two of them and interviewed one of them. I interviewed 11 Brazilian women who identified as *garotas de programa* while also spending time in bars and at the beach observing and talking to Brazilian women and tourists – but not to the same extent as in 2007–8 because the purpose of my research was more focused on the campaigners. I noticed, during this fieldwork, the drastic drop in European tourism and the absence of ambiguous spaces and areas for Brazilian women and foreign men to meet, whether at the beach or in the Alto – a sharp contrast to 2007–8, when Brazilian women and foreign men would flirt and engage in various forms of exchange along a continuum in open, amorphous spaces instead of in spaces exclusively reserved for prostitution. In 2014, these encounters were confined to an enclosed set of small open-air bars known as the *praça*, in the Alto de Ponta Negra, but they were hidden behind huge walls; this made *garotas de programa* and *gringos* completely invisible to passersby and clients in nearby bars and restaurants and transformed the ambiguous relationships into more straightforward exchanges of sex for money. While some women welcomed the clarity of the transaction, many others lamented the absence of undefined spaces to meet foreign men, as these had played a central role in their project of self-transformation and socioeconomic mobility. They also felt more pressured to leave right away with a man and more restrained in their ability to choose among them, given that fewer men would frequent these spaces more closely associated with prostitution – many men would come in and ask a woman to leave with them immediately, without having time to gauge one another.

During this visit, I was shocked by the drastic changes that had taken place during my absence, especially for women who sought to meet foreign men and make ends meet from these encounters. As I walked through Ponta Negra, I felt as if, to some extent, the anti–sex tourism campaigns of the past had succeeded in making prostitution (and other marginalized youths) disappear from Ponta Negra's public spaces, which further disenfranchised the women I had previously known. It seemed, therefore, important to tell the stories of the 2014 campaigns in the graphic novel and to acknowledge the ways in which shifting socioeconomic opportunities and constraints mediate experiences in sex tourism.

APPENDIX 3

THE CONTEXT FOR *GRINGO LOVE*

Sex Tourism

WHAT IS "SEX TOURISM"?

The response to this question is not a simple one, and while the graphic story provides some possible answers, the term's meaning is not necessarily agreed upon and is highly context-dependent. Commonly, the term "sex tourism" hints at prostitution that is geared toward tourists as clientele. The term is also usually gendered, like "prostitution" and "sex work," as implicitly the term refers to tourist *men* and local *women*; terms like "gay sex tourism" or "female sex tourism" point to the implicitly gendered meaning of "sex tourism." A common image of sex tourism in popular culture is that of an older, wealthier, whiter man sexually exploiting young, vulnerable, racialized, exotic women, an image that is possibly rooted in the origin of the term. Indeed, the term emerged in the 1980s to refer to practices involving an exchange of sex for material benefit in the context of tourism in Southeast Asia (Kempadoo and Ghuma 1999, 291). Since then, there have been many debates about what the term means, including how distinct/similar it is to both sex work or romance tourism (e.g., Sanchez Taylor 2001). Scholars have often described sex tourism as ambiguous and elusive (Brennan 2004; Cabezas 2009; Cohen 1982; Frohlick 2013; Fusco 1998; Padilla 2007; Stout 2014), including in Brazil (Cantalice 2011; Carrier-Moisan 2015, 2018; Mitchell 2016; Piscitelli 2007b; Silva and Blanchette 2005; Williams 2013). For many of them, what distinguishes sex tourism is precisely that it exceeds a straightforward exchange of sex for money (but for a fascinating exception, see Rivers-Moore 2016). In Ponta Negra, as shown in the graphic story, it is partly *because* relationships were not clearly defined by an exchange of sex for money that they appealed to both local Brazilian women and foreign men.

At the same time, in Ponta Negra "no sex tourism" often meant "no prostitution," although this was not always made explicit. Often, the term "sex tourism" was used because it evoked the image of young girls sexually exploited by perverted foreign men, but what many campaigners opposed in practice was the presence of women they perceived as not belonging in white, middle-class spaces. In this context, what people mean when they talk about sex tourism or engage in campaigns to curtail it matters deeply. As is visible in the graphic story, what comes to be known as sex tourism translates into state and non-state campaigns, police interventions, practices of surveillance, public reprobation, processes of discrimination, and stigmatization. Sex tourism can thus be understood as a domain of power/knowledge (Foucault 1991) in that it is productive and constitutive of the ways in which people relate to one another and to themselves. In what follows, I trace the making of sex tourism as a public concern in Natal through key moments and articulations, pointing to the specific ways that sex tourism came to be known there.

THE MAKING OF SEX TOURISM AS A PUBLIC CONCERN IN NATAL

The making of sex tourism as a public concern in Natal follows a similar pattern to the rest of Brazil.[1] It began with a focus on the sexual exploitation of children and adolescents in the context of tourism, which became a prominent issue worldwide in the late 1980s and early 1990s, especially following the influential work of international organizations such as End Child Prostitution and Trafficking (ECPAT). ECPAT views the sex trade as enabling child

---

1   Sex tourism was not always an issue of public concern in Brazil. Instead, during the 1960s and in the following three decades, Embratur, a state-owned agency of the Ministry of Tourism created during the military dictatorship (1964–85), promoted the image of Brazil as a tropical paradise. Known as the four Ss of international tourism – sun, sea, sand, and sex (Crick 1989) – in Brazil this marketing strategy drew on the image of the *mulata* (mulatta), seen as embodying the nation. Whether the state-owned agency was a "maker of images for the Brazilian nation" (Alfonso 2006; see also Gilliam 1998) or an "amplifier of pre-existing elements of identity" (Sacramento 2018, 199; see also Blanchette and Silva 2010), the Brazilian state was not, at the time, concerned with what came to later be known as "sex tourism."

sexual abusers, a vision that was, and continues to be, articulated in its campaigning activities and that led to the acceptance of anti-prostitution measures to fight the sexual exploitation of children by various states, including Brazil (Kempadoo and Ghuma 1999; Pothecary 2014). Yet Natal stood out nationally, to some extent, as it was the *first* Brazilian city to adopt ECPAT's Code of Conduct for the Tourism Industry against the Sexual Exploitation of Children, in 2001. While purportedly aimed at children, the code promotes ethical conduct targeting all forms of sex tourism (Resposta 2010). In Natal, especially in Ponta Negra, many establishments commonly displayed their adherence to the code, along with claims to repudiate sex tourism, often understood as prostitution. While this conflation is not unique to Natal or Brazil, it manifested in unique ways in the entertainment district of Ponta Negra, where owners of middle-class bars and restaurants used the opposition to sex tourism and ECPAT's code to ban *some* women, as shown in the graphic story.

The fight against sex tourism in Brazil also intensified with the international concern for human trafficking, and sex trafficking in particular, that gained momentum at the start of the millennium.[2] A key moment was the adoption of the Palermo Protocol to Prevent, Suppress, and Punish Trafficking in Persons, Especially Women and Children by the UN in 2000, which Brazil ratified in 2004. In contrast to the Palermo Protocol – where coercion, while open to interpretation, is understood as a necessary component of trafficking and where trafficking applies to various forms of labor exploitation (Oliveira 2008; Silva et al. 2013)[3] – the Brazilian penal code is framed in such a way that anyone helping a sex worker to move across borders could be considered a trafficker, and only exploitation in the context of the sex industry is recognized as trafficking (Piscitelli 2007a). This legal interpretation has led to a focus on the cross-border movement of Brazilian women seeking to work in the sex industry, and it is in this context that sites commonly associated with sex tourism in Brazil (like Ponta Negra/Natal) have come to be seen as the "gateway" (Williams 2011, 193) to sex trafficking, with which both sex tourism and human trafficking came to be conflated.

---

2 This concern is reminiscent of earlier anxieties about the traffic in women, known as "white slavery," of the late nineteenth and early twentieth centuries (Doezema 2010; Piscitelli 2004a; Silva et al. 2013).

3 This does not mean, however, that the protocol is exempt from conceptual problems – it does not specify what exploitation or coercion means; it emphasizes prostitution; and, as suggested by Silva et al., "it symbolically situates adult women as the equivalent, in rights and vulnerabilities, to children" (2013, 391).

During his first mandate as president of Brazil, Luis Inácio Lula da Silva intensified the fight against sex trafficking and the sexual exploitation of children through police-rescue missions that tapped into concerns for both human security and global humanitarianism, but they also targeted sex workers (Amar 2009; Grupo Davida 2005). These initiatives were part of the president's efforts to shift the image of Brazil as "one of the planet's most unjust, unequal societies to claim the status of a global role model of social justice, humanity, and safety" (Amar 2009, 514). These police-rescue missions paved the way for the public acceptance of anti-prostitution interventions as legitimate means to curtail both sex trafficking and the sexual exploitation of children, including in Natal.

However, as I have explored elsewhere (Carrier-Moisan 2013), the issue of sex tourism became a serious concern for Natal especially in the aftermath of an undercover media exposé by the national news network *Globo* in March 2006, disseminated widely in newspaper articles, on national television, and on the Internet (Globo 2006a, 2006b, 2006c, 2006d, 2006e). The media coverage also made waves in Europe and was featured in the Spanish newspaper *El Mundo* (Marin 2006), labeling Natal as a *europrostíbulo* (euro-brothel), an epithet that hurt the image of the city. In response to accusations of complicity (at worst) and inaction (at best), the municipality, along with the state of Rio Grande do Norte, suddenly became very active. It held a public hearing and designed a plan against sex tourism that included an operation called *Ponta Negra Livre*, or Free Ponta Negra (Dickson 2006). The operation, as featured in the graphic story, consisted of a series of raids and the spectacular deployment of police forces fighting sex tourism (itself left undefined and ambiguous). Almost everyone in Ponta Negra remembered those raids vividly the following year, when I conducted fieldwork. Both ends of the main street along the beach, Erivan França, were blocked while police officers searched the bars and restaurants and arrested several dozen foreign tourists. The raids were symbolically hailed as a success in the fight against sex tourism, even if the main offense committed by the detained foreigners had been to find themselves without their passports and no crime relating to the sexual exploitation of minors was uncovered (Bezerra and Lopes 2006). The fight against sex tourism in Natal thus occupied a gray zone, making it possible for local police enforcement to curtail prostitution (despite sex work not being illegal in Brazil).

The raids did not last long, but they left their mark on the cityscape as a symbolic display of state intervention against sex tourism. They formed part of a larger mobilization that included the municipal campaign "Stop Sex

Tourism," a campaign featured in the graphic story and whose aim was, once again, left ambiguous. Yet the state was not alone in its campaigning, as local residents, business owners, and activists with a wide range of affiliations also joined the effort. While motivated by various interests, their campaigning activities often manifested as anti-prostitution mobilization and, at times, implicitly, as anti-poor/black – an aspect I believe was made possible because the meaning of sex tourism was left ambiguous and undefined in most campaigns.

SEX TOURISM AS ANTI-POOR/BLACK

In Natal, the term sex tourism was not only gendered, it was also classed and racialized, as is possible to gather from the graphic story. It applied more to *some* local women than others; rarely, if ever, to local men or tourist women. In her ethnography of sex tourism in Salvador da Bahia, Brazil, anthropologist Erica Lorraine Williams (2013, 3) discusses "the broad and wide-ranging implications of sex tourism that go far beyond self-avowed 'sex workers' or 'sex tourists,'" what she terms the "specter of sex tourism." She suggests that in Salvador, sex tourism produces anxieties for both locals and foreigners because of suspicions about the nature of their relationships; these anxieties, however, are heightened by racialized and gendered presumptions about sexual availability – in particular, by the conflation of black female bodies with sexual promiscuity and disreputability (see also Fusco 1998). In Natal, too, suspicions were racialized and gendered, but also classed. My neighbor – a Brazilian woman about to travel on a boat cruise with her French boyfriend – once said to me "I hate this race," speaking of some women I had invited on my last night out in Ponta Negra; she assumed they were *garotas de programa*. This is a comment that we could interpret in various ways; it certainly points to her anxiety about sex tourism and her distancing from it. It also shows how she imagined *garotas* as "others" and how this imagining was linked to processes of racialization from which she sought to mark herself away (notably, she was avoiding the sun and had her hair colored in blond, in an effort to look more European or white). Bar, restaurant, and hotel owners also conflated "black women" and "sex tourism" and, in interviews, described their tactics to prevent local *garotas de programa* (read: women racialized as black or *morena* and working-class women) from entering their establishments under the guise of fighting sex tourism. As documented by scholars in different locations, the opposition to prostitution commonly points to spatial practices of inclusion and exclusion (e.g., Hubbard 1999;

Ross 2010). In mid-2000s Natal, the fight against sex tourism similarly led to exclusionary spatial practices. This mobilization was the precursor to further anti–sex tourism campaigns in the mid-2010s, as I discuss below.

THE 2014 WORLD CUP AND THE RENEWED CONCERN FOR SEX TOURISM

The public concern for sex tourism temporarily faded in Natal with the dramatic drop in European tourism that ensued in 2009 and afterward.[4] Faced with a tarnished image and seriously affected by the 2008 global financial crisis, Natal turned its attention to domestic and family-oriented tourism (Sacramento 2018). In part, the anti–sex tourism mobilization had been successful in decreasing the public visibility of practices associated with sex tourism in Ponta Negra.

Yet the advent of the 2014 World Cup in 12 host cities across Brazil, including Natal, revived public concern for sex tourism there. This renewed concern resulted from both Natal's particular history with sex tourism *and* the global circulation in the media of a presumed link between mega-sporting events and sex trafficking, even if the latter is not grounded in empirical evidence, as several studies have shown (GAATW 2011; Lepp 2013; Morrow 2008). In Natal, the global hype translated into campaigns linking sex trafficking to sex tourism.

At the same time, local middle-class residents and business owners saw a mega-event like the World Cup as threatening Ponta Negra anew, and thus a powerful remobilization against sex tourism in Natal spread rapidly. In Natal alone, there were at least ten different, simultaneous campaigns associated with the World Cup on the theme of sex tourism, sex trafficking, and/ or the sexual exploitation of children. Campaign materials included giant billboards, logos adopted by local businesses, pamphlets, T-shirts, posters, and ads in taxis. Several blitzes occurred in key locations, such as the newly built airport on the periphery of the city, shopping malls, key roads, official FIFA sites, and other locations specifically in Ponta Negra. There were marches, protests, public debates, and meetings to curtail sex tourism, in addition to intensifying police surveillance and repression.

---

4 The number of international tourists visiting Natal dropped by half between 2008 and 2014. Meanwhile, domestic tourism remained stable and even increased slightly (Aeroporto de Natal 2014; Infraero 2010, 2014; Mendes and Vasconcelos 2011).

As several scholars have argued, host cities of mega-events are increasingly invested in processes of image-making and "spectacular security" (Boyle and Haggerty 2009; Kennelly 2015), and Natal followed a similar trend. Now featured on a global stage of unprecedented scale, Natal sought to present the image of a respectable, safe city. This was accomplished through various processes, including the deployment of a massive security apparatus around the World Cup sites. In part, the fight against sex tourism provided a legitimizing discourse to justify the intensification of securitization. A panoply of state agents and police officers thus patrolled Ponta Negra – in helicopters, on foot, in cars, vans, or military-style trucks. The military police even participated in the anti–sex tourism campaign "*Estamos de Olho*" (We're Watching), led by the Catholic Church. The context in 2014 was thus one of intense policing and potential human rights violations. But Ponta Negra had *already* changed on the cusp of the World Cup. Indeed, the advent of this mega-sporting event made it possible to continue existing and ongoing state-led interventions, but with more intensity. While the anti–sex tourism campaigns of the mid-2000s had been "successful" in making Ponta Negra a more exclusive space, the new campaigns attempted to cement Ponta Negra this way, and the mobilizing had a stronger, more explicitly affirmed anti-prostitution tone (Carrier-Moisan 2019). This renewed and more forceful anti-prostitution stance marked a shift in the making of sex tourism as a public concern in Natal, as state repression and intensified policing became increasingly normalized and considered publicly acceptable to curtail prostitution. The Articulação Nacional dos Comitês Populares da Copa (the National Articulation of Popular Committees of the World Cup – hereafter, ANCOP, in its Portuguese acronym) published a special dossier on mega-events and human rights violations in Brazil. ANCOP (2014) identified the conflation between trafficking and prostitution as restricting the mobility of sex workers and the right to exercise their labor. It also pointed to the ways in which city-cleansing operations in host cities across Brazil by missionaries, anti-prostitution activists, and the state manifested as attempts to curtail the right of sex workers to work.

In response to the intense anti-prostitution repression that peaked around these mega-events, sex workers across Brazil have organized collectively, drawing on a long-standing, vibrant legacy of mobilization for the recognition of sex workers' labor and human rights (Leite 2009; Simões 2010). In particular, they have mobilized to denounce the raids and assaults in Niterói, a city across Guanabara Bay from Rio, and to counter the larger panic and repressive apparatus around sex trafficking and mega-events (Blanchette et al. 2014). In collaboration with sex work scholars and the sex workers' rights organization Davida, Observatório da Prostituição (Prostitution Policy Watch) dedicated several blog posts and reports to this issue across various cities. But in Ponta Negra's tourist district, this kind of collective organizing was not embraced by the women I spoke to during both periods of fieldwork. While many of the women identified as *garota de programa*, they commonly sought to distance themselves from sex workers working with local rather than tourist clients and did not organize collectively as sex workers. Given that the local association of sex workers, ASPRO-RN, was focused on the most vulnerable and marginalized workers, it also stayed away from Ponta Negra, which was seen as a lucrative tourist district for middle-class sex workers. This lack of collective organizing in Ponta Negra thus left a void in the cityscape and has allowed for anti–sex tourism mobilization to flourish with little organized opposition. Perhaps turning to Ponta Negra and the kind of social space it constituted may help to grapple with the larger context that made sex tourism a significant issue of public concern.

Ponta Negra

Ponta Negra – often referred to as the postcard of Natal – has also earned the nickname *Puta Negra* (Black Whore), an epithet that was pressed upon me several times as proof of the magnitude of the problem of sex tourism.[5] Indeed, the presence of both *gringos* and *garotas de programa* in Ponta Negra disturbed the local elite and middle-class residents and marked this urban beach as less desirable. As apparent in the graphic story, women who sought to meet foreign men were constantly reminded of their lower social status by middle-class *natalenses* (inhabitants of Natal) while they sought to access what this urban tourist beach had to offer. In what follows, I examine key aspects of the complex processes that have come to constitute – albeit never completely – Ponta Negra as a focal point in the making of Natal as an urban tourist beach for middle-class leisure and consumption (Lopes Júnior 2000).

---

5 While sex-worker activists in Brazil such as Gabriela Leite (2009) have reclaimed the term *puta* as a positive term of self-identification, the middle-class residents who used it in conversations with me did so derogatively, conflating blackness with disrespectable sexuality as if one indexes the other – a long-standing trope in Brazil (Caufield 2000; Goldstein 2003; Rebhun 2004).

THE MAKING OF AN URBAN TOURIST BEACH

Ponta Negra occupies, in the city's landscape and imaginary, a place of its own. Located 14 kilometers away from the city center, it is separated from it by the Parque das Dunas (Dunes Park), a 1,172-hectare protected reserve of sand dunes. It is also delineated by the Morro do Careca, a large, landmark dune on the southern end of the beach. Until the mid-twentieth century, Ponta Negra was a village that was peripheral to Natal. The main economic activities consisted of fishing and growing domestic crops on communal lands. These lands were illegally expropriated in the 1960s, with the complicity of the state, real estate sector, and the Catholic Church, in part to build the Barreira do Inferno military complex (SEMURB 2008). This process of land-grabbing initiated land speculation (Sacramento 2018).[6] During World War II, Natal served as a military base for the United States, and some commentators link the growing elite beach culture with American influence (SEMURB 2008). In the 1960s and 1970s, Natal's elite began to build second residences in Ponta Negra. Although the community remained relatively isolated from Natal given poor road connections to the city, it is during that time that the beach first turned into a site of commercial activity, as inhabitants from the Vila began to sell handicrafts or to retail at the beach, looking for other sources of income after experiencing land expropriation (SEMURB 2008).

In the late 1970s and early 1980s, larger state-sponsored economic policies meant to open the northeast of Brazil to tourism led to major infrastructure development and investment in the region (Maciel and Lima 2014; Sacramento 2018). Ponta Negra became a focal point in the tourism-focused urbanization of Natal, primarily through the construction of both (i) the Rota do Sol, a road linking Natal via Ponta Negra to the southern shoreline, and (ii) the Via Costeira, a roughly 10- to 12-kilometer highway along the Parque das Dunas, connecting Ponta Negra with the city center to the south (Lopes Júnior 2000).

Meanwhile, the resident population also grew significantly in part due to the development of a new middle-class residential area that eventually also included a shopping mall, the Conjunto de Ponta Negra, built in 1979 (Maciel and Lima 2014).[7] This new context significantly altered Ponta Negra and

---

6 This process of illegal land-grabbing is known as *grilagem*.

7 In the 1970s, the population of Ponta Negra was roughly 8,500 (Maciel and Lima 2014), while in 2007, when the first part of the graphic story is based, Ponta Negra counted 24,013 inhabitants (SEMURB 2008).

generated "multiple spatialities" (Sacramento 2018, 195) that are apparent in the graphic story: the grid-like, middle-class residential Conjunto and its shopping mall; the entertainment district known as the Alto; the more disorderly and impoverished Vila (where the old village was located), increasingly pushed away by the new residential development; and, finally, the beach, with its informal economy attracting not just beachgoers but also workers from the Vila and from other parts of the city and state. Spatially, this also marked the beginning of the process of "vertical growth of the built landscape" (Sacramento 2018, 195), as skyscrapers grew significantly and quickly in Ponta Negra, replacing the second residences of the local elite (see also Maciel and Lima 2014, 138, who referred to this as an "intense process of verticalization"). Between 1980 and 2000, the number of bars, hotels, and restaurants grew from six to 102 in Ponta Negra (Maciel and Lima 2014, 137), indicating the scale of rapid urbanization.

PONTA NEGRA AS A WHITE, MIDDLE-CLASS SPACE

Further developments in the early 2000s intensified Ponta Negra's tourism-focused urbanization. In 2000, the municipality revamped the waterfront, expanded the walkway, and began regulating the newly refurbished beach kiosks that, until then, had operated informally. Such regulation was part of a larger process of sanitization that made Ponta Negra more attractive to the middle class and elite of Natal. By 2000, while Ponta Negra had become *the* image of Natal for tourism, it also had "acquire[d] the status of icon for those who [could] enjoy the services offered there" (Maciel and Lima 2014, 137). Ponta Negra thus became a space of exclusivity associated with practices of middle-class leisure and consumption, such as sunbathing, walking/jogging on the beach, and frequenting bars and restaurants in an area known for its gastronomy, beach culture, and nightlife (Lopes Júnior 2000).

Yet the making of Ponta Negra as a space for middle-class consumption has never been completely accomplished. Fisherman and Vila inhabitants have continued to use the beach and engage with it as a place of work and source of income. Many informal workers have long offered their services at the beach (surf lessons, massage, buggy tours, sex, etc.) or sold food, drinks, and music from handmade sound systems. In particular, the women – especially those seen as poor and/or racialized as black or *morena* – who sought to meet foreigners became a key symbol of the degeneration of Ponta Negra and, as such, they experienced blatant forms of discrimination. Their presence has long generated tension with local middle-class residents, as well as with the business owners who contributed to the transformation of Ponta Negra into a middle-class space. These business owners have used various strategies to keep their clientele white and middle class, such as charging expensive entrance fees and enforcing a dress code. They also formed an association and joined AR-Ponta Negra (the local association of residents) in an effort to revamp the area and "cleanse" it from those considered undesirable. Their vision was partly realized in 2014, as their anti–sex tourism battle in the mid-2000s led to the quasi-privatization of the beach and the invisibilization of *garotas de programa* by the time Natal hosted the World Cup. These tensions are apparent in the graphic story and constitute the backdrop against which the experiences of Carol, Sofia, Ester, Luana, and Amanda are situated.

"PONTA NEGRA BELONGS TO THE EUROPEANS"

The urbanization of Ponta Negra that began in the 1980s also resulted in complex tensions between the more affluent local residents and foreign tourists – specifically, opposition to mass tourism and in particular to the Europeanization of Ponta Negra. For some local residents, Ponta Negra felt foreign, even invaded and owned by Europeans (see also Sacramento 2018). This was in part provoked by the advent of charter flights connecting Natal to various European destinations. In 1995, Natal had its first officially licensed weekly charter flight to and from Milan, paving the way for the emergence of a "marked presence of male Italian tourists in Ponta Negra" (Sacramento 2018, 197). Between 1995 and 2000, this number grew to six weekly charter flights, all connecting Natal to European destinations. In 2000, the end of the construction of a new passenger terminal at Natal's airport solidified Natal's capacity to offer international flights, including charter flights, to Europe. As Brazil's closest major city to Europe, Natal's popularity for European beach tourism boomed.[8] Drawing on images of racialized, exotic femininities imported from Rio de Janeiro, Natal promoted itself as a sun destination, boasting its 300 days of sun a year, its unique landscape, and spectacular sand dunes, while also reproducing the sexualization of Brazilian femininity (Sacramento 2018). The area – especially Ponta Negra – thus

---

8 Between 2002 and 2007, the number of international visitors almost doubled, while international flights (not just charter flights) grew to at least 23 per week (Infraero 2010; Chiquetti 2007).

became recognized as a site of heterosexual male pleasure that was frequented primarily by European male tourists.

During the mid-1990s and early 2000s, tourist-related real estate investment in Ponta Negra drastically increased, along with European residential tourism, which facilitated the development of long-term ties and transnational intimacies (Sacramento 2018, 194). By 2007–8, the presence of European tourists and expats was visible, as shops, bars, restaurants, hotels, travel agencies, and real estate became increasingly owned by Europeans. One could hear popular Norwegian music playing from one of the handmade sound systems or buy an Italian newspaper in one of the beachfront convenience stores. The Europeanization of Ponta Negra was mainly unwelcomed by the more affluent residents, who until then had considered Ponta Negra theirs and felt invaded. As Portuguese anthropologist Octávio Sacramento (2018, 195) suggests,

> the presence of foreign tourists and the fact that they may establish relationships of intimacy with local women creates disquiet among many local *natalenses*, who interpret this scenario as a new invasion, a sequel to colonial occupation. It is common to hear them claim that Ponta Negra is European (*Ponta Negra é dos europeus*) and expressing concern ranging from ambiguity to outright hostility with regard to foreigners.

In this context, the opposition to sex tourism became a catalyst to oppose mass tourism; this was evident in some campaigns, such as the protest featuring the sculpture of a white phallus in papier-mâché with various European flags on it, as shown in the graphic story.[9]

For women like Carol and her friends in the graphic story, unlike the middle-class residents and business owners, the Europeanization of Ponta Negra was very appealing. While excluded from urban planners' vision of Natal, these women were able, for a time, to make Ponta Negra *theirs* too. European men made it possible for them to realize their aspirations for social and economic mobility, if only temporarily or incompletely. Yet European tourism in Natal did not continue to grow endlessly. International tourism

---

9 For narrative purposes, in the graphic story the march appears in the summer of 2007, although it actually took place in November 2006.

(almost entirely European) dropped by *half* between 2008 and 2014 (Aeroporto de Natal 2014; Infraero 2010, 2014), in part as a result of the effects of the 2008 global financial crisis in Europe. The city, already struggling with its tarnished image due to sex tourism, sought to market itself as a safe, respectable destination for domestic and family-related tourism, an image that became difficult to maintain as the city also came to be increasingly associated with violence (Sacramento 2018). In this context, the idea that Ponta Negra belongs to the Europeans has lost some of its grip, especially as international tourism is moving to other urban beaches such as Praia do Forte, which was the chosen location of FANFEST (a festival associated with the World Cup). This new spatial configuration, alongside the drastic drop in European tourism after 2009, has led to a sense of desolation and decay in Ponta Negra, even as it simultaneously further gentrifies.

BETWEEN DECAY AND GENTRIFICATION

By the mid-2010s, the informal economy that was once iconic of the beach life had become further sanitized through new municipal regulations that required street vendors to obtain a license to sell their products (Globo 2012), while also regulating the activities that were possible (Martins 2014). The handmade mobile sound systems, a symbolic feature of Ponta Negra's beach life in the mid-2000s, were almost gone by 2014, also as a result of the new municipal regulations meant to control sonic, visual, and environmental pollution (Martins 2014). These handmade sound systems had played a key social role in the beach economy, including as meeting points for European tourists and Brazilian women given that women would come together to dance and display their bodies, seeking to catch men's attention. Furthermore, the beach had become increasingly privatized, and beachgoers had to pay to access the beach, through either food/drink consumption or beach chair rentals. The beach was also privatized through new forms of security, with private armed security guards on the premises of bars, restaurants, and hotels, chasing away "undesirables" such as ambulant sellers, people asking for money, or people seen as potential troublemakers. As a result, informal beach workers, including *garotas de programa*, have either disappeared or been displaced. Parts of the beach have also gentrified, with paddleboards replacing surfboards and with fancy shops replacing the iconic *jangadas* (wooden fishing boats). The advent of the World Cup also led to further state investment to revamp the beach, with night street lights installed along

Erivan França Street, a reconstructed waterfront, modernized kiosks, and public bathrooms; however, the revamping was incomplete when the World Cup began, giving the beach an appearance of decay that was intensified by the constant talk of crime and the presence of security guards and police officers on foot patrol and in helicopters, cars, and trucks.

This quasi-privatization of the beach aligned itself with a vision of Ponta Negra as a white, middle-class space, where the middle class may "safely" enjoy the beach and consume food or drinks (both health-wise, with sanitation regulation, and crime-wise, with the absence of those deemed undesirable). Many middle-class residents celebrated the "return" of Ponta Negra as *their* space; meanwhile, many casual beach workers lamented the new municipal regulation, as well as the absence of European tourists, blaming the drop in tourism to both the intense state crackdown on sex tourism in the mid-2000s and the 2008 global financial crisis. A sense of economic desolation was palpable among informal workers in tourism, as they commented on the absence of foreign tourists in town *despite* the World Cup. Similarly, several *garotas de programa* reported that the World Cup did not bring the much-anticipated economic benefits they thought it would. In 2014, Ponta Negra no longer stood as a stepping stone to Europe, leading many women to question its value as a place of futurities and aspirations, as can be gathered in the last part of the graphic story. Ponta Negra thus constitutes a complex, shifting social space, where relations of power exceed the simplistic dichotomy of locals and tourists.

Gringo Love

Why call this graphic story "gringo love"? Or you may ask, to borrow from anthropologist Denise Brennan's (2004) title of what is now a classic ethnography of sex tourism: "what's love got to do with it?" Gringo love – as an analytical concept – aims to capture the significance of intimate ties and forms of attachment that span transnational borders. It invites an engagement beyond understandings of love as a universal emotion individually felt or as the authentic expression of a "true" self. Instead, the concept hints at something collective, socially produced. Love is key in the graphic story, not because it is a great social equalizer, but because it *mediates* power differentials (Cheng 2010).

Gringo love, as a concept, may also be thought of as a form of emotional and embodied labor that women in Ponta Negra mobilize in different ways in their project of social and economic mobility. The concept is also tied to the imagined geographies implicated in the production of global sites of desires, as differences in power "become eroticized and commodified inequalities" (Brennan 2004, 16; see also Bloch 2017; Constable 2003, 2005; Kempadoo 1999; Manderson and Jolly 1997). As is apparent in the graphic story, in Ponta Negra, racialization cuts both ways: while Brazilian women were racialized by foreign tourists as tropical, hypersexual, traditional women, European men, too, were imagined by Brazilian women through long-standing racial tropes about whiteness, modernity, capital, and the West. In the context of these complex mutual racialized desires and inequalities, love may also be understood as a normalizing trope, allowing the insertion of unequal material-intimate exchanges as part of a gift (rather than market) economy. The concept of gringo love also hints at the ways in which value shifts in a transnational context like Ponta Negra, enabling practices of masculine and feminine distinction. In what follows, I draw on a long legacy of feminist and anthropological work to briefly point to some of the productive possibilities in thinking about the racialized, gendered political economy of love in Ponta Negra (Bloch 2017; Brennan 2004; Cheng 2010; Constable 2003; Faier 2007; Frohlick 2013; Padilla 2007; Padilla et al. 2007; Patico 2009; Stout 2014).

DESIRING THE "OTHER": IMAGINING AUTHENTIC BRAZILIAN WOMEN

Associations about Brazil's hypersexual women are such that tourists who come to Brazil expect to have easy sexual access to women – something that has become akin to a "souvenir" of Brazil, as reported by male foreign tourists in both Rio de Janeiro and Salvador da Bahia (Silva and Blanchette 2005, 262; Williams 2013, 95). Indeed, there is a long history of global circulation of images about Brazilian women: it began with Dutch, French, and Portuguese colonial representations of Brazil as an "earthly paradise, a kind of tropical Eden" (Parker 1991, 9), with descriptions of lascivious, sexually insatiable native women awaiting male newcomers, a trope that has persisted in the iconography of Brazil and eventually also included black women, following the Atlantic slave trade (Sadlier 2008; Parker 1991). While such representations have shifted over time and taken various expressions, they are intrinsic to the way the Brazilian nation came to imagine itself as a uniquely sexual nation due to its mixed heritage (Parker 1991). In the aftermath of the abolition of slavery (1888) and Brazil's independence (1889), Brazilian intellectuals and elite struggled to reconcile their racially mixed population with the eugenics that prevailed in Europe, and they adopted a national narrative about miscegenation that both celebrated hybridity and embraced the prevalent whitening ideology (known as *branqueamento* or *embranquecimento* in Brazil). This national narrative was popularized in the influential writings of novelist Jorge Amado (1958) and social historian Gilberto Freyre (1933), among others, who represented the *mulata* as a sexual seductress embodying a perfect racial mixture, erasing the history of colonial sexual violence (Gilliam 1998; Goldstein 2003). As noted by anthropologist Natasha Pravaz, this national narrative was anchored in state policies and practices, especially under President Getúlio Vargas (1930–45; 1951–4), when "samba would become the best indication of the hybrid character of the nation" (2003, 124) and the *mulata* the ideal personification of this racial mixture or "a representation of Brazil itself" (2003, 123). This image of Brazilian women was ingrained through state-sponsored tourist advertisements, as discussed above in this appendix, as well as through new technologies that included porn websites, rap videos, sex travel blogs, forums, and websites that eroticized Brazilian women (Gilliam 1998; Goldstein 2003; Piscitelli 2005; Pravaz 2003; Williams 2013). Now, Brazilian women in general are eroticized globally, as Brazil is typically imagined by foreigners as a tropical paradise full of exotic women who are readily available and sexually adventurous (Piscitelli 2007b; Williams 2013).[10]

Natal occupies a distinct place in local/transnational imaginaries, especially when compared to (i) Rio de Janeiro, the quintessential erotic paradise, with images of samba, carnival, and *mulatas* (Pravaz 2003); (ii) Salvador, a city long associated with Afro-Brazilian heritage, where cultural/black heritage tourism meets sex tourism (Williams 2013); or (iii) Manaus, in the Amazon, where images of exotic, authentic Indigenous women haunt the tourist imagination (Mitchell 2016). Natal, like other northeastern urban beaches such as Recife and Fortaleza, is primarily imagined as a tropical beach in the less "developed" northeast and is more closely associated with both *morenidade* (brownness) and poverty (Piscitelli 2005, 326). As reported

---

10 While this is the case, Brazilian women racialized as nonwhite are commonly seen as more hypersexual and readily available for sex.

in the context of transnational intimate relationships between men from the Global North/West and women from the Global South/East (Constable 2005), the European men in my study tended to imagine Brazilian women as traditional, not just hypersexual, and to contrast them with demanding, career-oriented, tainted-by-feminism-and-capitalism European women. In part, this racialization of traditional femininity was accentuated in Natal by the ways in which the northeast is imagined as more authentic and as less developed and modernized than the south or southeast, where Rio or São Paulo are located (Piscitelli 2004b). As is visible in the graphic story, many European tourists described explicit demand for money as a turnoff and imagined women who asked directly for money as *fake* and *inauthentic*. Most men, however, accepted the presence of material favors as long as it was part of the moral economy of the gift, based on reciprocity (Mauss 1967) – that is, they understood that poor, needy women could ask for money and even work as *garotas de programa*. Imagining Brazilian women in the sex tourist economy of Ponta Negra as poor provided these men with the possibility to reconstitute themselves as a benevolent provider, as I examine below.

"IT'S HELPING, NOT PAYING"

While the European men in my study did not constitute a fixed, stable, or homogenous group,[11] they shared a commonality in the way they presented themselves to me. They wanted me to know that they were "good" gringos, that they treated the women with respect, that they'd never have sex with underage girls, that they'd never pay for sex back home, and that they were helping a poor woman in need. While, from their perspective, what constituted the characteristics of a good gringo shifted and could be linked to nationalities (for instance, some men told me, "I'm not like Italian men") it often had to do with the idea of "helping, not paying" a needy woman, as

---

11 The European men in my study came from various countries (Italy, Portugal, France, Belgium, Germany, Ireland, England, the Netherlands, and Norway, to name but a few) but also from various socioeconomic means and situations. Some were married, others separated or divorced, and still others single. They traveled alone or in groups of two to three with their relatives, friends, or co-workers. Their ages also varied (among my interviewees, from 29 to 62, with an average age of 42). A few of them belonged to a business economic elite; some were expats who owned apartments, hotels, *pousadas*, restaurants, bars, nightclubs, travel agencies, or souvenir shops. But, importantly, they also consisted of lower-middle-class tourists traveling on cheap charter flights who had saved money for months or years and worked primarily in blue-collar jobs.

shown in the graphic story. Were these men simply trying to save face in front of a female Canadian researcher? It is possible to read their conception as the management of stigma, given that paying for sex is highly stigmatized even in the context of sex tourism and commonly understood as a masculine failure. In his landmark work on stigma, Goffman (1963) proposes that those who are stigmatized tend to express ambivalence toward their own selves as they, too, are subjected to social norms. Despite not conforming to given social norms, stigmatized people still apply these norms to themselves and to others. In this sense, by presenting themselves as good men helping a poor woman in need, European tourists likely sought to mitigate the stigma associated with paying for sex – an aspect that has been noted in the scholarship on sex tourism (see, for example, Padilla 2007). But there was more than the management of stigma in their claims to be helping poor women.

Helping may also signal the moral logic of a gift economy, based on reciprocal ties of interdependency (in contrast to a market economy), allowing men to position themselves as a benevolent provider (see Padilla 2007 for similar findings in the context of gay sex tourism). In this sense, the idea of helping works as a masculine practice of distinction, establishing them as good men. In Ponta Negra, many European tourists I spoke to came from relatively limited socioeconomic means and momentarily experienced social and economic mobility. They could easily afford to pay for women's drinks, invite them for dinner in fancy restaurants, or provide them with nice presents. These men had, momentarily, the economic power to be generous with women, which stood in sharp contrast to the limited economic means of a majority of Brazilian men. As gringos – coded for white and European in Natal – their body also signaled cultural capital, status, modernity, cosmopolitanism, and money (an aspect I examine further in this section). In this context, they experienced their masculinity as highly desirable and valued, and thus they commonly contrasted themselves to "bad gringos" (whom they saw as rude, uncaring sex tourists treating women as sex objects) or local "machos" (whom they saw as irresponsible men and violent drunks).

The production of racialized and/or classed masculinity is a common theme in the scholarly literature on sex tourism. For instance, in her work on sex tourism in the Dominican Republic, anthropologist Denise Brennan discusses the ways in which male tourists experienced their masculinity as more powerful given shifts in their social and economic status allowing them to be like "big men" (Brennan 2004, 29). Feminist sociologist Megan Rivers-Moore proposes that in Gringo Gulch, San José, Costa Rica, sex tourism constitutes a "relational economy" in which value is produced relationally and contextually, including masculine value. Drawing on Connell's (2000) landmark work on hegemonic masculinity and multiple, relational, contextual, and hierarchical masculinities, she analyzes sex tourism as a "masculinizing practice" (2016, 38). She suggests that American men experience themselves as "almighty" because of their temporary relative wealth in contrast to Costa Ricans, as well as their access to young, beautiful, sexy, and exotic women, a luxury they cannot afford at home. In Ponta Negra, men too experienced their masculinity as more powerful, both in racial and class terms, as well as in their desirability as men. This distinct masculine value and relatively higher economic and social status made possible the crafting of themselves as a good, generous, benevolent provider, exemplified through the idea of helping poor women.

Helping and othering are, to some extent, intrinsically tied, as, in their conception of women as needy and poor, European men drew on a geography of imagination (Trouillot 2003) that posits Europe as civilized, modern, educated, and developed and Brazil – even more so the northeast – as backward, traditional, and in need of saving. As Ann Stoler's (2002) work on colonial conquest, intimacy, and care has shown, helping and othering are thus connected, not separate, processes. Yet, as other scholars have discussed (see Mitchell 2016; Padilla 2007; Rivers-Moore 2016), male tourists' practices also transcend the simple search for imperial and misogynist domination that is popularly associated with sex tourism. While the men in my study drew on racialized imaginings, they were not commonly looking for dehumanized sex objects. Beyond their clichéd statements about hypersexual Brazilian women in the tropics, European men had complicated emotional attachments – whether real, imagined, ambiguous, temporary, or uncertain. In her analysis, Rivers-Moore points to the ways in which feminine value, too, is relational. In Gringo Gulch, local women were not produced as "disposable, but rather as highly valuable," even if their value derives from "their discursive production as hypersexual and poor" (2016, 62). This relational value in a transnational context like Ponta Negra had implications for women otherwise deemed disposable and abject in Brazil. As excluded, marginalized, and stigmatized locally, they found themselves desired by men who symbolized access to a better life, as I examine next.

GRINGO LOVE AS EMBODIED LABOR

Like masculinity, femininity is produced relationally in sex tourism (Rivers-Moore 2016). In Ponta Negra, this meant that while being poor and nonwhite was locally coded as disreputable, it had a distinct value in a transnational space where foreign men valued women's poverty and their racialized hypersexuality. Scholars have shown how women make strategic use of their racialization in the sex industry; for instance, Miller-Young (2010) examines how black women working in the adult entertainment industry "put their hypersexuality to work," and Williams (2013) analyzes how black women in Salvador, Bahia, do the same in sex tourism. This is akin to what Mitchell (2016) describes as performative labor in his work with *garotos de programa* (male sex workers), to hint at the racialized, embodied labor involved in stirring up desire in their foreign male clients. Their collective work, alongside the insights of sociologist Beverley Skeggs (1997, 2001) on femininity as embodied labor and class distinction, provide important cues to think about the embodied labor that exceeds the performance of love for profit and that is tied to the production of racialized/classed femininities. In Ponta Negra, producing oneself as both hypersexual *and* respectable was thus crucial for women's ability to secure long-term relationships with foreign men.[12]

In this process, women drew on existing racial scripts, as they identify primarily as *morena*, reflecting the way most Brazilians identified both nationally and in Rio Grande do Norte.[13] *Morena* (and its masculine equivalent, *moreno*) is an ambiguous term and polysemic category, whose meaning changes depending on the context, ranging from "a European brunette to a person with African and/or indigenous phenotype traits" (Edmonds 2010, 132). It may include both suntanned light-skin women and *mulatas* (Piscitelli 2007b; Williams 2013). Unlike the term *mulata*, it is not necessarily associated with African heritage and neither is it always sexualized; it can signal middle classness, as it is often understood as whiter than *mulata* (Maia

---

12 For more on this, see my detailed analysis of these aspects in Carrier-Moisan (2015).

13 While the Brazilian census gives the choice of five words for "color" terms, in everyday speech over 130 terms of identification have been discerned, with *moreno* and its variations being the most common (IBGE 1999). Yet *moreno* does not figure in the census, and in 2010, inhabitants of Rio Grande do Norte identified as follows: 59.2 per cent *pardos* (brown) followed by 36.3 per cent as *branco* (white), 4.4 per cent as *preto* (black), and none as *amarelo* (yellow) or *Indígena* (Indigenous) (IBGE 2010).

2009). In the Brazilian imaginary, to be "brown" is, in many ways, to identify with the national narrative on hybridity – it is to be, in some way, Brazilian. Yet, as suggested by anthropologist Alexander Edmonds in his ethnography of plastic surgery in Brazil, this celebration of *morenidade* (brownness) "reflects the persistence of eugenic thinking as well as informal hierarchies that stigmatize blackness. Brown is beautiful partly because it avoids 'Africanoid exaggerations'" (2010, 134). And, indeed, the term *morena* is increasingly seen as racist in Brazil, as was pointed out to me by Débora Santos, the graphic illustrator for this project, and as is more and more evident in public discussions around the term.

For the women in my study, *morena* constituted an in-between, ambiguous racial category. As such, women could produce themselves racially as *morena* along a continuum of what they imagined European men sought. At times, they tried to darken rather than whiten themselves; at others, they tried to emulate a complex racial hybridity signaling both hypersexuality *and* respectability. The graphic story points to some of these complexities, when we see Carol trying to look darker by suntanning while also straightening her hair, to simultaneously whiten herself. Carol sought to approximate the ideal, hypersexual-traditional woman imagined by European men – in this case, a feminine ideal distinct, even if tied to, the conflation of feminine beauty with racial hybridity in Brazil (Edmonds 2010). Carol sought to make herself racially legible to European men, which required her to engage in daily embodied work, but she also sought to display, in her bodily gestures and interactions with foreign men, what she thought would signal her feminine respectability and marriageability. As women labored to develop lasting intimate relationships with foreign men, they used their femininity as an embodied cultural resource, attempting to distinguish themselves from disreputable women (Skeggs 1997, 2001). Thus, appearing respectable and classy was key to their aspirational projects of social mobility, as there was more than just a negotiation of stigma involved in women's attempts to appear respectable. Women were also producing themselves as valuable, worthy, marriageable, lovable women (Carrier-Moisan 2015).

THE MAKING OF DURABLE TIES

The making of durable ties with foreign men was thus integral to the labor done by the women in my study. While the staging of attraction and affection certainly took place in Ponta Negra, the graphic story also shows that women like Carol had complex experiences with foreign men beyond the performance of love for profit and the alienation commonly associated with "emotional labor" (Hochschild 1983) and as assumed in some of the scholarship on sex work (for example, Hoang 2010).[14] By leaving the relationships open and ambiguous, and by moving through varying degrees of intimacies, the women drew on what other scholars have termed "incomplete commercialization" (De Gallo and Alzate 1976, cited in Cabezas 2009, 119), much like what anthropologist Amalia Cabezas proposes in the context of the Dominican Republic: "in using intimate labor that deemphasized the sale of sex, women were able to perform relational work that could open up the relationship to more stable and productive possibilities" (2009, 130). Mirroring men's practices of framing the exchange as "help," so, too, the women sought to locate their relationship with foreign men as part of the moral economy of the gift, to create practices of mutual obligation and reciprocity with them. This is similar to how Brazilian male sex workers integrate foreign men into their local kinship system as *padrinhos* (godfathers), as noted by Mitchell (2016).

In their attempts to transform temporary ties into lasting ones with foreign men, the women in my study thus drew on long-standing patterns of personalized reciprocity and intimate hierarchies. In the northeast of Brazil, especially in low-income households, material favors have historically been associated with the moral logic of a gift economy and the making of durable ties – including "ties of *ajuda*," or help (Cole 2013, 29; see also Rebhun 1999; Scheper-Hughes 1992). In this context, anthropologist Adriana Piscitelli proposes that "one important relationship is between a young woman and an older, richer, local man who provides money and different sorts of possessions. The *velho que ajuda* (old man that helps) is a widely known, long-lasting tradition all over Brazil, and a recognized means of social mobility for different social classes" (Piscitelli 2007b, 496). According to Piscitelli, the practice

---

14 Elsewhere, I expand on the notion of emotional labor as developed in the work of Hochschild (1983), especially on the ways in which the women in my study challenge the idea of a rigid distinction between the management of feelings in the private sphere (emotional work) and the commodification of feelings for profit (emotional labor), the latter seen as a form of alienation because the emotions do not belong to the worker. My analysis of the ways in which women sought to establish durable ties with foreign men in their self-making projects of social and economic mobility thus draw on insights from some of my previous publications (Carrier-Moisan 2015, 2018).

paved the way for ambiguous, affective sexual-economic exchanges with foreign sex tourists in Fortaleza, especially given that they could offer more benefits than the *velho que ajuda* (2007b). However, the *gringo que ajuda* is not simply a richer version of the *velho que ajuda*, given what the gringo symbolizes, as I will discuss. Indeed, intimate racialized hierarchies – a legacy of slavery and colonialism – have long been a feature of unequal relations of dependency and reciprocity (Furtado 2009; Goldstein 2003; Rebhun 1999; Scheper-Hughes 1992). Brazilian women have long sought to reinvent themselves through their intimate arrangements with wealthier and whiter men, but the figure of the gringo – coded for white and European – represents a distinct masculine figure.

IMAGINING GRINGOS AND PRACTICES OF SELF-MAKING

In Brazil, who is considered a gringo shifts in different locations and sociohistorical contexts. In Natal, the term (and its feminine equivalent, *gringa*) was commonly used as a shorthand for white Europeans, including groups that have been historically racialized as nonwhites, such as Italians. It also applied to Americans and Canadians, even though it was much less frequent to find these visitors in Natal. I also heard it in reference to Chileans and Argentineans, and in 2014, during the World Cup, the term was used synonymously with "foreigner" to refer to the many tourists attending the soccer games, including those who were Mexican, Japanese, Greek, and Uruguayan – pointing to its shifting semantic context. At times, it carried a negative connotation, given the power differential between tourists and locals as well as the massive presence of Europeans in Natal. Yet for many Brazilian women in my study, the term symbolized a distinct, racialized masculinity linked to whiteness, capital, modernity, mobility and the geographic space of the West/ North, especially Europe.

The phrase "gringo love" then also hints at the racialization of gringos, or foreign men, a process rooted in colonial tropes and produced anew in a transnational context such as Ponta Negra, where complex and competing racial valuations were at work. As shown in the graphic story, Brazilian women in Ponta Negra commonly contrasted *gringos* and *brasileiros* as distinct, racialized masculinities. They drew on racialized tropes about black masculinity in their conception of brasileiros as driven by their natural, animalistic, sexual urges and aggressiveness. They tended to see gringos as superior to brasileiros, and as scholars of sex tourism have noted elsewhere, they also distinguished between good and bad gringos (Blanchette 2011). As we saw in the graphic story, the women distinguished between different nationalities, or labeled the men unwilling to pay as *cafuçu* (local term for cheap and rude man). While they disagreed on which nationalities they preferred or disliked most, they frequently drew on a hierarchy of valuation whereby brasileiros were deemed worthless and gringos desirable.

This hierarchy of masculine valuation was key in the production of a distinct feminine subjectivity. Attempts to self-transform are also often tied to a modern identity in the feminist and anthropological scholarly literatures on transnational love and mobility (Bloch 2017; Cheng 2010; Constable 2003, 2005; Faier 2007; Hirsch and Wardlow 2006; Kelsky 2001; Padilla et al. 2007; Patico 2009; Schaeffer-Grabiel 2004). Another lens through which to think about these practices is offered in the work of Williams (2013) and her analysis of these experiences of global consumption in sex tourism as cosmopolitanism. She suggests that while the notion is commonly associated with those who occupy a privileged position in the global economy, exert global influence, transcend the nation-state, and approximate a globe-trotter with exhaustive knowledge of multiple cultures, it is helpful to think about the ways in which local people working in sex tourism also deploy a form of insurgent, alternative, grassroots cosmopolitanism (2013, 134). Similarly, for the women in my study, Ponta Negra, too, offered, for a time, possible access to forms of global consumption otherwise unavailable to them.

GRINGO LOVE AS A WEAPON OF THE WEAK

Gringo love can also be seen as a critique, as anthropologist Sealing Cheng proposes in a similar context: "intimate longing and relationships with the Other can also be critical commentaries on gender and regional hierarchies within the larger political economy" (2010, 10; see also Faier 2007; Schaeffer-Grabiel 2004). In her work with Filipina entertainers in US military camps in South Korea, Cheng suggests that in this context, love mediates inequalities and power differentials. Drawing on the important work of James C. Scott (1985), she conceptualizes love as a "weapon of the weak" that provides a "moral framework to negotiate their subordination and pursue their aspirational projects" (2010, 142) given that both the state and the market have failed them. I understand women in Ponta Negra similarly – I see gringo love as mediating various forms of power and inequalities based on race, class, gender, age, and nationality, including between Brazilian women and European men but also in the context of local hierarchies. Indeed, women's practices of feminine distinction cannot be disentangled from racial and class relations in Brazil, given the exclusionary practices that characterized the "differentiated citizenship" notorious to Brazil, a citizenship anthropologist James Holston depicts as "universally inclusive in membership but massively inegalitarian in the distribution of rights and resources" (2008, 284; see also De Castro 2006). The spatial phrase *sair dessa vida*, as shown in the graphic story, signals these complex, entangled experiences of social exclusion and aspirations for a better future (Carrier-Moisan 2018). In this context, the idea of *sair dessa vida* takes on a very distinct meaning from the one held by anti–sex tourism campaigners, who seek to make women exit sex work; rather, *sair dessa vida*, for most women, hints at the possibility of escaping the structural limitations of race, class, gender and sexuality, creating for oneself a more hopeful future.

Through its depictions of women's agency in terms of seeking upward mobility and projects of global self-making, the graphic story challenges common perceptions of women as in need of rescue and as oppressed either by the selling of sex or by their naïve love for foreign men, a vision held by the state and perpetuated by the campaigns against sex tourism. As the graphic story demonstrates, gringo love was part of a project of "global self-making" (Faier 2007) in a changing political economy, especially in the mid-2000s. Back then, women sought to establish durable ties with foreign men, which in turn enabled them to remake themselves as respectable, modern, upwardly and spatially mobile subjects with access to forms of middle-class consumption otherwise inaccessible to them; these ties also made it possible to disrupt the local hierarchies in which they occupied the bottom level. In the mid-2000s, Europe was imagined as a desirable destination offering the opportunity to refashion oneself and achieve economic and social mobility. This dominant imagining has been significantly altered since the 2008 global financial crisis – Europe is no longer envisioned uniquely as a space of economic prosperity.

Indeed, the Brazilian women I spoke with in 2014 seemed less hopeful about the possibilities of transforming their lives through gringo love. The capacity of local women to follow through with their desire to *sair dessa vida* (get out of this life) and to transform themselves elsewhere was circumscribed by recent shifts in both the local and global political economy. While Europe was no longer imagined as a place of futuristic possibilities, Brazil felt even more *sem futuro* (without a future), given the economic and political turmoil there. In this context, the bodies of gringos no longer unequivocally signal capital, global mobility, and cosmopolitanism to the same extent as they did in the mid-2000s, and both Europeans and Europe do not exert the same appeal, attraction, and sense of self-realization they once did.

As I am finishing writing these lines, I wonder about the implications of the most recently elected Brazilian president, Jair Bolsonaro, for women like Carol, Sofia, Ester, Luana, and Amanda, given the intensification of the militarization of public safety in Brazil and Natal that had already taken place in the last decades. I also wonder about the extent to which his presidency will exacerbate patterns long in the making, including the latent religious conservatism around gender and sexual minorities, the differentiated citizenships made possible by practices of sanitization, privatization, and securitization of public spaces, and the long-standing patterns of racialized, gendered, sexual, and classed-based inequalities. I am also troubled by one of his many homophobic and sexist statements – during an encounter with journalists in April 2019, Bolsonaro stated that Brazil cannot become the country known as a paradise for gay sex tourism: "If you want to come here and have sex with a woman, go for your life. But we can't let this place become known as a gay tourism paradise. Brazil can't be a country of the gay world, of gay tourism. We have families" (Phillips and Kaiser 2019). While seriously harming the LGBTQ+ community, he also legitimized the image of Brazil as a paradise for heterosexual male tourists and hinted at the sexual availability of Brazilian women.

When I began working on the graphic novel, I did not see these different nodes of power, but as I finish this project, it seems as if I can see traces and fragments in my ethnography of what Brazil is becoming. I feel as if I have been writing about another time. And it is: ten years is a long time, but the magnitude of the shift that has taken place in the political, economic, and social landscapes in Brazil is enormous. Ethnography is a slow process of documenting, but I am also conscious that it is partly history-in-the-making, even if the ethnographer is not entirely aware of it.

FURTHER READINGS

There are limits to any ethnographic study of sex tourism, and many inspiring, rich, exciting engagements complement my work. I've provided here some suggestions for readers interested in digging further on various issues, spanning from graphic novels to the study of sex tourism in Brazil. The list is not exhaustive and instead represents diverse sources that have inspired me, provoked me, or pushed me to think further, as well as those that relate closely to my ethnography and/or the graphic story.

Sex Tourism in Brazil

THE WORK OF ADRIANA PISCITELLI

Argentinean anthropologist Adriana Piscitelli, who has lived and worked in Brazil for decades, is a pioneer in the study of heterosexual male sex tourism in Brazil. Piscitelli has also conducted ethnographic research with Brazilian migrant women in the sex industry in Europe, as well as on the topic of intimate relationships between foreign women and local men in Brazil.

In English

- 2016. "Erotics, Love and Violence: European Women's Travels in the Northeast of Brazil." *Gender, Place and Culture* 23 (2): 274–87.

- 2016. "Sexual Economy, Love, and Human Trafficking – New Conceptual Issues." *Cadernos Pagu* 47: e16475.
- 2016. "Windsurfers, Capoeristas and Musicians: Brazilian Masculinities in Transnational Scenarios." In *Masculinities under Neoliberalism*, ed. A. Cornwall, F. Karioris, and N. Lindisfarne, 125–35. London: Zed Books.
- 2014. "Transnational Sisterhood? Brazilian Feminisms Facing Prostitution." *Latin American Policy* 5 (2): 221–35.
- 2008. "Looking for New Worlds: Brazilian Women as International Migrants." *Signs: A Journal of Women in Culture and Society* 33 (4): 1784–93.
- 2007. "Shifting Boundaries: Sex and Money in the North-East of Brazil." *Sexualities* 10: 489–500.
- 2004. "On 'Gringos' and 'Natives': Gender and Sexuality in the Context of International Sex Tourism." *Vibrant: Virtual Brazilian Anthropology* 1: 87–114.

In Portuguese

- 2013. *Trânsitos: Brasileiras nos mercados transnacionais do sexo*. Rio de Janeiro: EdUERJ.
- 2011. "Amor, apego e interesse: Trocas sexuais, econômicas e afetivas em cenários transnacionais." In *Gênero, sexo, amor e dinheiro: Mobilidades transnacionais envolvendo o Brasil*, ed. Adriana Piscitelli, Gláucia de Oliveira Assis, and José Miguel Nieto Olivar, 537–82. Campinas, SP: UNICAMP/PAGU.
- 2005. "Viagens e sexo on-line: A internet na geografia do turismo sexual." *Cadernos Pagu* 25: 281–327.
- 2004. "Entre a Praia de Iracema e a União Européia: Turismo sexual internacional e migração feminina." In *Sexualidade e Saberes: Convenções e Fronteiras*, ed. A. Piscitelli, M.F. Gregori, and S. Carrara, 283–318. Rio de Janeiro: Garamond.

THE WORK OF THADDEUS BLANCHETTE AND ANA PAULA DA SILVA

Thaddeus Blanchette and Ana Paula da Silva (an American-Brazilian couple living in Brazil) have conducted research together for decades on sex tourism and prostitution in Rio de Janeiro. They also contribute to Prostitution Policy

Watch, conducting research on mega-events and sex work, and are among the researchers forming the Grupo Davida (see below).

- 2017. "For Love or for Money? (Re)produtive Work, Sex Work, and the Transformation of Feminine Labour." *Cadernos Pagu* 50. http://dx.doi.org /10.1590/18094449201700500019.
- 2016. "Brazil Has Its Eye on You": Sexual Panic and the Threat of Sex Tourism in Rio de Janeiro during the FIFA World Cup 2014." *Brasiliana – Journal for Brazilian Studies* 4 (2): 411–54.
- 2014. "Cinderella Deceived: Analysing a Brazilian Myth regarding Trafficking in Persons." *Vibrant: Virtual Brazilian Anthropology* 10 (2). http:// vibrant.revues.org/1628.
- 2012. "The Myth of Maria and the Imagining of Sexual Trafficking in Brazil." *Dialectical Anthropology* 37 (2): 195–227.
- 2012. "On Bullshit and the Trafficking of Women: Moral Entrepreneurs and the Invention of Trafficking of Persons in Brazil." *Dialectical Anthropology* 36 (1–2): 107–25.
- 2011. "Prostitution in Contemporary Rio de Janeiro." In *Policing Pleasure: Sex Work, Policy and the State in Global Perspective*, ed. Susan Dewey and Patty Kelly, 103–45. New York: New York University Press.
- 2010. "Our Lady of Help: Sex, Tourism and Transnational Movements in Copacabana." *Wagadu* 8: 144–65.

ERICA LORRAINE WILLIAMS'S *SEX TOURISM IN BAHIA: AMBIGUOUS ENTANGLEMENTS* (2013, UNIVERSITY OF ILLINOIS PRESS)

This is the first full-length ethnography of sex tourism in Brazil. It is a superb, fascinating, engaging, and well-written account of sex tourism in the city of Salvador, Bahia. Unlike most studies (including mine), it is not solely focused on heterosexual male sex tourism, even if a large part of the study considers heterosexual encounters between local women and foreign men. Williams also examines relationships between local men and foreign women, as well as black gay sex tourism. The work's originality comes in great part from the ways in which the author documents the complex relations between cultural and sexual tourism – that is, how the commodification of Afro-Brazilian culture in Salvador is tied to the eroticization of Afro-Brazilian men and women in tourism.

GREGORY MITCHELL'S *TOURIST ATTRACTIONS: PERFORMING RACE AND MASCULINITY IN BRAZIL'S SEXUAL ECONOMY* (2016, UNIVERSITY OF CHICAGO PRESS)

This is a rich, provocative ethnography of gay sex tourism based in three distinct sites: Rio de Janeiro, Salvador da Bahia, and Manaus, in the Amazon. Mitchell cleverly proposes reframing the labor involved in sex work with tourists as "performative," a fascinating and compelling approach that illuminates the subtle, complex ways in which Brazilian male sex workers perform nationality, race, and masculinity in particular ways at the three sites, given what tourists are looking for.

THIAGO CANTALICE'S *DANDO UM BANHO DE CARINHO! OS CAÇA-GRINGAS E AS INTERAÇÕES AFETIVO-SEXUAIS EM CONTEXTOS DE VIAGEM TURISTÍCA (PIPA-RN)* (2016, PACO EDITORIAL)

This ethnography is based on research conducted in Pipa (a village located roughly 80 kilometers away from Natal), which has become a tourist destination for surfers, backpackers, and middle-class Brazilians in search of distinction. It is, to my knowledge, the only full-length ethnographic study in Brazil that examines the sexual-affective relationships between local men (known as *caça-gringas*, or *gringa*-hunters) and foreign women.

DOCUMENTARY FILM: JOEL ZITO ARAÚJO'S *CINDERELAS, LOBOS, E UM PRINCIPE ENCANTADO* (CINDERELLAS, WOLVES, AND A PRINCE CHARMING) (2008, 107 MINUTES)

This is a documentary on the topic of heterosexual male sex tourism in Brazil and the transnational migration of Brazilian women to Europe. Natal is one of the filming locations, and I had the opportunity to meet with the team and film director when they came to that city. The film goes beyond sensationalist representations of sex tourism and shows a range of contexts and experiences. It offers a critical lens into the sexual objectification of black women in Brazil while recognizing their sexual agency. While it could lead some viewers to lump together the sexual exploitation of children and sex trafficking with sex work, it does nonetheless challenge common representations of sexualized victims in sex tourism.

Mega-Events and Sex Work Activism in Brazil

The advent of the 2014 World Cup (held in 12 cities across Brazil) and the 2016 Rio Olympics led to many campaigns against sex tourism and sex trafficking, which targeted and impacted sex workers. In response, sex workers and their allies, including scholars, have documented the implications of these campaigns and the intensification of state repression with the advent of these mega-events. Sex workers have also produced various alternative narratives about their experiences during these events, drawing on a long tradition of activism. The following list is not exhaustive, but it gives a snapshot of the diversity and vibrancy of the sex workers' rights movement and its allies in Brazil, with a focus on mega-events and the main organizations advocating for sex workers' rights.

OBSERVATÓRIO DA PROSTITUIÇÃO

Part of the Metropolitan Ethnographic Lab at the Federal University of Rio de Janeiro, the Observatório da Prostituição (Prostitution Policy Watch) focuses on documenting sex workers' rights violations in Brazil and promoting their human, sexual, and labor rights. It was very active during the 2014 World Cup and 2016 Rio Olympics under the Red Light Rio project, which involved collaboration between sex workers and academic researchers, filmed interviews with sex workers about their experiences during the World Cup and Olympics (some of which are available online: http://redlightr.io), and the production of various reports on the impacts of mega-sporting events for sex workers. Prostitution Policy Watch works in collaboration with the sex workers' organization Davida, as well as with the Rede Brasileira de Prostitutas (Brazilian Network of Prostitutes); it is led by anthropologist Soraya Silveira Simões while also involving the participation of many academic researchers, including Thaddeus Blanchette, Ana Paula da Silva, Laura Murray, Amanda de Lisio, and Gregory Mitchell, among many others. One of the initiatives of Prostitution Policy Watch includes *O que você não vê: A prostituição vista por nós mesma* (*What You Don't See: Prostitution Seen by Us*), a photo exhibit done by sex workers in Rio de Janeiro that also includes a virtual exhibit: http://www.oquevcnaove.com.

DAVIDA AND GRUPO DAVIDA

Davida is a sex workers' rights association based in Rio de Janeiro and funded by the late activist Gabriela Leite. It leads various vibrant, creative, and provocative forms of mobilization for the rights of sex workers. For instance, in 2005, under the leadership of Leite, the organization created the designer label Daspu (shorthand for *das putas*, which means "of the whores") to challenge stereotypes about sex workers and give visibility to their movement in a wicked, tongue-in-cheek manner while also financing their activities. Grupo Davida is a group of academic researchers associated with Davida who also study sex work. Some of their publications include the following:

- Grupo Davida. 2014. "Trafficking as a Floating Signifier: The View from Brazil." *Anti-Trafficking Review* 4: 161–6.
- Grupo Davida. 2005. "Prostitutas, 'traficadas,' e pânicos morais: Uma análise da produção de fatos em pesquisas sobre o tráfico de seres humanos." *Cadernos Pagu* 25: 153–84.

GABRIELA LEITE

Gabriela Leite was a leading figure of the sex workers' rights movement in Brazil until she died in 2013, and she continues to be an inspiration for many sex workers and allies. It is impossible to do justice here to her immense legacy and contributions; for readers interested in knowing more about her life, in 2009, she published her biography in Portuguese, *Filha, Mãe, Avó e Puta* (*Daughter, Mother, Grandmother and Whore*). Laura Murray, another prominent figure and academic researcher involved with the sex workers' rights movement in Brazil, made a documentary film about her called *A Kiss for Gabriela* (a play on the name of the magazine that Leite founded, *Beijo da rua*, or *Street Kiss*). The documentary film is accessible in Portuguese with English subtitles: http://www.akissforgabriela.com/?cbg_tz=240&cat=3.

PUTAFEMINISTAS (FEMINIST WHORES)

Gabriela Leite was one of the most vocals activists who reclaimed the term *puta* (whore) in Brazil. Following her legacy, there are now many sex worker activists who strongly identify with feminism and who challenge versions of feminism that conflate prostitution with women's oppression. The most publicly visible self-identified *putafeministas* are Monique Prada, who, in 2018, published a book called *Putafeminista*; Amara Moira, who published the 2016 book *E se eu fosse puta?* (*What If I Were a Whore?*) and writes a blog of the same name; and Indianare Siqueira, who ran for municipal election in Rio in 2016 and got an alternate seat, using the slogan "a whore for councilwoman" while also narrating her experience of police abuse as a trans woman in a Facebook post. These *putafeministas* have been very active in publicly denouncing the moral panic that surged with the advent of mega-sporting events in Brazil.

ANCOP

The Articulação Nacional dos Comitês Populares da Copa (National Articulation of Popular Committees of the World Cup, hereafter ANCOP) released a report in 2014 addressing human right violations during the 2014 World Cup. In a section on rights violations in the context of work, the report addressed city-cleansing practices undertaken by the state, missionaries, and anti-prostitution activists during the World Cup that targeted sex workers and curtailed their mobility and labor rights under the guise of fighting trafficking. The full report, titled *Dossiê Mega Eventos e Violações dos Direitos Humanos no Brasil*, can be found here (Portuguese only): https://comitepopulario.files.wordpress.com/2014/11/ancop_dossie2014_web.pdf.

Comics, Graphic Novels, and Sex Work (in Canada)

CHESTER BROWN'S *PAYING FOR IT: A COMIC-STRIP MEMOIR ABOUT BEING A JOHN* (2011, DRAWN AND QUARTERLY)

There are not many comics or graphic novels addressing the topic of sex work, especially in ways that challenge the victimization of sex workers or the image of prostitution as tied to underground, sinful criminality. Chester Brown's *Paying for It* is a rare gaze into the world of a male client of sex workers in Canada. It is autobiographical and engages the author's intimate thoughts and experiences as a john. While his drawings may be seen as dehumanizing the sex workers he portrays (he never shows their faces and tends to portray them as generic – he claims he wants to avoid outing them by drawing them in this way), he also depicts himself in unflattering ways, at times bordering on creepy. Still, the graphic novel challenges some assumptions about depraved, abusive clients of sex workers and sexualized victims in prostitution. *Paying for It* also documents a shift in the North American sex industry with market-mediated intimacy and the search for the girlfriend experience for male clients – what sociologist Elizabeth Bernstein describes as the search for "bounded authenticity." It would be an interesting complement to her 2001 article "The Meaning of the Purchase: Desire, Demand and the Commerce of Sex" (*Ethnography* 2 [3]: 389–420), or to her 2007 ethnography *Temporarily Yours: Intimacy, Authenticity, and the Commerce of Sex.*

SYLVIE RANCOURT'S *MELODY: STORY OF A NUDE DANCER* (2015, DRAWN AND QUARTERLY)

This graphic novel is fascinating – both in the stories written in its pages as well as the story surrounding its publication. In 1985, Sylvie Rancourt, a woman in her mid-twenties, began to create comics based on her experiences working as a dancer in Montreal's strip clubs, which she did for about ten years. She had moved to Montreal with her boyfriend from rural northern Quebec (Abitibi), and both were struggling to make ends meet when she began dancing. While it was autobiographical, she used an avatar – Melody – based on one of her stage names and began making comics (in French) about her experience, which she sold as a zine to clients in the bars where she worked. She later self-published it as a magazine, which was translated into English and distributed in the United States and Canada, where it became an underground cult comic. *Melody* almost disappeared in the late 1990s due to Canadian censorship laws and was only published as a book in 2013 (in its original French), almost 30 years after its creation (which means that *Melody* would be one of the first autobiographical Canadian comics). *Melody* grips readers because of its confessional, frank, taboo-breaking personal tale and minimalist drawings. It is not voyeuristic, victimizing, moralizing, or sensationalistic. Instead, *Melody* captures us because it feels real, intimate, and raw, and it cleverly recreates the everydayness of nude dancing. For instance, we see Melody a little awkward and nervous in her debut, even falling off her stool; we recognize greedy bosses, we witness exchanges of advice between dancers, we see her boyfriend selling cocaine in the clubs where she worked, and so on. *Melody* provides a unique window into the world of strippers in 1980s Montreal, and it is a fascinating tale about women's ability to define and use their bodies – even when objectified or sexualized – as sites of pleasure and/or labor.

BIBLIOGRAPHY

Aeroporto de Natal. 2014. "Estatísticas." http://www.natal.aero/br/o
-aeroporto/estatisticas/.

Alfonso, Louise Prado. 2006. *EMBRATUR: Formadora de imagens da nação Brasileira*. Master's thesis. Department of Anthropology, State University of Campinas.

Amado, Jorge. 1958. *Gabriela, Cravo e Canela*. Sao Paulo: Companhia das Letras.

Amar, Paul. 2009. "Operation Princess in Rio de Janeiro: Policing 'Sex Trafficking,' Strengthening Worker Citizenship, and the Urban Geopolitics of Security in Brazil." *Security Dialogue* 40 (4–5): 513–41. https://doi .org/10.1177/0967010609343300.

ANCOP. 2014. *Dossiê mega eventos e violações dos direitos humanos no Brasil*. Articulação Nacional dos Comitês Populares da Copa e Olimpíadas (ANCOP).

Azevedo, Sheyla. 2005. "ONG E UFRN criticam vereadores." *Diáro de Natal*, September 9, 4.

Bechdel, Alison. 2006. *Fun Home: A Tragicomic*. Boston: First Mariner Books.

Behar, Ruth, and Deborah A. Gordon. 1995. *Women Writing Culture*. Berkeley and Los Angeles: University of California Press.

Bezerra, Augusto César, and Wagner Lopes. 2006. "Ofensiva Policial fecha Bares em Ponta Negra." *Tribuna do Norte*, April 6.

Blanchette, Thaddeus G. 2011. "'Fariseus' e 'gringos bons': Masculinidade e turismo sexual em Copacabana." In *Gênero, sexo, amor e dinheiro: Mobilidades transnacionais envolvendo o Brasil*, ed. Adriana Piscitelli, Glaúcia

Oliveira de Assis, and José Miguel Nieto Olivar, 57–102. Campinas, SP: UNICAMP/PAGU.

Blanchette, Thaddeus G., Laura Murray, and Julie Ruvolo. 2014. "Sobre Futebol e Pânicos Morais: Prostituição no Rio de Janeiro durante a Copa do Mundo 2014." *Percurso Acadêmico* 4 (8): 188–209. https://doi.org/10.5752/P.2236-0603.2014vonop188-209.

Bloch, Alexia. 2017. *Sex, Love, and Migration: Postsocialism, Modernity, and Intimacy from Istanbul to the Artic*. Ithaca: Cornell University Press.

Boyle, Phillip, and Kevin D. Haggerty. 2009. "Spectacular Security: Mega-events and the Security Complex." *International Political Sociology* 3 (3): 257–74. https://doi.org/10.1111/j.1749-5687.2009.00075.x.

Brennan, Denise. 2004. *What's Love Got to Do with It?: Transnational Desires and Sex Tourism in the Dominican Republic*. Durham: Duke University Press.

Cabezas, Amalia L. 2009. *Economies of Desire: Sex and Tourism in Cuba and the Dominican Republic*. Philadelphia: Temple University Press.

Cantalice, Tiago. 2011. "Turismo, sexo e romance: Caça gringas da Praia de Pipa-RN." In *Gênero, Sexo, Amor e Dinheiro: Mobilidades Transnacionais Envolvendo o Brasil*, ed. Adriana Piscitelli, Glaúcia Oliveira de Assis, and José Miguel Nieto Olivar, 141–83. Campinas, SP: UNICAMP/PAGU.

Carrier-Moisan, Marie-Eve. 2013. "Saving Women or (Re)inscribing Exclusion? New Protagonists in the Public Spaces of Sex Tourism." In *Contesting Publics: Feminism, Activism and Ethnography*, ed. Lynne Phillips and Sally Cole with Marie-Eve Carrier-Moisan and Erica Lagalisse, 48–75. London. Pluto Press.

———. 2015. "'Putting Femininity to Work': Negotiating Hypersexuality and Respectability in Sex Tourism, Brazil." *Sexualities* 18 (4): 499–518. https://doi.org/10.1177/1363460714550902.

———. 2018. "'I Have to Feel Something': Gringo Love in the Sexual Economy of Tourism in Natal, Brazil." *Journal of Latin American and Caribbean Anthropology* 23 (1): 131–51. https://doi.org/10.1111/jlca.12243.

———. 2019. "'A Red Card against Sex Tourism': Sex Panics, Public Emotions, and the 2014 World Cup in Brazil." *Feminist Formations* 31 (2): 125–54. https://doi.org/10.1353/ff.2019.0019.

Caufield, Sueann. 2000. *In Defense of Honor: Sexual Morality, Modernity, and Nation in Early Twentieth-Century Brazil*. Durham: Duke University Press.

Cerwonka, Allaine, and Liisa Malkki. 2007. *Improvising Theory: Process and Temporality in Ethnographic Fieldwork.* Chicago: University of Chicago Press.

Cheng, Sealing. 2010. *On the Move for Love: Migrant Entertainers and the US Military in South Korea.* Philadelphia: University of Pennsylvania Press.

Chiquetti, Taciana. 2007. "Cai o número de passageiros para Natal neste trimestre." *Correo da tarde*, April 30.

Cohen, Erik. 1982. "Thai Girls and Farang Men: The Edge of Ambiguity." *Annals of Tourism Research* 9 (3): 403–28. https://doi.org/10.1016/0160 -7383(82)90021-4.

Cole, Sally. 2013. "Autoconstructed Feminist Publics: Household Matters in Northeast Brazil." In *Contesting Publics: Feminism, Activism, Ethnography*, ed. Sally Cole and Lynne Phillips, 17–42. London: Pluto Press.

Connell, R.W. 2000. *The Men and the Boys.* Cambridge: Polity.

Constable, Nicole. 2003. *Romance on a Global Stage: Pen Pals, Virtual Ethnography and "Mail-Order" Marriages.* Berkeley: University of California Press.

———. 2005. *Cross-Border Marriages: Gender and Mobility in Transnational Asia.* Philadelphia: University of Pennsylvania Press.

Crick, Malcolm. 1989. "Representations of International Tourism in the Social Sciences: Sun, Sex, Sights, Savings, and Servility." *Annual Review of Anthropology* 18 (1): 307–44.

De Castro, Lucia Rabello. 2006. "What Is New in the 'South'? Consumer Culture and the Vicissitudes of Poor Youth's Identity Construction in Urban Brazil." *Young: Nordic Journal of Youth Research* 14 (3): 179–201. https://doi.org/10.1177/1103308806065815.

Dickson, Ricardo. 2006. "Câmara discute o Turismo-Sexual em audiência pública." *Tribuna do Norte*, March 14.

Doezema, Jo. 2010. *Sex Slaves and Discourse Matters: The Constructions of Trafficking.* London: Zed Books.

Edmonds, Alexander. 2010. *Pretty Modern: Beauty, Sex and Plastic Surgery in Brazil.* Durham: Duke University Press.

Faier, Lieba. 2007. "Filipina Migrants and Their Professions of Love." *American Ethnologist* 34 (1): 148–62. https://doi.org/10.1525/ae.2007.34.1.148.

Foucault, Michel. 1991. *Discipline and Punish: The Birth of a Prison.* London: Penguin.

Freyre, Gilberto. 1933. *Caza Grande e Senzala: Formação da Familia Brasileira Sob o Regimen da Economia Patriarchal.* Rio de Janeiro: Maia & Schmidt Ltda.

Frohlick, Susan. 2013. *Sexuality, Women and Tourism: Cross-Borders Desires through Contemporary Travel.* New York: Routledge.

Furtado, Junia Ferreira. 2009. *Chica da Silva: A Brazilian Slave of the Eighteenth Century.* Cambridge: Cambridge University Press.

Fusco, Coco. 1998. "Hustling for Dollars: *Jineterismo* in Cuba." In *Global Sex Workers: Rights, Resistance, and Redefinition*, ed. Kamala Kempadoo and Jo Doezema, 151–66. New York: Routledge.

GAATW. 2011. "What's the Cost of a Rumor? A Guide to Sorting Out the Myth and Fact about Sporting Events and Trafficking." Global Alliance against Trafficking in Women (GAATW). http://www.gaatw.org /publications/WhatstheCostofaRumour.11.15.2011.pdf.

Galman, Sally Campbell. 2019. "Not a Mirror, but an Icon: Ethnographic Comic Art in Three Acts." *American Anthropologist*, August 18. http:// www.americananthropologist.org/ethno-graphic-galman/.

Gaspar, Maria Dulce. 1985. *Garotas de Programa: Prostituição em Copaca-bana e Identidade Social.* Rio de Janeiro: Zahar.

Gilliam, Angela. 1998. "The Brazilian *mulata*: Images in the Global Economy." *Race and Class* 40 (1): 57–69. https://doi.org/10.1177/030639689804000105.

Globo 2006a. "Aqui se vende sexo." *Jornal da Globo*, March 6. http://g1.globo .com/jornaldaglobo/0,,MUL890637-16021,00-AQUI+SE+VENDE +SEXO.html.

———. 2006b. "Estrutura para o turismo sexual." *Jornal da Globo*, March 8. http://g1.globo.com/jornaldaglobo/0,,MUL890622-16021,00 -ESTRUTURA+PARA+O+TURISMO+SEXUAL.html.

———. 2006c. "O triste destino das menores prostitutas no Nordeste." *Jornal da Globo*, March 9. http://g1.globo.com/jornaldaglobo /0,,MUL890618-16021,00-O+TRISTE+DESTINO+DAS+MENORES +PROSTITUTAS+NO+NORDESTE.html.

———. 2006d. "Para acabar com o turismo sexual no Nordeste." *Jornal da Globo*, March 10. http://g1.globo.com/jornaldaglobo/0,,MUL890611 -16021,00-PARA+ACABAR+COM+O+TURISMO+SEXUAL+NO +NORDESTE.html.

———. 2006e. "Troca-se sexo por esperança." *Jornal da Globo*, March 7. http:// g1.globo.com/jornaldaglobo/0,,MUL890630-16021,00-TROCASE +SEXO+POR+ESPERANCA.html.

———. 2012. "Camelôs precisam de licença para vender em Natal, diz Secre-taria." *Jornal da Globo*, August 23. http://g1.globo.com/rn/rio-grande-do-norte

/noticia/2012/08/camelos-precisam-de-licenca-para-vender-em-natal-diz
-secretaria.html.

Goffman, Erving. 1963. *Stigma: Notes on the Management of Spoiled Identity*.
New York: Simon and Schuster.

Goldstein, Donna. 2003. *Laughter Out of Place: Race, Class, Violence and
Sexuality in a Rio Shantytown*. Berkeley: University of California Press.

Gordon, Avery. 1997. *Ghostly Matters. Haunting and the Sociological Imagination*. Minneapolis: University of Minnesota Press.

Grupo Davida. 2005. "Prostitutas, 'traficadas,' e pânicos morais: Uma análise da
produção de fatos em pesquisas sobre o 'tráfico de seres humanos.'" *Cadernos Pagu* 25: 153–84. https://doi.org/10.1590/S0104-83332005000200007.

Hamdy, Sherine, and Coleman Nye. 2017. *Lissa: A Story about Medical Prom-
ise, Friendship and Revolution*. Toronto: University of Toronto Press.

Haraway, Donna. 1988. "Situated Knowledges: The Science Question in
Feminism and the Privilege of Partial Perspective." *Feminist Studies* 14
(3): 575–99. https://doi.org/10.2307/3178066.

Hathaway, Rosemary V. 2011. "Reading Art Spiegelman's 'Maus' as Postmod-
ern Ethnography." *Journal of Folklore Research* 48 (3): 249–67. https://doi
.org/10.2979/jfolkrese.48.3.249.

Hecht, Tobias. 2006. *After Life: An Ethnographic Novel*, with portions based
on the narrations of Bruna Verissimo. Durham: Duke University
Press.

Hirsch, Jennifer, and Holly Wardlow. 2006. *Modern Loves: The Anthropology
of Romantic Courtship and Companionate Marriage*. Ann Arbour:
University of Michigan Press.

Hoang, Kimberly Kay. 2010. "Economies of Emotion, Familiarity, Fantasy,
and Desire: Emotional Labor in Ho Chi Minh City's Sex Industry." *Sexualities* 13 (2): 255–72. https://doi.org/10.1177/1363460709359224.

Hochschild, Arlie Russell. 1983. *The Managed Heart: The Commercialization
of Human Feeling*. Berkeley: University of California Press.

Holston, James. 2008. *Insurgent Citizenship: Disjunctions of Democracy and
Modernity in Brazil*. Princeton: Princeton University Press.

Hubbard, Phil. 1999. *Sex and the City: Geographies of Prostitution in the
Urban West*. Aldershot, UK: Ashgate.

IBGE. 1999. "What Color Are You?" In *The Brazil Reader: History, Culture,
Politics*, ed. Robert M. Levine and John Crocitti, 386–90. Durham:
Duke University Press.

————. 2010. *Síntese de indicadores sociais: Uma análise das condições de vida da população brasileira*. IBGE (Instituto Brasileiro de Geografia e Estatística). https://www.ibge.gov.br/estatisticas/sociais/trabalho/9221 -sintese-de-indicadores-sociais.html?edicao=17068&t=publicacoes.

Infraero. 2010. "Anúario Estatístico Operacional 2010." Infraero. https:// transparencia.infraero.gov.br/wp-content/uploads/2019/02/anuario -operacional/2010.pdf.

————. 2014. "Estatísticas." Infraero. https://transparencia.infraero.gov.br /estatisticas/.

Kelsky, Karen. 2001. *Women on the Verge: Japanese Women, Western Dreams*. Durham: Duke University Press.

Kempadoo, Kamala, ed. 1999. *Sun, Sex and Gold: Tourism and Sex Work in the Caribbean*. Lanham: Rowman and Littlefield.

Kempadoo, Kamala, and Ranya Ghuma. 1999. "For the Children: Trends in International Policies and Law on Sex Tourism." In *Sun, Sex and Gold: Tourism and Sex Work in the Caribbean*, ed. Kamala Kempadoo, 291–308. Lanham: Rowman and Littlefield.

Kennelly, Jacqueline. 2015. "'You're Making Our City Look Bad': Olympic Security, Neoliberal Urbanization, and Homeless Youth." *Ethnography* 16 (1): 3–24. https://doi/10.1177/1466138113513526.

Leite, Gabriela. 2009. *Filha, Mãe, Avó e Puta. A História de uma Mulher que Decidiu ser Prostituta*. Rio de Janeiro: Objectiva.

Lepp, Annalee. 2013. "Repeat Performance? Human Trafficking and the 2010 Vancouver Winter Olympic Games." In *Selling Sex: Experience, Advocacy and Research on Sex Work in Canada*, ed. Emily van der Meulen, Elya M. Durisin, and Victoria Love, 251–68. Vancouver: University of British Columbia Press.

Lopes Júnior, Edmilson. 2000. *A Construção Social da Cidade do Prazer: Natal*. Natal: EDUFRN.

Maciel, Ana Beatriz Camara, and Zuleide Maria Carvalho Lima. 2014. "Uso e ocupação de Ponta Negra, Natal/RN: Uma análise multi-temporal." *Sociedade e Território* 26 (2): 127–47. https://periodicos.ufrn.br /sociedadeeterritorio/article/view/5302.

Maia, Suzana M. 2009. "Intersections of the Transnational: Brazilian Erotic Dancers in Queens, New York." *Vibrant: Virtual Brazilian Anthropology* 6: 37–64. www.vibrant.org.br/issues/v6n1/suzana-maia -intersections-of-the-transnational/.

Manderson, Lenore, and Margaret Jolly, eds. 1997. *Sites of Desire, Economies of Pleasure: Sexualities in Asia and the Pacific*. Chicago: University of Chicago Press.

Marin, Héctor. 2006. "Soy menor, el condón te saldrá caro." *El mundo*, September 17. http://www.elmundo.es/suplementos/cronica/2006/568/1158444004.html.

Martins, Nadjara. 2014. "Natal/RN – Comércio irregular em Ponta Negra terá multa de até R$ 5 mil." *Tribuna do Norte*, July 27. https://fiscalambiental .wordpress.com/2014/07/27/natalrn-comercio-irregular-em-ponta -negra-tera-multa-de-ate-r-5-mil/.

Mauss, Marcel. 1967. *The Gift: Forms and Functions of Exchange in Archaic Societies*. Trans. Ian Cunnison, with introduction by E.E. Evans-Pritchard. New York: W.W. Norton.

McCloud, Scott. 1993. *Understanding Comics: The Invisible Art*. New York: HaperCollins.

Mendes, Andriell, and Sara Vasconcelos. 2011. "Turismo de Natal aposta na copa." *Tribuna do Norte*, August 7. http://tribunadonorte.com.br/noticia /turismo-de-natal-aposta-na-copa/191392.

Miller-Young, Mireille. 2010. "Putting Hypersexuality to Work: Black Women and Illicit Eroticism in Pornography." *Sexualities* 13 (2): 219–35. https://doi.org/10.1177/1363460709359229.

Mitchell, Gregory. 2016. *Tourist Attractions: Performing Race and Masculinity in Brazil's Sexual Economy*. Chicago: University of Chicago Press.

Morrow, Katherine L. 2008. "Soccer, Sex, and Slavery: Human Trafficking in the World Cup." *Tulane Journal of International and Comparative Law* 17: 243–66.

Oliveira, Marina Pereira Pires de. 2008. "Sobre armadilhas e cascas de banana: Uma análise crítica da administração de Justiça em temas associados aos Direitos Humanos." *Cadernos pagu* 31: 125–49. https://doi.org/10.1590 /s0104-83332008000200007.

Padilla, Mark. 2007. *Caribbean Pleasure Industry: Tourism, Sexuality, and AIDS in the Dominican Republic*. Chicago: University of Chicago Press.

Padilla, Mark, Jennifer S. Hirsch, Miguel Munoz-Laboy, Robert E. Sember, and Richard G. Parker, eds. 2007. *Love and Globalization: Transformations of Intimacy in the Contemporary World*. Nashville: Vanderbilt University Press.

Parker, Richard. 1991. *Bodies, Pleasures and Passions: Sexual Culture in Contemporary Brazil*. Boston: Beacon Press.

Patico, Jennifer. 2009. "For Love, Money, or Normalcy: Meanings of Strategy and Sentiment in the Russian-American Matchmaking Industry." *Ethnos* 74 (3): 307–30. https://doi.org/10.1080/00141840903053097.

Phillips, Tom, and Anna Jean Kaiser. 2019. "Brazil Must Not Become a 'Gay Tourism Paradise' Says Bolsonaro." *Guardian*, April 26. https://www .theguardian.com/world/2019/apr/26/bolsonaro-accused-of-inciting -hatred-with-gay-paradise-comment.

Piscitelli, Adriana. 2004a. "Entre a Praia de Iracema e a União Européia: Turismo sexual internacional e migração feminina." In *Sexualidade e Saberes: Convenções e Fronteiras*, ed. A. Piscitelli, M.F. Gregori, and S. Carrara, 283–318. Rio de Janeiro: Garamond.

———. 2004b. "On 'Gringos' and 'Natives': Gender and Sexuality in the Context of International Sex Tourism." *Vibrant: Virtual Brazilian Anthropology* 1: 87–114. http://www.vibrant.org.br/issues/v1n1/adriana-piscitelli-on -gringos-and-natives/.

———. 2005. "Viagens e sexo on-line: A internet na geografia do turismo sexual." *Cadernos Pagu* 25: 281–326. https://doi.org/10.1590/s0104 -83332005000200011.

———. 2007a. "Brasileiras na indústria transnacional do sexo." *Nuevo Mundo Mundos Nuevos*, Debates (Online), 1–47. https://doi.org/10.4000 /nuevomundo.3744.

———. 2007b. "Shifting Boundaries: Sex and Money in the North-East of Brazil." *Sexualities* 10 (4): 489–500. https://doi.org/10.1177/1363460707080986.

Pothecary, Sam. 2014. "A Darker Side to the World Cup: Child Exploitation at Brazil 2014." *Argentina Independent*.

Pravaz, Natasha. 2003. "Brazilian Mulatice: Performing Race, Gender and the Nation." *Journal of Latin American Anthropology* 8 (1): 116–47. https://doi.org/10.1525/jlca.2003.8.1.116.

Rebhun, L.A. 1999. *The Heart Is Unknown Country: Love in the Changing Economy of Northeast Brazil*. Stanford: Stanford University Press.

———. 2004. "Sexuality, Color and Stigma among Northeast Brazilian Women." *Medical Anthropology Quarterly* 18 (2): 183–99. https:// doi.org/10.1525/maq.2004.18.2.183.

Resposta. 2010 [2001]. *Code of Conduct for the Tourism Industry against Sexual Exploitation of Children*. Natal: Resposta.

Rivers-Moore, Megan. 2016. *Gringo Gulch: Sex, Tourism, and Social Mobility in Costa Rica*. Chicago: University of Chicago Press.

Rohter, Larry. 2006. "She Who Controls Her Body Can Upset Her Country-men." *New York Times*, April 2. http://www.nytimes.com/2006/04/27/world/americas/27letter.html.

Ross, Becki. 2010. "Sex and (Evacuation from) the City: The Moral and Legal Regulation of Sex Workers in Vancouver's West End, 1975–1985." *Sexualities* 13 (2): 197–218. https://doi.org/10.1177/1363460709359232.

Rutherford, Danilyn. 2012. "Kinky Empiricism." *Cultural Anthropology* 27 (3): 465–79. https://doi.org/10.1111/j.1548-1360.2012.01154.x.

Sacramento, Octávio. 2018. "The Production of Tourism in Ponta Negra, Northeast Brazil: Policies, Representations and Logics of Desire." *Journal of Tourism and Cultural Change* 16 (2): 191–207. https://doi.org/10.1080/14766825.2017.1324862.

Sadlier, Darlene Joy. 2008. *Brazil Imagined: 1500 to the Present*. Austin: University of Texas Press.

Sanchez Taylor, Jacqueline. 2001. "Dollars Are a Girl's Best Friend? Female Tourists' Sexual Behaviour in the Caribbean." *Sociology* 35 (3): 749–64. https://doi.org/10.1177/S0038038501000384.

Satrapi, Marjane. 2007. *The Complete Persepolis*. Pantheon: New York.

Schaeffer-Grabiel, Felicity. 2004. "Cyberbrides and Global Imaginaries: Mexican Women's Turn from the National to the Foreign." *Space and Culture* 7 (1): 33–48. https://doi.org/10.1177/1206331203256848.

Scheper-Hughes, Nancy. 1992. *Death without Weeping: The Violence of Everyday Life in Brazil*. Berkeley: University of California Press.

Scott, James C. 1985. *Weapons of the Weak*. New Haven: Yale University Press.

SEMURB. 2008. *Conheça melhor o seu bairro 2007: Ponta Negra*. SEMURB (Secretaria Municipal de Meio Ambiente e Urbanismo) Natal.

Silva, Ana Paula da, and Thaddeus Blanchette. 2005. "Nossa senhora da help: Sexo, turismo e deslocamento transnacional em Copacabana." *Cadernos Pagu* 25: 249–80. https://doi.org/10.1590/s0104-83332005000200010.

Silva, Ana Paula da, Thaddeus Blanchette, and Raylane Bento. 2013. "Cinderella Deceived: Analyzing a Brazilian Myth Regarding Trafficking in Persons." *Vibrant: Virtual Brazilian Anthropology* 10 (2): 378–419. http://ref.scielo.org/8drfy7.

Simões, Soraya Silveira. 2010. "Identidade e Política: A prostituição e o reconhecimento de um métier no Brasil." *Revista de Antropologia Social dos Alunos do PPGAS-UFSCAR* 2 (1): 24–46.

Skeggs, Beverley. 1997. *Formations of Class and Gender: Becoming Respectable*. London: Sage.

———. 2001. "The Toilet Paper: Femininity, Class and Mis-recognition." *Women's Studies International Forum* 24 (3–4): 295–307. https://doi.org/10.1016/S0277-5395(01)00186-8.

Sousanis, Nick. 2015. *Unflattening*. Cambridge, MA: Harvard University Press.

Spiegelman, Art. 1991. *Maus*. New York: Pantheon Books.

Stoler, Ann. 2002. *Carnal Knowledge and Imperial Power: Race and the Intimate in Colonial Rule*. Berkeley: University of California Press.

Stout, Noelle M. 2014. *After Love: Queer Intimacy and Erotic Economies in Post-Soviet Cuba*. Durham: Duke University Press.

Trouillot, Michel-Rolph. 2003. *Global Transformations: Anthropology and the Modern World*. New York: Palgrave Macmillan.

Williams, Erica Lorraine. 2011. "Moral Panic: Sex Tourism, Trafficking, and the Limits of Transnational Mobility in Bahia." In *Policing Pleasure: Sex Work, Policy and the State in Global Perspective*, ed. Susan Dewey and Patty Kelly, 189–200. New York: New York University Press.

———. 2013. *Sex Tourism in Bahia: Ambiguous Entanglements*. Urbana, Chicago, and Springfield: University of Illinois Press.